ANIMAL
HAPPINESS

ANIMAL HAPPINESS

VICKI HEARNE

HarperPerennial
A Division of HarperCollins*Publishers*

All the pieces in Part 1, except for "Sarah, Who Hated Holidays," appeared in the *Los Angeles Times Sunday Magazine*. "The Airedale: A Case of Genial Fraud" appeared in *Dog World*. "Oyez à Beaumont" appeared in *Dog World* and *Raritan*. "Beware of the Dog!" appeared in a slightly different form in *Harper's*. "Wittgenstein's Lion" appeared in *Common Knowledge*. "Why Dogs Bark at Mailmen: A Theory of Language" appeared in *Harper's* under the title "What's Wrong with Animal Rights?" and in *Best American Essays, 1992*. "The Case of the Disobedient Orangutans" appeared in a different form in *Harper's* under the title "How to Tell an Ape a Joke." It also appeared under the title "How to Tell an Ape a Joke" in *Best American Essays, 1993*. "Job's Animals" appeared in slightly different form in *Common Knowledge*.

"Utterings," by Donald Davie. Copyright © 1983 by Donald Davie. Reprinted by permission of the author.

Designed by C. Linda Dingler

The Library of Congress has catalogued the hardcover edition as follows:

Hearne, Vicki, 1946–
    Animal happiness / Vicki Hearne.
    p.   cm.
    ISBN 0-06-019016-7
    1. Pets—Anecdotes. 2. Animals—Anecdotes. 3. Hearne, Vicki,
1946– . 4. Animal trainers—United States—Anecdotes. I. Title.
SF416.H375 1993
636—dc20   92-53349

ISBN 0-06-092606-6 (pbk.)
95 96 97 98 99 ❖/RRD 10 9 8 7 6 5 4 3 2 1

For my father
and in honor of Bill Koehler

Some things, niño, some things are like this
That instantly and of themselves they are gay
And you and I are such things, O most miserable . . .

—Wallace Stevens,
"Of Bright & Blue Birds & the Gala Sun"

Contents

Introduction

We do not live in the best of times. Animals and people are in terrible trouble, all kinds of trouble. Miseries abound, and there are no good reasons for them in most cases.

And anyway, how can there be a book about happiness even in the best of times, from the happiest of writers? For that matter, how can there be happiness? Freud says that it is love and work; others have had other descriptions. Jack Schaar, in an essay called "... And the Pursuit of Happiness," is at pains to list some of the bewilderingly different accounts that have been given of happiness, and to note that accounts or definitions of happiness tend to be merely accounts of the preferred or most valued activities and states of being of the person in question—except for Ben Franklin, who said that happiness is release from pain, from which it follows that happiness depends on suffering.

Schaar takes seriously the fact that happiness (like justice, I sometimes think) is a side effect, an accident, not something that can be pursued directly but something that comes while you are after something else, have your mind and heart invested elsewhere. He also makes a point that should trouble Americans, which is that Thomas Jefferson, who penned that bit about the pursuit of happiness, not only performed an act of dubious authority in "guaranteeing" a right to the pursuit of something that cannot be guaranteed, but also had a limited idea of happiness as indolence, a good supper, and so on— creature comforts.

Schaar's questions are important, but he wants, with good reason, to bring his readers to doubt their assumptions about happiness, especially in this political system, whereas I want to look more closely at the not always reassuring nature of various happinesses rather than doubt them, so I will simply commend his essay to my readers and in many other ways leave the scholarship of happiness, if there is to be any, to them.

A scholar of happiness would have to be a very delicate taxonomist indeed. Happinesses include creature comforts, relief from suffering, love (sometimes), friendship, ability and accomplishment, aesthetic experiences, and simple moments of inexplicable serenity, well-being, frivolity, perhaps of drunkenness, destructiveness. In the case of animals, happinesses also include fighting, hunting, chewing up the sofa, digging in the freshly planted garden, tipping over the garbage pail, and a host of others that often, when they come to the attention of a human being, lead to the death of the animal. The kinds of happiness are nearly as numerous as their occasions, and as unreliable in the long run, or so the darkness tells us—which is why some happinesses, and acceptance of them, come to require courage.

Each happiness is peculiar to the species and to the individual, so no one can own someone else's happiness. Of course, in friendship there can be the shared happinesses of, say, watching a horse race or discussing the proofs of rare mathematical theorems or shopping, but even so it is a mistake, and in some cases an illness, to imagine that your friend's happiness is yours.

My own happiness tends to have a lot to do with Airedales these days (an acquired taste, some say, a symptom, others say), especially the young fellow named Texas. Like the Airedale Derry in a children's book I once read, Texas is always encouraged by the success of his last encounter. Derry at one point in the story is heading down a river, having sundry adventures. He meets his first porcupine and dives in immediately, fiercely, to show that piggy what a True Airedale is made of. And instantly bolts, shrieking, tail between his legs, face full of quills. Soon he meets a mother bear and her cubs. Derry should have learned some caution from the porcupine, but the book tells us that he plunges in to investigate, "encouraged by the success of his last encounter."

This is not, I believe, the trait of the ideal family companion, but it is for me glorious, irrepressible essence of Airedale.

When I first got Texas at five or six months, he had been yard-raised, playing heedlessly with his mama and siblings, so there were two ideas that had never crossed his mind. One was the idea of self-control, and the other was that anyone could or would leave him alone for so much as five minutes. So he barked, and barked, and barked. A tremendous noise. "They gotta have good voices!" cackled his breeder, cheerfully and unsympathetically.

Our house is constructed so that Texas's operatic energies did not penetrate to my study but carried nicely into my husband Robert's study. Robert, driven to distraction, did what he knows better than to do, which was to yell at Texas, "Shut UP!" (I heard that.)

Texas was delighted, for now he was not alone. He had a friend, a playmate. There were Robert and Texas, barking at each other.

Robert then did something else I do not advise anyone to do, but please remember that Texas has quite a voice and Robert was severely stressed. He picked up a chunk of wood about the size of Texas's head and threw it, straight at the head.

Texas simply caught it neatly (Airedale jaws open very wide) and threw it back, barking, overjoyed, urging Robert to play the wonderful game again.

Robert reported this to me in high dudgeon, came into the room shaking with rage. "Do you know what *He* did?"

Sometimes Robert calls Texas "Himself." Not in admiration.

Now Texas is a bit older and has started to settle as much as he is ever going to, and to show that he is, as my friend Bill Koehler put it one time, "a dog you could ride the river with," a dog who won't leave you in the lurch. This makes me happy, but what makes me unreasonably happy is simply that he is always encouraged by the success of his last encounter, and that there is in this dog not an ounce of the trait that is becoming more and more highly valued under the influence of a group of people calling themselves "behaviorists," submission. Texas is on top, and his way of obedience is a way of owning the work for his own. Hence, the day of his breakthrough on retrieving was the day he bit the dumbbell in two. After that, he had no objections to retrieving—the work became his to control. He's not that interested in pleasing me except insofar as pleasing me is another way to articulate his powers over the world.

Not everyone likes this sort of thing. A friend of mine who runs training classes in another state asked me how my Airedales were doing, and I reported various successes, and she said she was glad someone was doing something about Airedale temperament, because she kept running into these Airedales who only wanted to play and get up to mischief and didn't care about pleasing their handlers. No submission, I suppose. I kept mum, but it sounded like a reasonable sort of Airedale temperament to me—if not carried to extremes, of course—and I didn't want my friend to guess too much about my own temperament.

But when Texas is not working, his manners, though they are improving, are not all they should be. This pup who is a happiness for me might drive someone else to drink, break up marriages, or, more likely, end up with a lethal injection. It is pretty much a matter of chance that I have him, that he is alive, that I am alive, that I am healthy enough to work him, that he inherited the working ability that motivates me to work him. It is a matter of unhappy chance for my older Airedale Drummer, who is a far more solemn, conscientious chap—as Airedales go. Drummer doesn't like all that acrobatic pizzazz. There are as many hearts and minds out there, animal and human, as there are faces, and at least twice that many possible scholarships of happiness.

I alluded in my opening to darknesses and promptly invoked the name of an Airedale who for me is all light, perhaps as a talisman, for myself and my reader, against those darknesses—and perhaps that is one thing happiness is. Darknesses include this one: There is cruelty and ruthlessness, and above all, there are failures of the imagination, unhappiness caused by someone's being unable to imagine what it would be like to be someone else. And there are other ways that one creature's happiness is another's torment—the owl, for example, happy in the moon-dazzling excellence of swoop on the hapless field mouse. If Texas wins a competition, other dogs, many of them in general of equal merit, lose that day.

Some people try to live without causing suffering, but this is impossible. No one—not the field mouse, not the vegetarian—escapes being in lethal competition with other creatures. If the field mouse gets the bit of grain, some other field mouse does not, and the farmer not only destroys habitats but kills vermin in the course of maintaining the fields that grow the tomatoes and the wheat bran and the tofu. To be alive, to breathe, is to have the freedom to live at the expense of others, to impinge on others; and our freedom, says the French philosopher Emmanuel Levinas, can never be justified. He goes on to say that it *can* be rendered just, that we can earn the right to our happiness, by luck as often as not, the luck of character and circumstance. The word "happiness" comes from the Middle English "hap," meaning "chance" or "fortune."

Dostoyevsky gives us Ivan Karamazov, who will not accept the happiness of the entire world if it is based on the suffering of so much as a single babe—that is, he rejects the Christian possibility, not for being impossible, but for being intolerable. This is a distinctly human option, not a position any animal in my ken has it in his or her power to take, one reason some traditions hold that animals are "innocent," and possibly the reason that Aristotle, in his ignorance, denied to animals, women, and children the possibility of happiness. But there are aspects of human ethics—nowadays largely confused with morality—that overlap matters that can occupy animals, or some animals. Animals are capable of conscientiousness, of a fastidiousness about what matters to them and their fellows, including their human fellows, that in some cases puts us to shame, or at least often puts me to shame, but as far as I know there are no brooding Ivan Karamazovs among the nonhuman animals, who may therefore have a greater gift for accepting happiness than we do.

A greater gift for accepting happiness, but not a greater *capacity* for happiness. A human being may experience joy as a result of doing something that an animal cannot do—producing a beautiful mathematical proof, for instance, or running a successful training class at the end of which the dogs and handlers are in harmony with each other, moving with (moral?) grace—but all happiness is animal happiness, even the happiness of the philosopher or the poet or the scientist flush with discovery. It may be that some forms of unhealthy glee and triumph are unique to our species—which is not to say that animals cannot rejoice in triumphing over enemies for the sheer sake of unholy triumph, but rather that human beings are capable, I suspect, of certain perceptions of what counts as triumph that are alien to animals. We are, or some of us are, capable of, call it *twisted* happiness, and I do not know whether the happiness of someone who writes a cranky letter to the editor is or is not on a continuum with the twisted happiness of the mass murderer, say there is such a thing—I do not even know that. (Though I do know the dubious happiness of the writer of the letter to the editor.)

This book leads to a discussion, in the last essay, of the Book of Job, where the Voice from the Whirlwind celebrates itself, its happiness, in terms of animals, terms that are beyond, or at least not to the point of, morality, questions of suffering. It leads there by way of various pieces written in various moods, some of them simply light-hearted, such as the sketches and tales in Part 1, many of which I wrote for the *Los Angeles Times Sunday Magazine*.

This book leads to Job also by way of "Josephine Trainer," the advice columnist of Part 3, whose voice is probably the least innocent of the voices heard here. She's hard-bitten, and gives her advice in the ironical awareness of the hopelessness of advice in a world that needs the salvation of imagination, vision, emotional courage. But I do not think that she is bitter; her mocking of the people who write to her is by and large gentle, or so I found when I wrote to her wondering whether Airedales ever take up the cosmic perspective.

This book is also an account of some things that make me happy—the mysteries of connection between different kinds of mind, and above all the mysteries of those different kinds of mind. I mean, that there should be so many different kinds of mind, animal and human.

I have not always managed to write in as celebratory a manner as my topic deserves, to be reliably merry in my railleries, but I have tried, for the convenience of readers who do not wish to know too much about why I get so grumpy, to separate the grumpier passages from the blither ones, and having done that, can do nothing more beyond begging the reader's indulgence. Also the reader's faith in this: The deepest happinesses are side effects of knowledge, including especially the simple and astounding knowledge that others exist, and this book is offered as an attempt to honor that knowledge and all of its mysteries. The idea is not so much to contribute to that knowledge as to begin to reveal that there is such knowledge to be had, precious beyond imagination, and in many cases beyond our ordinary powers to grasp it even as we live in the radiance that is sometimes possible, the radiance that happens when reality and knowledge come into congruence, provoking, as Wallace Stevens has it, "a laughter, an agreement, as if by surprise."

1
$\mathcal{P}$ROFILES

Parrots and Philosophers

*H*uman philosophers tend to talk strangely when the topic of parrots comes up, as if they believe their stature depends on the diminished stature of parrots. I would tell you some of the bizarre things I have heard otherwise rational philosophers say about parrots, but it would probably be actionable if I did so in print, and they would deny it anyway. A human philosopher thinks that no one notices when she starts putting on airs.

A parrot doesn't think this way. You may say that a parrot puts on airs. Well, a parrot does. But a parrot *knows* he's putting on airs; he's not like a blue jay that way, it's completely different. A blue jay gets all mixed up in his thinking because he starts believing his own PR, but a parrot is more cool-headed than that, which is why you can win an argument with a blue jay and never with a parrot.

Of course, some philosophers know this about parrots and don't try to argue with them. John Locke, for example, in *An Essay Concerning Human Understanding*, tells a story about a parrot summoned by an apparently philosophical prince who was wondering how smart parrots were. The prince asks the parrot where he comes from, and the parrot tells him, and he asks who he belongs to, and the parrot says to a Portuguese, and he asks what he does at home. The parrot replies that he takes care of the chickens. The prince is taken aback: "You take care of the chickens?" Parrot: "Yes, and I'm very good at it, too." And he makes "the Chuck four or five times that People use to make to Chickens when they call them." It seems that a chaplain who was present "would never from that time endure a *Parrot*, but said, they all had a devil in them."

I can see why that chaplain was upset. The parrot had coolly kept control of the exchange, turning what started as a condescending IQ test into a conversation on a topic of his own choosing. That is very much like my general experience of parrots—even a cat isn't as good at keeping control of a conversation as a parrot is. Locke has better sense than to try to argue with a parrot, even from the relatively safe distance of his massive book, and tells the story without much comment.

There is a parrot living in a bar in Tijuana—I have this on excellent authority—who causes people to order more drink than they intended by sidling up to them, cocking his head, and asking, "Can you talk?" And there was Napoleon, a parrot from Brazil, who put on airs at Riverside's Mission Inn from the time in 1907 when he was given as a gift to Frank Miller, the inn's founder, until 1956. Napoleon held his own with more dignitaries than any other parrot in history, so Riversiders say, including Andrew Carnegie, Henry Ford, Albert Einstein, William Howard Taft, Teddy Roosevelt, Emperor Hirohito, and Carrie Jacobs Bond. All of them attempted in various ways to introduce their own topics of conversation, but Napoleon prevailed over what were for him wits no better developed than a blue jay's, and he was not thwarted until June of 1956, when the Mission Inn was taken over by Benjamin Swig, a hotelier from San Francisco.

I have heard a rumor that Swig attempted to deny that Napoleon was "really talking," that Swig read *French* philosophy, people such as *Descartes,* and would say that parrots only *appear* to be talking because they are possessed by devils, and as a result, on July 3, 1956, exactly one month after the arrival of the San Franciscan, Napoleon died of a heart attack, thus, I think, maintaining his southern Californian refusal to let usurpers from the north ruin the conversation. I can see how it was, how frustrated Swig must have been when he tried to engage Napoleon about the beauties of the Golden Gate Bridge. Napoleon died with his conversational boots on. He was buried on Mount Rubidoux, and is commemorated in tiles on the second floor of the Mission Inn, outside the room called El Loro.

Napoleon's story makes me suspect that human resentment of parrots, especially all the talk about their having devils in them and so on, springs not from their startling ability to utter human phrases but from their aggravating refusal to let you choose the topic. You know how it is. You go up to a parrot, and he's probably in a cage and you're not, so you feel pretty superior, maybe you even think you can feel sorry for the parrot, and you ask the parrot how he is, and he says something gnomic like, "So's your old man," or "How fine and purple are the swallows of late summer." Then the parrot looks at you in a really interested, expectant way, to see if you're going to keep your end up. At first you think you've been insulted, but a parrot is too cool to throw insults around, unlike a blue jay, and once you notice that, you start trying to figure out what the parrot means by it, and there you are. You haven't a prayer of reintroducing whatever topic you had in mind. *That's* why philosophers keep denying that parrots can talk, of course, because a philosopher really likes to keep control of a conversation.

Too Much Leopard

I was sitting with my husband Robert, a tall logician, in a waiting room on Ventura Boulevard in Sherman Oaks. With us were Dr. Max MacElroy, D.V.M., and Cinder, a black leopard six months old, who weighed around forty-five pounds and was leaping for Robert's back as Robert was trying and failing to figure out what was happening to him. (Exactly how scholars and philosophers end up in such enviable situations is a trade secret.)

I knew what was happening to him. Cinder, like any good kittycat, is intensely interested in people, and especially in figuring out which person in a given situation would be the most interesting one to unsettle. Robert qualified because he's tall (the big cats are especially alert to height: tall people read as enemies and short people read as prey) and because he was the only one in the room who had never before found himself suddenly in the presence of a young, energetic, and intelligent leopard, so he was sending out brain waves that made Cinder curious—logicians, especially deep ones, have brain waves the rest of us wot not of. You know about cats and curiosity? The old saying has it wrong. It is usually the mouse that is killed by the cat's curiosity, not the cat, and even if the mouse is a scholar, satisfaction doesn't bring him back.

Robert wasn't killed, and in fact lost his heart to Cinder. This sort of thing happens with leopards, which is why Dr. MacElroy has big cats in the first place. It started with Rocky, a lion who was brought to him with virtually every bone in his body broken—"pathological fractures caused by rickets." There was a bobcat with a similar story, and Cinder's mother was another. Dr. MacElroy fixes them up, and that's how they become his pets. I was interested in Dr. Max and his leopard cubs because Cinder is well handled and didn't eat up Robert. An enormous amount of attentiveness is required in order to end up with a mentally and physically healthy leopard in captivity.

Leopards, I was told by Bob Wagner at the American Association of Zoological Parks and Aquariums, are considered the most cunning of the big cats. They are unlike lions, for example, in that they spend a lot of time in trees and can carry their kills—up to forty-five pounds, about half their adult size—into treetops and consume their dinner in the branches. "Cunning" is, of course, the sort of term you use if you are a zookeeper worried about staying whole, but I am uneasy with the adjective because most people have forgotten its true meaning, which is "knowing," not "dishonestly knowing," though I must admit I had the feeling there were a minimum of two or three leopards in the room all the time, and when Cinder's brother was brought out, it seemed like a herd of leopards.

What Cinder is like to look at: The paws express Cinder the mischievous kitten, playing innocently, and the eyes and mouth reveal the lovable kittycat, the one who wants to sit in your lap, and the whole leopard reveals something else. The affectionate kitten is real, the mischievous kitten is real—and so is the leopard.

Who, as I said, didn't eat the logician. But she terrified him. "I wasn't *scared*," he said, "but it's hard to explain. I was terrified, not scared. She was uncanny—one moment landing as light as thistle-down, sitting on my shoulder and weighing nothing. The next moment she made herself weigh six hundred pounds, or that's what it felt like." (Cinder, you recall, actually weighed about forty-five pounds that day. Now she weighs more.)

The usual fate of a captive leopard is a small cage or a zoo, when it isn't rickets and early death, or so I am told by people who may know. Cinder's fate, thanks to Dr. MacElroy, was not so bleak. In fact, she was slated to be a working cat, an actress, so you may have seen her on movie and television screens, though the big cats rarely get decent credits. She may one day play the part of a lovable pet, and you may be moved to want a leopard. Don't do that. Leave the big cats alone.

If you are tempted, then *look* at the extraordinary intelligence in

Cinder's eyes, at how dangerously that intelligence flames there. Think of the thinness of your own skin, the thinness of your own mind. Think of the vanity involved in presuming that you could ever own or control what goes on in those eyes.

And then think about the handlers and trainers of the big cats— people who can collaborate with that flame.

Honcho de Dedeaux

*L*ouis Dedeaux says his Rottweiler Honcho is a good working dog. "Everything I've tried works with him. He gets a little stubborn sometimes, tries to outsmart you, which makes him that much more fun. You gotta stay one step ahead of this guy."

When Dedeaux says, "Everything I've tried works with him," that's saying something, because Dedeaux tries just about everything with dogs. He's been breeding Rottweilers for eleven years, grew up in a Louisiana French family, and had a father who fancied coonhounds—"Black-and-Tan, Redbone, you know, water races and all that." Dedeaux has also worked with Greyhound racing and drag hunts. When he was nineteen he opened a guard-dog kennel in Whittier but then got into Schutzhund because "I like that a lot better than just guard-dog work. You have to have a lot more control on the dogs, and they have to be real versatile to do something like a building search." ("Schutzhund" means "protection dog." Originating as temperament tests for young dogs, puppies really, who were police and war-dog prospects, Schutzhund tests developed into sports in their own right. A sound Schutzhund prospect is also a sound family-dog prospect, so long as the family in question doesn't think buying a dog is like buying a microwave that you operate by pushing buttons.) Dedeaux is doing things like Schutzhund work because, "well, coon hunting is fun, but it's not real practical."

Dedeaux bred Honcho himself. He's from a good working line, but he didn't look like much in the beginning. He was one of only two surviving pups in his litter, about a third the size of his brother, but Dedeaux kept him "because he was all there, he looked good, everything was there. And his attitude was right."

His *attitude* was right. He stood tall, regarding the world with humor and friendly curiosity, fearless and without resentment or anger. Such a pup will forgive you your errors in handling and will not bail out on you when the going gets rough.

Then, at three months of age, Honcho got parvo. "He had it bad. The vet said he hadn't seen a dog with such a high titer reading, much less one with a reading that high who lived. The vet said, 'Go ahead and put him down now. You'll be out a friend, but if you try to treat it you'll still be out a friend, and the money, too.' But I said no, to put him on an IV. He's tough, he had the will to live, didn't get depressed like most pups do with parvo, and you could always get him to do something, like you could get him to eat. The vet said it was unbeliev-able, and in all that he showed his workability, and he started tracking right after he got over the parvo."

Dedeaux gets calls for his Rottweilers from celebrities because his dogs are well known, but he gets repeat calls for his dogs because they are *sound*. He doesn't breed so much for show, he says, because although he thinks breed standards are of course important, he believes that especially with a large, tough breed like the Rottweiler, workability is more important. (Honcho, incidentally, is on his way to a breed championship.) Dedeaux also worries a great deal about the specter of inherited hip dysplasia in his pups, because "you're not going to get the seven to fourteen years of companionship if your dog can't walk when he's two."

You can't get one of Dedeaux's Rotts just by having enough money in the bank to cover the check. "I don't worry about do they want one of my pups. I worry about do I want them to have one of my pups?" But Dedeaux has advice for prospective buyers. "They do need time, some money, and attention, and I don't sell to anyone who just wants a dog running around the backyard barking. But I tell people, too, not to buy a puppy from anyone who says, 'You can't see the mother, because if I don't leave her back in the kennel she might bite you.' That may not be the dog's fault, and the pups may be fine, but the average person looking for a pet doesn't know how to judge that."

Rottweilers are one of the breeds coming under attack as vicious dogs. Honcho himself is "real good with kids." Well, all breeders say that about their favorite dogs, but Honcho's soundness has been tested. "Honcho had a bit of a rough time. He's been teased by kids, but he came through that and still really likes kids. Some other dogs go through that, well, they'll just hang back when kids come over, but Honcho introduces himself to new kids on the block. When my six-year-old, Adam, goes outside, I have him take Honcho. Then I know he'll be safe."

Some dogs, of course, whether they are Bearded Collies or Rottweilers, become afraid of children and adults if they are teased, which is why some state legislators, responding to dog people, have attempted to pass legislation that would not hold a dog responsible for biting anyone over seven years of age who teased or tormented the dog in question. That legislation is important, because teasing dogs is a popular activity among some people, just as teasing voters is a popular activity among politicians. In both cases, teasing dogs and teasing citizens, it often turns out that the tormentor doesn't realize what he or she is doing and has to learn the hard way.

Such legislation is important because we need more good dogs like Honcho, who started tracking right after he got over the parvo that was supposed to kill him, who didn't get depressed when sicker than any pup should have to be. Like Dedeaux says, "Everything I try seems to work with this guy."

English Riding, Western Style

*I*n my dream life in those days I was in Vienna, Virginia, or England, about to introduce elegantly groomed and bred horses and their equally elegantly groomed and bred riders to the high arts of dressage and stadium jumping. But my eyes, once open, found it impossible to evade the hard, hot, high desert light and what it revealed—forty mongrel versions of dusty western tack on forty different versions of horse and puzzled western rider. While I was desperately trying to close the vast imaginative gap between the scenery of Twenty-nine Palms, presided over by Sand Mountain, and the white-fenced and well-ordered Arcadia of my dreams, a large red-shirted man ambled over to me.

"Reason I came here," he was saying, as if to himself, "we got this mare won't do nothing but jump out of her corral. But my little girl, that's Mary Pat, says she can ride Peggy, that's short for Pegasus because she won't stay in her corral—anyway, we heard maybe you could do something with her."

Escaping from her corral was Peggy's only distinction. Her mother was a hundred-dollar Indian pony from the Morongo Reservation, and her father was uncertain. But I agreed to look at her, and Mary Pat's father, Dave Nelson, signaled toward the group of horses, from which emerged an undersized mare with a more or less black, mottled coat. She was almost entirely hidden under sixty-plus pounds of roping saddle. On her back was Mary Pat, thirteen, anxiously clutching the reins and the saddle horn. There was nothing for it but to try the mare out, but my ignorant heart sank as I went to get my jumping saddle from the trunk of my car. I thought wistfully of the horses I could have in training if only I had a bit more money. If only I lived in Virginia. Or in England, or Europe, or in a different century and in another language and so on.

I headed Peggy toward an improvised jump made of stacks of old tires. She had never been asked to jump. Indeed, she didn't know the basic gaits—walk, trot, and canter—and she weaved and "squirreled," as horsemen say, seeking any avenue of escape, until she found that I was firm and that there was no escape.

So she jumped the tires. Simply folded up her knees like she was praying and jumped, demonstrating textbook form.

There I was, with a mare I knew I could do anything with—but the owners! Mary Pat had never even seen a jumping saddle. Her father had no conception of what goes into the making of a show jumper. But there is a lot of heart in that family, apparently a heredi-tary condition, for Mary Pat started surprising me. She was the first student I ever had who actually *did what I told her to do.* Older train-ers had warned me that there would be such students, but I hadn't believed them until now. Watching Mary Pat and Peggy, alone in the California desert, I thought of the diary of one nineteenth-century traveler who had said of southern California, "The mountains cut the land off from sympathy with the East." I sometimes felt that God was whispering things into the landscape, in the breathing of that child and that horse.

Then there was the day, very early in Peggy's career, when a Santa Ana was blowing. While she and Mary Pat were on a course of jumps, the wind had blown the second fence of one combination just far enough so that there was no room between them for a horse to man-age a proper landing and takeoff. Any rider would have been forgiven for pulling up, but Mary Pat just got this *look* on her face and headed her little mare into that fence. Peggy took them both at once, as one fence.

After that, when we went to horse shows, instead of hearing snotty remarks about Peggy such as "I think a hunter should look like a hunter, don't you?" we heard a new sort of remark. Things like, "Watch out for that little girl in the blue coat on the Appy. She can jump that horse out of a box!"

One day, at the L.A. County Fairgrounds, Mary Pat and Pegasus came in first in a huge open jumper class against seasoned profession-als. But Mary Pat was unhappy, depressed, frustrated, because even though they had won, her mare wasn't going right. I said reassuringly, "Cheer up. There are at least fifty pros here who would be delighted to be going home with the purse you won today!"

Mary Pat set her chin, glared at me through angry tears, and said, "My *mare* isn't happy. You always told me that what mattered was the horse!" Pegasus seemed to agree. She nodded her head vigorously a few times and stuck her eye next to my eye, regarding me meaningfully.

I remembered Gervase Markham, a sixteenth-century thinker, who opens his treatise on riding by saying, "Of all creatures, the horse is the noblest."

Love and Responsibility

D̲r. Helen Anderson and Dr. Helen Ranney have a noble Dober-
man Pinscher named Bismark. He is a splendid representative
of the first dog ever bred specifically for companion-dog work. That
means that Dobies are bred for the kind of courage whose other
names are gentleness and love.

Unfortunately, not all of Bismark's neighbors know this. Dr.
Anderson takes him on a morning walk each day. On their route are a
number of other dogs who have seen the wrong movies about Dobies
and tend to make accusatory remarks to Bismark. These dogs are not
stupid; the fear of Dobermans is all too easy to understand in light of
the bad press they've received.

One of the dogs who used to disaparage Bismark was a female
Golden Retriever. Bismark never returned the insults; he is a nobleman and forgives people for their poor judgment. Besides, male dogs
usually know that when a female starts taking pains to insult them, it
means she's interested. I have tried to explain this to a number of
male humans, in attempts to bring peace to certain relationships. I
usually fail, but this little Golden succeeded.

One morning the Goldie was in the house instead of the backyard
when Anderson and Bismark came by, and the front door was open. The
Goldie charged out, and her owner was terrified, both because she was
sure Bismark would kill her dog and because if Bismark should fail to kill
her quickly, she was bound to be hit by a car—there is a lot of traffic on
that street. What happened was that Bismark fell instantly in love and
leaped forward to hug the Goldie around the neck with his front legs,
thus simultaneously saving her life and establishing a deep relationship.

But the thing is that Bismark's nobility doesn't always manifest itself quite the way you might expect. Bismark is a trickster. At least, that's what some say. I say he worries about the moral soundness of his human charges. He feels that people should be up and about bright and early, so he sometimes reconnoiters the house, poking any exposed bits of sleeping human he finds with a cold, wet nose and insisting that he needs to go outside, that it is *urgent*. As soon as everyone is up, Bismark goes back to his own bed and relaxes.

Some of his detractors say that he isn't as honest as he ought to be. When Dr. Ranney is undressing, Bismark waits alertly by the bed, hoping that she will leave some piece of clothing there. Quite often she does, and he nabs it and takes it to his bed, for extra cushioning as well as entertainment. The reason he doesn't wait around for Dr. Anderson's discarded sweaters and socks and so on is that this habit of his caused her to become much tidier. Bismark explained to me that he believes that his beloved Dr. Ranney would also be a happier person if she kept her wardrobe in better order. Dr. Ranney claims that she is quite happy as she is, but as I said earlier, Bismark is from a line bred for serious companionship.

Bismark's bloodlines are also American from almost the word go, and his breeders, Judy and Edward Weiss of Levittown, New York, tend to breed for a somewhat "softer" dog than German breeders do. Germany is the location of some splendid dog training, and German breeders and trainers tend to prefer a dog who is "sharper." This doesn't mean that German-bred Dobies are nasty—far from it.

The truth is a funny thing. I was talking with a friend who was asking my advice about what sort of dog to get. She wanted a large dog that would be easy to train and groom, safe around her children, and a good protector. I said she was describing a Dobie. She believed me but said that she couldn't get over her irrational terror of the dogs. She grew up in Nazi Germany and remembers Hitler spreading propaganda to the effect that Dobies were of impure blood and therefore vicious and unstable. His generals used Dobermans in World War II, of course, as did the U.S. Marines; he apparently made his anti-Dobie speeches before the war broke out.

In any event, a good Dobie is the dog I would choose if I had a child who needed a reliable pal and lived in an atmosphere of risk—but I emphasize that a lot more is captured than I can go into here by the expression "a good Dobie."

Living Jewels

*J*apanese concepts sometimes translate into English in funny ways, with the result (in my experience) that a conversation between an American and a Japanese often begins with the Japanese trying to get the American to realize that the American doesn't understand.

One aspect of Japan's complicated culture has to do with the keeping and breeding of koi, or ornamental carp. As near as I can gather, this is an artistic discipline; the word "koi" means "living jewel." Breeders look for a myriad of perfections of shape and symmetry or asymmetry of pattern and color. The very serious breeders are keenly conscious of an ancient complex of philosophical and artistic meanings of the patterns besides, but I am still too bewildered by my glimpse into their world to say more than this.

What matters most about koi to most koi keepers is the patterns they make in the pond. So, as one pond keeper in Santa Barbara told me, though you can never know how many koi you have at a given moment, if you are properly attentive, you can tell that one of your fish is gone, even out of the corner of your eye, by the changes in the patterns. Standing at the edge of his koi pond, I found this easy to believe.

That pond used to house an ogohn (solid-colored) koi named Von Hindenburg, whose death revised a work of art—that is to say, the patterns in the pond. His name, all by itself, was interesting as a name for a fish, but it was the fact that he *had* a name that captured my attention, for he belonged, not to the man in Santa Barbara, but to the man's pond. It seems that if there is a belonging of koi, it is to their ponds rather than to a person. (And the ponds can be extraordinarily difficult to set up, since they must be not only beautiful but also safe from raccoons and greater blue herons, who tend to regard koi as lunch, not art.) What was different about Von Hindenburg was that he was the only koi in the pond who would eat out of a person's hand. Though this is not unusual for koi, it was unusual in that pond. When Von Hindenburg came up for a treat, his fellow koi would follow, so he was the focal point of the ever-changing work of art, the leading element of the design, so to speak.

I am hopelessly American, and having learned that baby koi must be culled carefully, I was intrigued that some koi keepers fail to take this responsibility seriously. In culling, the most beautiful survive in all cases where human judgment replaces the connoisseurship of raccoons and greater blue herons. I found myself particularly interested in some casual southern California koi breeders who couldn't keep their minds on this sort of thing. There was a young fish that failed to display any of the proper, traditional beauties. Also, he swam at a funny kind of tilt. His owners, instead of culling him, named him Robert Geometry, which was the nickname of a friend of theirs who was always studying branches of geometry in which the symmetries elude the mathematician at every turn.

Robert Geometry didn't survive very long anyway, thus possibly affirming the wisdom of culling. I still can't figure out how it is that even though you cannot count your koi, you can name them. But I learned, standing at the edge of a beautiful pond and at the edge of an ineluctable mystery, talking quietly of koi, that you can name a fish, or a tree—or a human being—even though it is literally countless and unaccountable.

How American—or how interesting—to love the one that doesn't fit in and so requires a name.

Four-Legged Therapist

$\mathcal{E}$llie had to sit out the Christmas party because she was in full season, and that makes life rough for even the noblest of her male friends. Ellie's friends are mostly working dogs with careers to attend to.

Fortunately, the fact that Ellie was on the sidelines didn't mean that she wasn't still on the job, operating from behind the scenes. What she did was continually check things out, making sure no one was getting into any trouble. For example, at the December obedience demonstration, which Ellie also had to sit out, there was a child who became momentarily frightened, and his lower lip started to tremble because he thought he was lost. Ellie said, "Oops!" and attracted the child's attention. He came over to Ellie, got a lick and a pet from her, and giggled because the beautiful dog had made friends with him. That meant that Mama and Papa didn't have to console an upset child, which in turn meant that they were free to keep their attention on the stars of the show, who were educating the public about the extraordinary abilities of dogs.

Ellie is opinionated about dog behavior; she's a mother and has had to raise some unruly sons. That's why she ended up refusing to allow Bobbie Morris, her owner, to let a houseguest, two-year-old Fallon, play with a new toy. Fallon had just been given one of those stuffed dogs that bark and run around when you clap your hands, and then stop barking and stand still when you clap again. To the Morris family and their friends, the dog was a delightful toy, but to Ellie it was just more nuisance barking. Since Bobbie Morris is a volunteer animal control officer, Ellie goes, "Oops!" when she hears nuisance barking, because she knows that dogs who are ignorant enough to do nuisance barking can end up in the pound. She learned to turn the toy dog off by barking at it.

Ellie's hobby is therapy. She's one of a team of therapy dogs, some of whom work at hospitals and convalescent homes full-time. Ellie is just part-time, but she's especially effective, for the same reason she's so good at controlling nuisance barking and calming children at Christmas parties. She can sense when a patient starts to shift into an unhappy or depressed mode of thought. When that happens, Ellie says, "Oops!" and gets on the case. She's so good at it that I haven't any idea what she does or how she does it.

Did you know that a twenty-pound Pembroke Welsh Corgi can save both her son and an upset animal control officer who can't swim? During the big storms in February, the creek near Bobbie's home became a raging flood, and Ellie's son R.C. dashed happily out into what he had known as a shallow creek. He panicked and started swimming rapidly downstream, away from shore. Morris panicked and plunged into the creek herself, dressed in heavy winter clothing. In three strides she was suddenly up to her chest in water, "screaming hysterically, because I thought I was watching my puppy drown, and then I was drowning." Ellie, who hates so much as to get her feet wet, said, "Oops!" She leaped into the flood and swam to Morris. With Ellie in her arms, Morris was able to think properly again, and when Morris started to think properly, R.C. was able to think properly, and with his last strength he turned around and swam back to shore and Mama.

People who know Ellie tell many conflicting stories to account for her abilities. All of them are true, including the one I like—the one about her registered American Kennel Club name, which is Lost Hills Ellie Oop.

A Tom Sawyer of a Hound

*B*efore I met Blandford, I thought I would know how to recognize the lead hound in a pack. The lead hound has all this *presence*. When you watch a pack of hounds return from galloping over hill and dale, there will be one hound who has a lot of lonely dignity about him, like Abraham Lincoln during the war years, and you will say, "That's the lead hound, I'll bet."

What I said when I first caught sight of Blandford was, "That's the clown in the pack, I'll bet." Blandford is a foxhound with the Santa Fe Hunt, which carries on an aristocratic tradition, but he keeps being not quite consonant with this tradition. He has, for one thing, an odd way of moving, more like the rawboned, loose-limbed critters of the yarns told in the American South than like the elegant hounds in English paintings, with their smoothly articulated appearance. He has an odd way of looking at you, too. Flave Pisciotta, who with her husband, Alex Pisciotta, Jr., sees to the care of the hounds, calls it "a spaced-out look."

When I met him, the riders, horses, and hounds were returning from a morning spent clattering across a rocky but inviting landscape just inland from the coast. All were thirsty and eager to cool off. The riders were impatient to get to the elaborate picnic lunch known as the hunt breakfast. The hounds and the horses were cooperating happily in this project, part of which entailed Alex Pisciotta, the master of foxhounds on this hunt, taking them down to a shaded pond to swim and splash. After the hounds were refreshed, they all—all but Blandford—responded enthusiastically to the cry calling them in to food and rest.

Blandford was thinking things over. I was there with my camera, hoping for some nice shots of a sleek hound streaking up the hillside. Blandford, reading my intentions correctly, stopped to pretend to scratch a flea ungracefully every time I got ready to click the shutter. Blandford doesn't have fleas. He just enjoyed seeing how exasperated he could make me, and how excited he could get the master of foxhounds, who was redoubling his efforts to call him in.

The other hounds had come up out of the pond and were back in position around the master's horse. Blandford was sitting at the edge of the water, on the other side, inaccessible, his head tilted as he watched my efforts and everyone else's with interest. He had just about pushed us to the exact moment when lesser people like me would start using bad language. Then, as though it had suddenly come to his attention that there were people on the other side of the pond, he waded over amicably and joined the rest of the hunt. I got a couple of nice shots of him, but they won't go into my book on the nobility of the foxhound. They'll go into my book on the amazing fact that certain hounds survive to old age without being hung, drawn, and quartered.

Blandford, who was still in his adolescence when I met him, hadn't been with the Santa Fe Hunt long; he was one of six hounds drafted from the Los Altos Hunt the previous October. He was initially shy to a ridiculous point, and Flave Pisciotta tells me, "We couldn't even get to him at first. He just dug in and hid. I've never seen an animal that melted into walls like he does—I don't know how he does it, he just melts." (Imagine Abraham Lincoln cowering at the sight of visitors.)

He is also one of their better hunting hounds; once, in fact, when the Los Altos Hunt struck the trail of a boar—a large and fierce animal—Blandford took the lead. He is good at picking up a line, and at sounding it, and what is more, the other hounds honor him when he announces a line (which means that if he says he's found something, the other hounds believe him and follow even if they can't scent directly). This tells me a lot about Blandford. It also confuses me, since foxhounds who have what it takes to strike a line and hold it are supposed to be bold and friendly critters, and Blandford has shown himself to be other than that.

Then I remembered that a foxhound is a kind of detective, nosing things out, and that this is, after all, America, and that our national heroes include Tom Sawyer, who as a lad was not famous for his cooperative spirit. Friends and neighbors of the young man used to say things like, "Tom will be president someday, but only if he doesn't get hung first." Tom didn't become president, but he did become a detective, and Blandford the hound does strike a line and hold it, and the other hounds honor his call.

Horses Without Landscapes

I was at the National Horse Show in Madison Square Garden, in New York City, thinking back to when I had been a trainer of hunters and jumpers in southern California and about how I hadn't noticed, there, what a strange and necessary thing a horse show is. In California, most horse shows have landscapes, backgrounds, settings. At the National Horse Show at Indio, which went with the Date Festival, you could look up anytime you liked at the spectacular way the desert was edged by the San Bernardino Mountains.

In New York there is nothing like that, of course. There are the arena, the barn area, and the practice ring, and outside there is Manhattan. Inside the building, you think about the horses and riders. Outside the building, you think about the statistics you read as you rode the subway to get to the Garden, concerning your chances of being murdered, depending on your race and gender.

I was thinking about California because I hadn't been keeping up with Grand Prix jumping, so I didn't know who the new international-quality riders were. Back in California, there had been this kid named Rob Gage, and I would wonder about him, as I wondered about all the junior riders, whether he would turn out to be for real. When they're young, it's hard to tell just by watching them whether they've got the real stuff, because they can get by with being merely superbly athletic, and because they haven't yet learned about morality.

And suddenly it was 1985, and I was in New York, and the announcer was saying that the next horse on the course was Largo, ridden by Rob Gage. As I watched them take the massive and deceptive fences of that course, I saw that at least one of those kids had learned how to ride. The kid was gone. Here was a grown-up who had acquired the genuine authority of the true horseman while I wasn't looking. He and Largo had a clean go, met the standards set for them.

The next morning, I learned that Gage had won the title Grand Prix Rider of the Year. It turned out that he'd won it with only two horses, Largo and Sage, instead of a whole string of horses, as is more usual. I decided I'd better go ask Gage how he had done that. But first I read through my program again, because I didn't remember seeing his name there. In fact, it wasn't there; as I later learned, the copy was already at the printer's when Gage rode the Grand Prix course at Baltimore, the show in which he would either win or lose, not only the one class, but also the title and thus the chance to ride at the Garden.

Gage was then thirty-three, still too young for one to be able to see in his face what one sees in the faces of the older horsemen of authentic hearts and minds. But here is something I learned about horses and horse shows at the Garden that I never noticed in the appropriately landscaped shows in southern California: A horse show is an uneasy place for anyone who is sensitive to the difference between real horsemanship and fake variations. Because the deeply true and the deeply false meet there, in pressured situations, the authentic becomes more visible, at least to anyone with real eyes.

At the Garden, things are all crowded together, and as I have said, there is no background at all. The genuinely great riders and horses must warm up for the most difficult events in a tiny, stuffy practice area. Here, the riders and horses must create out of nothing more than the material of themselves the whole of art of riding, because here there is nothing in the way of setting, no landscapes to help horse or rider enlarge the meaning and beauty of their motions.

So with Largo, Sage, and Rob Gage. They make their own landscapes. Largo is a very powerful and talented horse, but he was ridden stupidly for a while and was given up as crazy until Gage started riding him. Sage is steadier, but he doesn't have the power Largo has. Yet it was Sage that Gage chose to ride at the Grand Prix in Baltimore, where the fences required a great deal of power.

When Gage was asked why he had chosen Sage rather than Largo, he said, "Well, I keep being told I have this attitude problem. Every time I go into the ring I am absolutely convinced that I'm going to jump clean. I'm always astonished when I collect faults. So I forgot to tell Sage that the fences were too big for him."

This is, I think, a characteristically California attitude. Californians don't get proper upbringings, by and large, which is why Easterners regard us suspiciously as lacking tradition, with the consequence that someone forgets to tell our horses and our kids that the fences are too big for them, and somebody forgot to warn Largo and Sage that Madison Square Garden has no landscapes.

By a Frog's Own Light

I was first alerted to frogs and light by Josephine Miles, a poet and scholar raised in southern California, mostly. One of my favorite poems is hers about a psychic metaphysician, what we would call a fortune-teller these days, who had a small house where he told his fortunes on a road between Rialto and Riverside. The poem is called "Seer," and in it Jo speaks of how the metaphysician's hand, indeed all the objects of the South Coast, "so take the light"—take the light and make it their own.

When I told her how much I liked the poem, she spoke to me of a frog she had seen once by that same road. She said that what she saw, suddenly, was that a frog sees by a frog's own light, and that happiness is just that—seeing by one's own light, taking the light and making it one's own. "But," she added, looking out of a room that was not in southern California, "first there must be light."

I remembered Jo's poem about light when my friend Sara Suleri told me her frog story. The frog in this story did not live in Los Angeles, or even in the South Coast Air Basin, but rather in Pakistan. But it is a story about light, so it is thereby a story about southern California.

Sara told me that the bathrooms in Pakistan are sunken and beautifully tiled affairs, or at least hers was. Frogs sometimes came into them, I suppose, because the tiles were smooth and cool and wet, unlike the rest of Pakistan. No one minded, because the frogs, like the tiles, were elegant and therefore not out of place.

But this frog came in and caught sight of his reflection in one of the tiles. And would not leave his reflection, but stayed there in rapt contemplation, hour on hour, day on day. Ovid tells the story of Narcissus, who, catching sight of his reflection in a pool, could not leave it. This story is usually told as a tale about the origins of one form of pathology of the soul, but I used to think that was quite odd, for in virtually every other case in which someone gives their life over to the contemplation of beauty, we admire them and think up a taxonomy of virtues to describe them. After all, we remember Narcissus not for his looks but for his looking.

So the frog remained in his trance. Sara worried about him and would pick him up and take him to another part of the bathroom, hoping that he would eat and drink and get a little rest. But no. He always returned to that tile and to his reflection, and in the end he died, perhaps of starvation, although it may be that he simply ascended willingly, as mystics sometimes do, into the realm of the gods.

I thought that if the frog had been returned to his family, put back in touch with the psychic and domestic actualities of things, perhaps his life might have been saved. So I said, "But Sara, why didn't you take him outside?"

She said, "Well, I didn't know, you see, what he was thinking about, but it seemed to be important to him, and I thought that degree of commitment and perseverance deserved respect. If it had been me, I would not have wanted to be deprived of my vision."

I asked her what sort of frog it was, and she said, "It never came up between us. He was a frog-sized frog, smallish but not tiny when he sat in the palm of my hand. Of a clear eloquent color, somewhere between green and brown, that spoke of the coherence of the quest. And he was very neat and tidy, a frog well put together. I did not ask him his name or his species."

She went on to say that she had once met a very great poet, and that she had not asked him his name or where he got his degree, because being a poet *is* a poet's credentials. My old friend Josephine Miles, who saw by her own light, would have understood. She would perhaps insist, if she were here watching over my shoulder as I write, that we all see by our own light, take our own light.

But if she were here to say that, I would remind her that she had once said, although not in print, "But first there must be light."

Justice in Venice Beach

I was with my dog Annie on the boardwalk in Venice Beach when I discovered that there is something to the notion that it is a complex fate to be an American. Annie is a registered American Staffordshire Terrier (AmStaff, for short) and at the moment this was interesting, because that year, 1986 as I recall, the *American Kennel Club Purebred Dog Gazette* conducted a poll to find out which breed would be voted the all-American dog. The AmStaff won. AmStaffs, like pit bulls, English Bull Terriers, and some others, are among the breeds and lines of dog various groups in this country are proposing to muzzle, outlaw, generally abolish, or at least require special licenses for, on the grounds that they are vicious and un-American. The enthusiasm in question has spread, so that there are now breeds that are un-Irish, un-English, un-Norwegian, un-German, and un-Australian.

The day Annie and I were at the beach—it was June, and everything sparkled—I wasn't thinking about all that, Venice Beach not being a place where I worried too much about running into members of the House Un-American Activities Committee. Annie was walking formally at heel, the kites were flying, the peddlers were peddling various things legal and illegal, the skaters were skating, the lovers were loving. I must say that Annie was a bit nervous about the whole situation, since she does worry about the moral lives of those around her.

Suddenly, from behind a kiosk selling entrancingly unwearable garments, appeared two excited American males, respectable, each with a dog, a Collie and a German Shepherd. They asked me what sort of dog Annie was. I said she was a pit bull, which is the answer I give when I am alarmed, and it is in any case true from certain points of view. Respectable-looking American males who are excited always alarm me.

One of these gentlemen—he had a distinctly Santa Monica lawyerish look about him—started howling about people like me with vicious dogs like Annie being responsible for the ruination of the country. His friend, a Stanford alumnus as it seemed, added that if it weren't for people like me the Stanford football team wouldn't have had to change its name from the Indians to the Cardinals, thus betraying everything Stanford stands for. (There may be something to this.)

Now, you have to understand that Annie is definitely a matriarchal sort of dog. She thinks people and dogs should behave themselves, and she also thinks that she is in charge of seeing to this, so she was looking very much like an alert and ready-to-move version of Mount Everest. This caused the Stanford man to move threateningly toward me. Annie growled at him. He retreated, while his Collie, Lad, responded to the excitement by attacking Cracker, the German Shepherd. (Both dogs were males.)

This was too much for Annie. Coming as she does from a long line of noble fighters, she disapproves of street brawls the way a great boxer might. So she leaped in between the snarling pair and performed the acrobatic feat of simultaneously grabbing in her mouth one of the ears of each. The snarling became screeching, and a policeman of sorts appeared to break up the fight. But there was by now no fight, of course, because both dogs had instantly apologized profoundly, promising Mama never to do it again.

Annie said, "See that you don't!"

Cracker and Lad recognized genuine authority. They sat down obediently, symmetrically and formally, putting all they had into announcing their intention to go forth and sin no more. They were dogs, of course, and dogs know what people rarely do—the female is in charge. Always. The respectable male *Homo sapiens,* however, were confused and muttered something uncivilized about feminists. Annie looked at them with a Look of Meaning, and they quieted down.

So the breed that is to be outlawed, muzzled, etc., because of its fighting history, was the one that broke up the fight and restored order. And this is the breed voted the all-American dog. Which tells me that to be authentically American is exactly to be misunderstood. There is justice in America, just as Thomas Jefferson hoped there would be, but her true name and nature is a secret.

Beauty and Terror on the Wing

The great poets and artists, the ones who see beauty plain, unmediated by reason, and who mercilessly show it to the rest of us if we give them half a chance, tend to come up with variations on the idea that beauty is the beginning of terror. The reasons for this are not hard to understand, at least partially; one could even define a genuinely beautiful thing (as opposed to a merely pretty or cute one) as something whose loss strikes genuine terror into the soul.

Most animals can be made to look merely cute to us. In fact, I sometimes think that the plethora of cute pictures of kittens and puppies forms a kind of buffer zone that protects some of us from being confronted too directly with their genuine beauty. But there is one creature who seems to resist the cowardly human impulse to reduce genuine beauty to the merely pretty, and that is the hummingbird. I doubt that there is a resident of California unobservant enough to have escaped at least a momentary glimpse of the terrible swiftness and directness of the beauty of hummingbirds.

Everyone I know has at least one hummingbird story. Mine is that when I was young and dumber than I am now, I had a friend, Wes Weathers, who was writing a dissertation at UCLA on some especially gruesome and scientific aspect of hummingbirds. Wes was ambitious, with plans to become a "hard-core" scientist. His research entailed his having a lot of hummingbird corpses, so he went hummingbird hunting, and I once in a while accompanied him. One day we were standing in one of southern California's canyons, and Wes had his rifle fixed on a bird of a species he needed more specimens of. He was taking a long time to aim and fire.

Suddenly he lowered the gun. "You can't shoot someone who puts on a display like that," he said.

Wes went on, by the way, to become a hard-core scientist and these days doesn't hunt hummingbirds or anything else. Among the things his reputation rests on is a technique he devised using a centrifuge to study the metabolism of free-ranging animals.

I was reminded of Wes the other day when I heard Colin Campbell's hummingbird story. Campbell is now a reporter for a New York paper, but he wasn't always, and this story took place while he was living in a cabin in California. Once he walked into his cabin to find a hummingbird frantically trying to escape. He threw a blanket over it and carried it outside, in his hand. The bird, he said, played dead as soon as the blanket covered it, and continued to play dead in Campbell's hand. Until, with a straight suddenness only an observer of hummingbirds could believe, the bird darted to the very top of a tree. "Its flight was so beautiful I was frightened," he said.

Another day he came into his cabin to find a dead hummingbird on his desk. This time, he thought to himself, there would not be any of those fine accurate clashes between feathers and air to scare him. He thought that he would pluck a few of the bird's feathers before disposing of the tiny corpse. And he pulled one out, and then another, and then a third or fourth. As he pulled the last one, the bird fell apart on the desk, and turned out to be completely filled with maggots. Campbell says that he is not sure which moment was more terrifying—the perfect flight of the first bird from hand to tree, or the maggoty vision forced on him by the second. He does know that the only comparably terrifying experience he had was when, as a reporter on some awfulness in Lebanon or Southeast Asia, he came on a pile of human bodies eaten by maggots.

I remembered the day, now two decades ago, when I first saw hummingbirds with an unmediated eye. It was a hot August day, but I felt lost in the icy knowledge of beauty and said so to Wes. He said, "That's what hummingbirds are for, so we can know beauty entire." I thought then and sometimes think now that it is a good thing hummingbirds are tiny and swift, so that we can only see them for a second or so at a time. But I also wish they would reveal themselves more mercilessly to the statesmen who give the orders that result in piles of bodies.

Straight to the Heart

Wayne Roberts lives in an apartment on Venice Boulevard with his discus fish and his black Labrador Retriever, Arrow. Roberts can talk at length without ever boring you about the curious ways baby discus fish feed, and the funny and fascinating ways discus fish establish their pecking order. He can also tell engaging anecdotes about the reasons raising discus fish is a fine hobby for a quadriplegic, which Roberts is.

But the word "hobby" does not come up when Roberts discusses his relationship with Arrow. Words that do come up are "work," "bonding," and "conversation." I cannot begin to tell you the work that goes into establishing a relationship with a dog that makes "conversation" the right word to use to describe human-dog exchanges, but I can give you a couple of examples.

One of the difficulties for a dog who belongs to a quadriplegic is that it is hard for the person to give the number of pettings and cuddlings the dog wants. Arrow is an educated dog, and so for him as for us, conversation is a form of intimate contact. Nonetheless, a dog likes a pet, so it sometimes happens that Arrow looks up at Roberts out of the corner of his eye and says, "Look here, Wayne, I love you and I'm really lucky that I get to be your dog, but would you mind if I went over to Deena and had a little tickle-and-cuddle fix?" (Deena Frank is Roberts's girlfriend. It was Arrow who introduced them.) Roberts, of course, says, "Sure, just don't forget to come back on duty."

Once one of the human helpers who come to Roberts's apartment twice a day to get him in and out of bed and fix dinner failed to show up. Roberts got out the phone numbers he calls in such a situation, but they slipped from his hand and, in the aggravating way of important pieces of paper, slid under the bed. This could have meant a help-less night and perhaps longer in the wheelchair. It didn't. Arrow hadn't then been trained to look for things under beds, but when Roberts called him and asked him to find the list and bring it to him, Arrow did.

The amount of work and money that goes into training a dog like Arrow is enormous, though not as enormous as the amount of work, and sometimes psychic trauma, that goes into learning to handle a dog like Arrow if you are disabled. When Roberts first showed up at the training school to meet Arrow and learn to work with him, after hav-ing gone through a lengthy application and screening procedure, he was totally unprepared for what he had to do. "I always had dogs, and liked them," he said, "but I was full of misconceptions about how you talk to a dog. I thought you just had to be friendly, sort of make small talk. But a dog like Arrow doesn't care for small talk, and he just ignores you if you try that with him. In order to talk to Arrow, you have to say what you mean and mean what you say. That's *hard* if you aren't used to it." It is hard indeed. If you succeed with your service dog and manage to graduate, you have been through a great deal, a kind of boot camp for novice dog handlers that entails eight hours a day and more of training. But the hardest part is that when you try phony flattery and small talk on a dog like Arrow and he ignores you, it hurts. It goes straight to the heart.

That's the bad news for anyone reading this who is handicapped and interested in a service dog. These dogs aren't gadgets; you have to earn the right to tell Arrow to do any of the several hundred services he can perform. Furthermore, there aren't yet enough dogs and train-ers and funds to supply the disabled who can make the grade.

The good news is that all of the trouble is worth it, because what you learn from Arrow is the reason the English word "courage" has the French word *coeur*, or "heart," hidden in it. Because when you do make the grade and a dog like Arrow becomes willing to talk to you, that too goes straight to the heart, and stays there.

Part of my conversation with Roberts and Arrow took place out of doors and drew the attention of a neighbor who had a nice but untrained dog with him, off lead and out of control. He approached me as I was leaving, saying that he was in trouble because his landlord insisted that he either move or get rid of his dog. He wanted to know what I advised, how come Roberts got to keep his dog with him and other people didn't, and he then went on to talk about his having been twice burgled, about a woman in the apartment complex who had been raped, and so on. I felt divided on the issue. On the one hand, husky and healthy men whose dogs aren't given so much as basic obedience and who complain because they don't have it easy the way people like Wayne Roberts do tend to make me feel unfriendly. On the other hand, I sympathize with anyone who is afraid of crime and wants to keep a dog. The advice I gave him was, "Find an obedience class, and take the trouble to find a good one."

That may have been less than helpful advice. It's tougher than it looks, finding good training, especially since good training for any of us means training a dog to the point of being a full partner, a friend. A dog, or a person, has to earn the right to friendship, however. When I say that, I am thinking of Kathy Kaegel and her Golden Retriever, Remington, trained at Support Dogs in Saint Louis, Missouri.

Kathy Kaegel has no arms or legs. Her dog therefore has an extra-tough task opening doors for her, and an extra degree of responsibility, since she cannot correct or control Remington even to the extent that Wayne Roberts can with Arrow. So it may look on the face of it as though Remington is a slave—some have said that all dogs are slaves. But you get a different picture watching Kathy Kaegel brush her dog every day, not merely patiently but with pleasure, with a brush held in her teeth.

Watching dogs like Arrow and Remington, and thinking about the mutual autonomy and mutual dependence that is the miracle of our friendship with dogs, I have this advice for anyone who wants a dog. Before you get the dog, find a good trainer. One who gives you the feeling that he or she knows what it is for a dog to be reliable enough to cooperate with someone who has no arms and no legs, and one who also knows what it might be to honor and motivate so reliable a companion by brushing her with a brush held between the teeth.

The degree of knowledge that goes into such a project is not easily come by, but knowledge is, I sometimes think, the only form of justice available to us.

Properly Pigheaded

*B*laze was in every way I know of a satisfactory pig. The poet Fred Lape says, "Nothing can make a pig look sad; his face / is built wrong for it." The poem goes on to say that "the soil's good humor runs inside his veins" and that, "maybe the earth herself had a good belly laugh / the era that she first gave birth to pigs." I happen to know that this isn't so; pigs can look ill-tempered, depressed, tired; they can suffer and show it. But of course satisfactory pigheadedness entails a pig living up to the way the eyes and mouth are formed into a grin, and the way the nose wrinkles as with laughter with every move the pig makes. This Blaze did. It isn't pigs that are unsatisfactory, it's civilization.

Caleb Trainer had always wanted a pet, but he was allergic to every form of dander nature and man between them have contrived. Pigs, however, aren't allergenic, it turns out, even though some people think they look as though they ought to be. And there was a book, of course, which Bertie Lewis, Caleb's wife, described as "visionary, don't you see, for Caleb." The book was a children's story about a wonderful, intelligent, heroic pig. Caleb had visions of the whole hog, and one day Bertie was cooking when she suddenly realized there was a small burlap sack hopping around on the floor. She knew what it was.

The difficulty with the civilized world, of course, is that it is the wrong size for pigs, although it's about right for piglets. Caleb had gone looking for a runt and found one, a runt who was rejected by other buyers because he was too small. But "too small" was just right for Caleb, who said so to the farmer, who responded by suggesting that perhaps a shot of Southern Comfort spread over his evening grain would stunt his growth.

Well, as Bertie explained, "We gave that up in two or three weeks. They grow a little bit every day, and you notice this right off."

Blaze was housebroken in three weeks. Caleb said, "He was playful and pigheaded. When he found our hardwood floors were a problem, he learned to work up a good speed, set himself, and slide on them. Also, he liked to take your shoes off and run away with them. Or when I was working in the yard and he thought I should be doing something more interesting, he would take my tools and run off with them. After a while, he was two years old, and more than half-grown, and getting pretty big."

This changed things, because "he became uncomfortable about being in the house. One day he stood up under the kitchen table, and it came off the floor, and there were dishes broken and noise and clatter. After that, he felt that the house wasn't fit for him."

I queried Caleb on this point, not sure that I had heard right. The usual result of such a situation is for the *humans* to be uncomfortable about the animal being in the house. No, Caleb was quite clear: Blaze was uncomfortable. Though perhaps so were Caleb and Bertie, especially when Blaze would come into the house while they were gone and rummage through drawers and things, leaving hoofprints and noseprints here and there. This can be hard on a marriage, as in the case of the time Caleb accused Bertie of coming inside with muddy shoes.

David Martin, novelist and admirer of pigs, says that on the farm you don't have to do any philosophy to figure out which are the animals and which are the humans. You don't go by behavior—you just take note of the fact that the humans are the ones in the house.

This wasn't the farm. Caleb said, "Of course, by now he was big enough to open all the gates and doors, and could come and go at will. But he just stopped coming inside."

Then Blaze went to live with Jeryl Cleary, a neighbor and friend of Caleb and Bertie's in Desert Hot Springs. Caleb and Bertie moved Blaze because he was lonesome. There were no other animals because of the allergies, and Blaze liked to play with dogs. Jeryl has quite a collection at her place, goats, horses, cats, dogs, and so on, and Blaze was welcome. He fit fine at Jeryl's, even once he was full-grown, not the size of a prize-winning domestic pig, but still about the size of a razorback, too big for a lap animal.

Circumstances in the form of worries about Bertie's career in sculpture took the two of them to San Francisco. This may sound like the familiar story of an animal being abandoned when ambition interferes. I wouldn't be telling you this tale if that were the case. The way I knew it was not the case was by looking at Blaze. He was still, at eight years old, pigheaded and smiling proof that the soil's good humor ran in his veins.

For a Song

*P*eople who know Carol Connors know her mostly through her songs, and that is how she knows her cats, Minstrel and Maestro. They are Abyssinians, and were young when I met them, but already practicing their music. That's what Carol Connors calls it, their music, and I do not advise that anyone come between a cat owner and her heeding of her cats. Abyssinians are not particularly talkative, but they *sing,* say Connors and other admirers, making variations on a kind of meow-chirp, or whirl-chirp, or twirl. (Honesty prompts me to report that Maestro has added a growl he learned from keeping company with some leopards. Whether this is a matter of his having learned bad habits from low company or high company I leave it to the reader, or to an expert, to propound on.)

There was a time when Carol Connors hadn't made it. Virtually no one but her creditors knew her name, and she was preoccupied with questions about whether she would be able to eat and fix her car. At the time of her first encounter with an Abyssinian, she was standing at the end of a dock on the bay in San Diego, listening to the songs she wanted to write. She became aware that there was also a song behind her—"one of the loveliest sounds on the planet." Turning, she saw a creature as exquisite as the song it made. Initially, Connors says, she was frightened, despite the creature's beauty, or perhaps because of it.

She followed him home—the first instance in my ken of a human following a cat home—and met his owner, from whom she learned the breed of the cat, his name (Pharaoh), and the fact that Abyssinians are expensive. She immediately conceived a desire to have an Abyssinian, which, she says, was like other people's having an ambition to own a Mercedes or fly first-class to Paris.

She loves these cats because they are unlike her: "They are contained in their regality in a way I am not."

Eventually she got her first Abyssinian, named Songbird. And said to herself, and probably to most of her friends, "Can you believe it! I own an Abyssinian! I must have arrived!" This isn't what people usually mean by having "arrived." She was still poor, and had to choose between Songbird and repairs on the car.

I am used to stories about people spending the grocery money on fine dogs or on horses—there is even an expression, "horse-poor," so common is the latter phenomenon. This is the first case I've encountered of someone being cat-poor, though there must be others. I can understand it easily enough, though. All cats contribute to domestic harmony; Abyssinians do it by making room in the house for music, or so the story and the song go, and we don't often have much else.

Consider Minstrel and Maestro. Despite the fact that they are half-grown males and therefore share a certain endearing clumsiness with the adolescent male of every species I know of, one or the other or both of them will suddenly move into poses as graceful as the trills they make, like lace turned into liquid sound. Their song, though, is only the most obvious instance of a psychic harmony that in fact led Connors to name one of their forebears Harmony—"not for her music per se, but because when I got her I was in such discord with myself. Harmony put harmony back in my life. She made room in my house for harmony."

Minstrel is the larger of the two, and the one who doesn't have the show points, so like the minstrels from whom he got his name, he is a lover, the one visitors are taken with. Maestro, more majestic in name and markings, though smaller, has taken Napoleon as his hero and practices holding authoritative poses.

You might think that now that she can afford to repair her car, Connors has become sensible about Abyssinians. Not so. When she heard of a litter of kittens, she drove 110 miles, in the dead of night, with her boyfriend, Martin Kraus, to look at them. She tried to be sensible and get just one kitten, but Kraus is from Brooklyn, so he said, "You don't break up brothers!" Connors protested—she had, I guess, been too long without an Abyssinian and was getting into a discordantly practical frame of mind. Fortunately, her Brooklyn knight said, "Tell you what. If you'll take both of them, I'll buy one for you. But if you only take one, I'm buying the other one!"

So the Brooklyn visionary prevailed, and here are Minstrel and Maestro, making room in the house for songs.

Max into Maximilian

Mary Stockstill has long put her trust in the Good Book. The two great Braille volumes beside the chair in which she might be found knitting a multicolored blanket or entertaining her grandchildren are a source of light in her life. There is also her dog Max, in whom she believes, and the typewriter in which she has come to believe, the Braille one I used to ask her questions about Max when I went nosing over to her house. Max, a chocolate Labrador, her eyes and ears.

Not just her eyes. Her eyes and ears. Mary Stockstill is both deaf and blind.

Max is in "limited service." Most of the blind who use dogs can communicate through the harness about what they hear in the way of dangers, especially traffic dangers—a matter of some moment, since a dog who is concentrating on avoiding obstacles, particularly obstacles a dog is not naturally given to worrying about, such as overhanging branches, is distracted from auditory cues. Hence, normally, handler and dog guide each other. Guide dogs are justly famous for their "disobedience"; a good guide dog should refuse to obey a command that will take the handler into danger. Similarly, the blind handler should refuse to follow the dog if he or she hears danger. Since Mary Stockstill can't hear, she and Max cannot negotiate traffic, hence the expression "limited service."

But this is some kind of limited service. I watched Stockstill work Max at night, alone on a residential street. He took her safely down the street—skirting a pile of weeds and branches left carelessly on the sidewalk, which could have meant a nasty fall—and stopped at the curb. He also glanced back nervously at me. Stockstill didn't know why he was hesitating, only that his halt wasn't the usual firm halt that signals the presence of a curb. He continued looking back at me each time she urged him forward.

When we got back to the house and could talk again through her Braille typewriter, she wondered if Max had been distracted by barking dogs—if, that is, he had not worked responsibly while I watched.

I thought he had worked beautifully. There had been something suspicious for him to worry about: me, following the two of them in the dark as I scribbled in my notebook and muttered into my tape recorder. Not many young dogs would have kept their cool with such conflicting messages. How would you feel if the person you were supposed to be guiding and watching out for was being trailed by a dubious-looking stranger talking into a tape recorder? I would want to call my mother, or the cops—or Max.

Instead of calling his mother, Max just kept doing his job, which at that point had entailed keeping Stockstill out of the street, not letting her get lost, and watching me. She, deciding to trust Max, asked him to guide her home, which he did, still keeping a wary eye on me.

So Max thinks for himself, but his human handlers don't always appreciate his wisdom. There was the time, for example, out shopping, when Max decided it was too warm in the store and simply led Stockstill out, without being requested to do so. Her husband, Chuck, panicked, then found them outside the door. He said in the somewhat cross relief one feels under such circumstances, "I wasn't through shopping!"

Mary said, "Well, Max decided you were."

Stockstill became blind in 1939 at the age of ten. Her deafness "bottomed out" in 1959, which was also the year she thought she had to give up on having a dog, because there were no facilities then that trained dogs to deal with people who were both deaf and blind. It was nearly three decades before she got Max—years of I don't know what grief, frustration, and despair that go with being housebound and pretty much cut off. I don't know about all that because Mary Stockstill wouldn't tell me about it. "Just make Max look good."

Well, that isn't hard. He used to be, as Stockstill said, "just a puppy named Max. Now he's Maximilian."

The Philosopher's Cat

*J*ack is of the breed American Silver Short-Haired Tabby, according to the posters one sees here and there showing various breeds of cat, though he looks a great deal like sundry cats of my acquaintance who have more dubious—or more vigorous, if you prefer—lineages. He belongs to Larry Wright, a philosopher, and would thus seem to be in an ancient tradition: the cat who beguiles the careworn thinker. Montaigne said that he was grateful to his cat for reminding him that a cat may play with a philosopher. That isn't exactly how Montaigne put it, but he talked along those lines.

Jack hasn't read Montaigne. In this way he resembles a lot of cats, but in important ways he doesn't resemble them.

Jack is a pretty macho cat. If you are among those he favors by approaching your shirt collar along the back of the couch when you visit Wright to discuss the logic of truth-conditional inverted vague predicates (LOT-CIV), it doesn't mean that he wants a friendly rubdown but that he senses in you sufficient wit to think up something *interesting* for him to do. Sliding the vase softly across the coffee table for his delight? Sliding it noisily and clumsily for his condescending amusement? That sort of thing. But Jack isn't often condescending.

And he *cares*, a lot, about whether the household remains well ordered. Jack's household consists not only of the philosopher, but of the philosopher's wife, Gerry, and his daughter, Emily, seven. Recently, mother and daughter went off to Ohio for a visit. (People do these things, unaccountably to cats.) In this event, something may have been disclosed about the true nature of cats. Whenever I went to the Wrights' house, it was Larry who was properly appreciative of Jack. Also, Jack was always responsive to Larry. Larry had concluded from this that Jack respected his intelligence. His conclusion turned out to be false, counterfactual, just plain wrong.

Wright told me that during the absence of Jack's women, the cat yowled in a primal way up and down the hallway, swore vigorously, and once even attempted entrance to the bedroom—a thing unimagined in the eleven years of Jack's life. Further, this cataclysmic female absence gave Wright occasion to find out what Jack thought of his general competence. On the first morning, Wright fed Jack for the first time in a decade. Jack's usual response to his food is to dig in. This time, however, he approached the dish suspiciously, stared at Wright, and spat angrily before stalking away with his tail high.

Being a philosopher, Wright of course meditated on Jack's comportment, wondering What It All Meant. In the course of meditating, he recalled that Jack had declared Wright's study off limits. He never entered that room, the one with the heavy-duty books lining the walls. Wright had supposed this was more evidence of Jack's respect for him, and he tried to console the cat for the loss of Gerry and Emily by inviting him into the study—offering, as he thought, special privileges. So he whistled to Jack in the way they have agreed on between them.

Jack did indeed climb the stairs, and Wright reports that a large gray tabby head poked cautiously into the room. Wright was at the time reading a massive tome. Jack looked at the book, and at Wright. His hair stood on end, and he *backed* down the stairs, warily keeping his eyes on the dangerous philosopher at work.

Wright consulted Plato, Nietzsche, and Montaigne, wanting to know whether Jack's behavior suggested respect for philosophers. As a result of his researches, he concluded that the fact that human beings do philosophy is evidence that unlike cats, they are irrational and may even lack a concept of self. When he asked Jack about this, Jack said that Wright was trying to do philosophy with him and that the whole point of being a cat is that you don't descend to such nonsensical behavior.

Companion Dog Excellent

I hear a lot of people talk about how they don't want "all that show-dog, robot training" for their dogs. Some people say this because they make good money saying it on TV. Other people say it because they've heard someone say it on TV.

And some people say it when they meet Debbie Ryan and her Golden Retriever, Major. They say, "That's a nice dog! Not like those robot-trained show dogs, but a natural dog!"

This is about as bizarre as the world gets, because Major was fourth in the 1985 Superdog trial, a competition to determine which are the best of the nation's best "robot-trained automaton show dogs." And Debbie Ryan is one of the nation's top amateur handlers of doggie automatons. When she isn't being a top handler, she works as a checker in an Alpha Beta near her home in Sunnymead—not exactly wealthy and influential.

"Show dog" is not right either. Obedience trials are often held in conjunction with dog shows, at which dogs are judged on appearance alone, but they are trials, not shows. As in "Olympic trial." Developed athletic ability is involved—for example, jumping hurdles one and a half times a dog's height at the withers, or doing a broad jump twice as long as the hurdles are high. But the sport is more comparable to dressage with horses than to contests of sheer speed and power; the ideals are like the ideals of dance: balance, smoothness, harmony, symmetry, straightness, energy. Like any ideals, these go wacky from time to time—I have seen some very strange things going on in places where people and their dogs are striving for perfection in performance—but there is nothing wacky about Major.

Dogs like Major are capable of nearly perfect understanding of the formal movements, and the informal ones, too. Major is best known under the name Major, but he is entitled on formal occasions to use the name OTCH Ryan's Golden Major. Before that his titles were Ryan's Golden Major CD, Ryan's Golden Major CDX, Ryan's Golden Major UD. Written out, that's Ryan's Golden Major Companion Dog, Ryan's Golden Major Companion Dog Excellent, Ryan's Golden Major Utility Dog—and at last, Obedience Trial Champion Ryan's Golden Major. However, that's quite a mouthful when you're laughing either at Major or with him, so when Ryan comes home and is greeted by an eager dog who is carrying something in his mouth (he takes greetings seriously) or showing his unique grin when he can't find anything to grab and take to the door, she just says, "Howdy, Major. How's tricks?"

Or, "Major! The mailman's here." Ryan used to have a mailman who knew Major, so when the mail truck pulled up, Major would be sent out to bring in the mail. There's a new mailman now, and Ryan doesn't know if he's nervous about the dog or not, so Major is having to learn to open the mailbox by himself.

I of course wanted to know if we were dealing with a *real* Companion Dog Excellent and not one of those phony show dogs, so I said, "Well, that's pretty good about the mail, but what about slippers and newspapers?" Ryan said, "Newspapers? Sure. The only problem is that when we go out for walks and he sees someone else's newspaper, he wants to fetch that too. In fact, he'll retrieve anything. When I ask him to get his leash, he brings back a whole mouthful of leashes, and at a dog show I can ask him to bring me equipment and things from the tackle box." She paused and then confessed, "Of course, he doesn't always bring the thing I asked for, but he always brings something."

I asked, "What about tricks?"

Ryan laughed and said, "Oh, yes, tricks. Let's see. . . . He sits up like a Poodle, crawls on command, and I'd like to teach him to grin on command, but he hasn't got it yet. He only grins when he wants to."

Only grins when he wants to! Major was sounding less and less like a robot, so I asked about further ambitions.

"Well, we're doing a little field work now, just for the exercise, but I guess we'll show him. And we're waiting for Bill Koehler's next tracking class."

They were doing field-trial work "just for the exercise." Remember that the next time you hear that field-trial dogs are toys of the wealthy. And the next time you hear that competition dogs of any sort are toys of the wealthy, remember Major, whose record of triumphs I could perhaps get down in detail if I had the whole of this book to do it in.

I met Major at the annual Christmas party. He and Ryan were at the American Legion Hall in Pomona, along with other top working dogs and handlers from the Orange Empire Dog Club, putting on a show for the children. This is an old tradition; I used to be involved. Sometimes the show is at a children's hospital, sometimes at Juvenile Hall. The object is to inspire joy in the faces of children while showing them what a trained dog is like. Nobody, so far as I know, has ever gotten any money from this activity, and Dick and Bill Koehler, who sponsor the show, don't even invite Hollywood talent scouts. They have no sense of PR whatsoever.

As if that weren't bad enough, Ryan doesn't have an agent. I asked her why in the world she was putting all that time into a dog who has nothing fancy in the way of pedigree. "Oh, I guess I just like him," she said.

Ordinary Wonders

I sometimes have occasion to hear people trashing California in general and southern California in particular. I used to worry about this, especially when I was fond of the trasher, but events have since shown me that there isn't anything to worry about. California has a way of getting its own back, just by being California.

About twenty years ago, I was camping around and about the state with Shimshon Lerman, then my husband, an Israeli. At its best the Israeli temperament is a splendid one, but with the odd flaw here and there. Now, Shimshon was and is a fine man, there is no doubt about that, which is one of the reasons I was married to him, but with Israelis the general rule of thumb seems to be that the more admirable and lovable they are, the more they make up for it by infuriating you. The same is sometimes true of artists, poets, and great dogs and horses.

Shimshon was given to infuriating me by insisting that thin-skinned, mushy-brained Californians don't know anything about real life in general and the out-of-doors in particular, because there's no danger to speak of in California, so no tests of survival. (This was more than mildly hypocritical, coming as it did from a man who was as tenderly careful of the well-being of those around him as anyone I have ever met, for all his classically sabra prickly exterior.) The latest of these conversations was occurring as we drove into a campground at Big Sur. We were late getting there—I don't remember whose fault this was—and were thus the only cooking fire going; the other campers were bedded down. It was a clear night, and the smell of the meat on the fire was sheer happiness.

There was a small closet for trash, and inside the closet door was a

Smokey the Bear poster with stuff on it about taking care of your forest friends. Smokey's presence suggested that perhaps there are dangers out of doors in California, I thought, but did not say. Smokey grinned from the center of the poster, and around the edge were pictures of various native critters, including a raccoon. In those days you did not instantly fly into a panic about rabies and think of calling Animal Control or Agriculture or Fish and Game when you saw a raccoon, you just went ahead and either enjoyed or were irritated by the wonders of nature.

I was depositing a trash bag when Shimshon came up behind me and said, alarmed, "What in the world is that?"

"What is what?" I said, looking around to see if there was an army on the way or something.

"*That,*" he said, pointing at the poster.

"That's Smokey the Bear."

"No, no. I mean that!" He pointed at the raccoon portrait. I told him it was a raccoon. He said there couldn't be an animal that looked like that. I said there was, and that they liked terrain of just the sort we were on. He said that southern California had addled what few brains I had to begin with, and no wonder the world was so weird if grown women could believe in creatures from outer space. Then I said—well, we fell to quarreling for a bit, until the thought of supper recalled us to our senses and we went back to sit peacefully eating. I suggested that we store our food chest either in the car or in the closet so the raccoons wouldn't get at it.

Shimshon started laughing at me—protecting our food from creatures from outer space or Walt Disney Studios!—but his laughter was cut short, for in front of us, on a log about fifteen or twenty feet from the fire, was a raccoon, putting on a show that included dancing, acrobatics and juggling. Once again he said, "What in the world is *that?*"

I said, a little smugly (but please don't judge me by this, think of how you would feel if all your life you had to listen to people knock California), that that, my dear, was a raccoon. Shimshon said it was a bear. I said it was a raccoon. This time our bickering was interrupted by the coon himself, who was performing so charmingly that one simply had to watch.

I was as entranced as Shimshon was, but briefly, because I suddenly remembered that raccoons are clever and that they have hands.

I said again that we ought to put the food chest away, and would he help carry it. This led to a repeat of the scene above, with the lines about addled southern Californians.

I retaliated with lore about coonhounds and raccoon hunting and how rough that sport can get if the human beings and dogs don't cheat. This elicited more talk about scaredy-cat Americans, tall tales, and Paul Bunyan. Just in time, I had sense enough to get the flashlight and look round at the food chest. There, of course, were the raccoon's two buddies, happily piling into our food. This time, Shimshon was the one to get scared.

"What are we going to do? We're sunk. We don't get to eat tomorrow, we spent all our money on gas, what are we going to do?"

What we did was to use flashlights to keep the coons at bay for a while, until we could get the food locked away. I was the one who had that bit of woods lore, about using flashlights on raccoons. (I hope it still works, but the coons have probably figured it out by now.)

The other thing we did was to sleep in the tent rather than under the starlight, listening unhappily to the sounds of various creatures outside, arguing, no doubt, about how best to get at our food chest.

That is the one and only time I have ever come close to winning an argument with an Israeli, and of course he refused to admit that I had won. What he said was, "Well, you don't understand, because people in California get so accustomed to wonders that raccoons seem ordinary to you." I refrained from telling him that raccoons are found throughout most of North America. After all, he got the important part right. Southern Californians are the way they are because they are so used to wonders.

A Prince Among Dogs

I was listening to Harry Lawton, an old friend of mine who writes southern California history, telling me about Amy Congers and a poster celebrating local history. He was complaining that Professor Congers, an art historian, refuses to acknowledge that the most important facts about southern California are things like the beaches, the citrus industry, UCLA, and so on. Southern California's most important intellectual, cultural, artistic, philosophical, and moral contribution to the resources of the world's mind, she insists, is Rin Tin Tin. I asked, "Does she have a dog?"

Not only does she have a dog, but he's a German Shepherd, and he's named Prince. Since Amy is an art historian, people like to think the name is a pun on "prints," but it turns out that Amy has memories from when she should have been too young to have memories, of a family dog named Prince; therefore corny as it is, she had to call him Prince, because she so deeply honors history. I knew immediately that Prince would turn out to be an admirable dog, because of his owner's deep insights into history.

He is. She got him when she was living in Albuquerque. He is not only as noble as a statue but has had professional experience, specifically in narcotics, and can detect drugs and drug dealers infallibly. He's not overly moralistic about it, though; he doesn't care about marijuana, only the hard stuff.

Prince made life unbearable for a former neighbor of Amy's who was a big-time dealer and had lots of visits from other dealers. Prince didn't approve of any of this. The day the dealer came knocking on Amy's door to complain about the dog, Prince went for him, fast and serious. And fast and serious was the way the dealer made tracks for home and safety. That, Amy said, was the only time Prince ever went for a visitor, except for one guy who was not only boring Amy but giving her advice. Well, Prince knows as well as Rin Tin Tin ever did that you don't bore ladies and you don't give them advice. Prince showed him firmly to the door and out.

That's the sort of thing that makes some people extol Shepherds as the dogs who remind us that etiquette is the lubricant of society. I said as much to Harry, who is not only a California historian but one who has been covered with honors, and suggested that Prince was evidence that Harry, in not honoring Rin Tin Tin as the source of all that is good about southern California, wasn't doing his scholarly duty. He said, "Social lubricant indeed! At my last Halloween party he got the prize for best costume by threatening to eat the jury, and this in the face of the rule I insist on, which is that the contestants must bribe the jury, not threaten them."

I went back and asked Amy about this, because she had also told me about the time a judge awarded damages to Prince without even examining the evidence or hearing the witnesses. That story seemed to conflict with Harry's.

Amy said, "Well, in the first place, you don't expect an heir of Rin Tin Tin's to *bribe* people, do you? But there were plenty of arguments in Prince's favor. First, he had the most authentic costume." It seems that he came carrying a Frisbee with "Rin Tin Tin" written on it. "Also, because no one could possibly resent a celebration of Rin Tin Tin, no human's feelings would be hurt if he won, which is connected with the next argument, that giving the prize to Prince was a statement about local history. And all this while Prince sat there looking angelic."

I believed Amy, because as even Harry admits, though gloomily, Prince always looks angelic. However, looks can be deceiving, so I said, "And there was nothing about eating people?"

"Well, of course I said that I couldn't guarantee the health and happiness of the jury if he lost. Prince really believes in the importance of historical truth."

Amy loves to brag about Prince, who has what dog people call presence—loads of it. Consider the story about the judge. At one point Prince was in a fight with a dog twice his size. The Lab had started the fight, so Prince took the Lab to court, not because he and

Amy find court battles entertaining, but because the Lab's owner refused to apologize for her dog and refused to pay vet bills. The Lab was also in the habit of attacking children and grandmothers, and at this point Amy may have been getting just a tad righteously combative, which can happen if there are enough assaults on the character of one's dog—but that is speculation on my part.

Amy said that she had carefully researched the law and brought the relevant documents, as well as witnesses to the fight, character witnesses for Prince and against the Lab, Polaroid pictures of Prince's wounds, and so on.

She also brought Prince into court. And Prince made the documents and witnesses and legal precedents irrelevant; the judge took one look at him and ruled in his favor. "The glare from his halo in that courtroom," said Amy, "was blinding."

Peppy the Wonder Horse

gile as a snake!" my partner said one day, trying as usual to figure whether he was disgusted or impressed. On this occasion Peppy had wriggled out of his stall, squeezing himself under the top half of the door, and bolted.

When I met Peppy (registered name Peppermint Twist), he was for sale cheap because everybody in the county was afraid of him. I bought him because he could jump like nobody's business. I had a recurring dream when I was first training him, a dream in which Peppy and I had won the gold medal at the Olympics, and I was being interviewed by reporters about what kind of horse he was, and in my dream I found myself saying, with enormous admiration and fondness, "He's still the same ornery son of a bitch he was when I bought him!" It was the orneriness, see, that got him over those fences—that was his sanity, but he had insanities as well.

I got his chart done by a horse astrologer. She called me back in a state of high alarm. She said, "You know he's an Aquarian? Well, that's *all* he is. Everything in his chart is air signs. That horse is no good. The only thing he'll ever understand is about four feet of air under him. Sell that horse!" Well, I'm an Aquarian too (the sign that rules genius and insanity), so I said to the astrologer what I said to a lot of people in those days, when the advice "Shoot that horse!" or "Sell that horse!" came my way frequently. I said, "But he loves to jump!"

We began going to shows. As soon as Peppy found out that a horse show is a place where you get to jump even more than at home, he became peaceful about shows and everything connected with shows.

At one show there was a huge spread fence, called an oxer, followed by a tight turn into a five-foot upright. Peppy came in hard to the oxer and jumped it clean but fell to his knees when he landed. I lost the reins. I had just time either to get them back and try to force him over the upright or to ask him, with my legs only, to turn, set himself for the formidable fence, and take it. I did the latter. He took the fence, and during the wide turn to the next fence I was able to collect the reins. Since American Horse Show Association rules define a disqualifying fall as one in which the horse's shoulder touches the ground, and since Peppy had only fallen to his knees, we got the trophy and I went around saying worshipfully, "O puppy!" (In strict circles, you say, "O Puppy!" to a horse only at the most exalted moments.)

Peppy became, in time, such a reformed character that he was my most reliable school horse. He became kind. I could trust him with the safety of little old ladies, babies, and in one case a blind rider. He never became calm about trucks after the day he smashed into one and caused five hundred dollars' worth of damage, and the only other thing he couldn't learn was standing quietly in the middle of a trail ride, but I'm not into trail rides either and didn't care about that.

Peppy in time retired and was in the care of Mel Opotowski, one of his many fans. Mel called me one day to say, with a combination of grim energy and innocent excitement, "I've got a Peppy anecdote. I felt sorry for the hoss, because every so often he remembers that he's the great and fabled Peppermint Twist, and he runs around suddenly doing inspired athletic things and pulling muscles. So I thought I'd take him out and get a little condition on the hoss. At one point I decided to stop and rest."

I knew what was coming. It came.

"So I suggested to Peppy that he stop and rest too. But resting is not an idea he responds to readily. He argued about it. I argued back. He settled the matter by rearing, and I fell and broke two ribs."

I told Mel, who had not known Peppy in the days of his early out-lawhood, about the astrologer and about how everyone used to say, "Shoot that horse!"

Mel said, "I am no Aquarian, so 'Shoot that hoss!' was one of the things that occurred to me as I lay on the ground looking up at him. Other things came to mind. Various long, slow, painful ways you can kill hosses if you put your mind to it. The next day, though, there he was practicing Grand Prix movements out in the pasture. There isn't anything you can do with a hoss like that. You can't even shoot him."

So Peppy the Wonder Horse rides again.

The Nordic Nerd

George is a magnificent Samoyed. His owner, Colleen, has put a great deal of time into training him and has ambitions for him in competition. She loves him as only someone who trains a dog can. But George has also taught her more than a young girl should know about why the language has swear words. Samoyeds just don't seem to have read the stories about faithful dogs, and they don't especially want to please you. Very few dogs want to please you, but the Nordics, including Samoyeds, will often make a point of bringing your attention to this fact.

One night in August, in a training class in Riverside, she was still unsuccessful, twenty minutes after giving the command, "George, Down!," in eliciting anything remotely resembling obedience from George. Dick Koehler, the trainer, came by and asked cheerfully, but with deep sympathy also, "How's the Nordic nerd doing?" Colleen recognized the aptness of the description instantly.

George was originally a stray, and would still be one if he had his way about it. Colleen told me that one day when she was out for a walk with George—on leash, of course!—she came across a Samoyed breeder who was quite impressed with the dog and asked her about his breeding. She reluctantly confessed that she didn't know his breeding, that he had been a stray. The man was at first astonished that such a good representative of the breed should have been out loose, but then he said, "Of course, a good Samoyed like that, why should he hang around?" So in Samoyed metaphysics, hanging around—anywhere—is just not living up to your heritage. When a Samoyed goes roaming, looking no doubt for desolate regions of ice and snow, it is nothing personal against whoever happens to think they own the dog, it is just destiny.

There is some evidence that Nordic breeds (including Huskies,

Malamutes, and so on) aren't really fulfilled in southern California. Circumstances separated Colleen and George for a year, and he spent a winter in the frozen Northeast. Temperatures dipped below zero, icy winds blew, and when you did see a dog out of doors, attending to necessity, you saw heroic canine attempts to walk without touching the frigid ground. Except for George. The colder and icier it got, the happier he was, eschewing the protection of his cozy doghouse for snowdrifts, unsheltered from the wind. In the summer he was willing enough to come inside into the air conditioning, but if there was snow, if there were blizzards, he would pace and whine, agitating to go out. He would sit for hours and gaze with his dark eyes, listening to whatever tales of his forebears the wind brought him.

Colleen wrote to me about walking the streets of Omer, a desert town in Israel, and seeing posters advertising a lost female Samoyed. A week or so later, she ran across a loose Samoyed and took the dog to the address on the posters. The owners greeted the dog with joy, and Colleen, who is nothing if not gallant, offered to take the posters down for them now that the dog was home. They said, "Oh, no, leave them up. In fact, we had several thousand printed, and every so often when we've nothing better to do, we put up a few more, because we know that even if she isn't missing at the moment, she will be in a few days!"

And Colleen finished this story by saying, "Oh! It made me so lonesome for my Nordic nerd!" One may wonder if this sentiment on the part of a warmhearted and loyal Californian, for a dog whose heart seems to be elsewhere, in some alien snow-swept plain, isn't wasted. Perhaps it is.

But there is something else to know about Samoyeds. Quite a few of them have remarkably flexible and expressive voices, and sometimes imitate the rhythms and intonations, if not the consonant sounds, of human speech. And the friend who was caring for George during Colleen's absence tells me that one day George was appealing to him for attention, and he turned the dog down.

George lifted his head and throat in that way that sometimes reminds Samoyed owners of the awesome history of the breed, but instead of a chilling arctic howl, George pronounced a clear and heartfelt "Coollleeeen!"

This is a true and solemn story of a Nordic nerd who became lonesome for southern California.

Far Fierce Hours and Sweet

*T*omorrow is Epiphany, the day, as tradition has it, that the Magi arrived in Bethlehem and beheld the child of Mary and Joseph. This means that they were still there, sharing the stable with their donkey, which in manger scenes is usually depicted as humility and sweetness incarnate. I never used to question the accuracy of that rendering.

Then I *got* a donkey and learned that they have many fine traits, but that humility has nothing to do with it. Mine came with a suitably biblical name, Jeremy. The manner of his coming into my life was possibly not so biblical. My parents owned a printing and bookbinding shop that did both fine work and job work. There was a tenderhearted but not always clear-thinking fellow named Bill who came into the shop from time to time with printing orders connected with various (generally doomed) grand promotional schemes. One day Bill brought in an order for a promotional brochure announcing the grand opening of, as I recall, a new housing development. Bill had been given a donkey, and had had the idea of raffling the donkey. I objected strenuously—donkeys live a long time, people aren't likely to take good care of their raffle prizes, etc.

Bill said what was he to do, the raffle was already announced. I opened my mouth once too often and said, "Rig the raffle so that I win him." And that's what we did.

My friends worried. "What can a donkey be *for?*" I didn't know. Very few people do know much about donkeys, because they live so long and because we're still blinded by our inheritance of a horse culture in which we laugh at the aphorism "A donkey is a horse translated into Dutch."

My horse, Peppy, didn't know how wrong written Dutch looks to a native speaker of English, but he knew right away how wrong that donkey looked. If he had known Chesterton's poem in which the donkey says the part about "With monstrous head and sickening cry / And ears like errant wings, / The devil's walking parody / On all four-footed things," he would no doubt have agreed, although he would have been unprepared to assent to the feeling at the end where the donkey talks about his "far fierce hour and sweet; / There was a shout about my ears, / And palms before my feet."

Peppy, on first seeing Jeremy enter his domain, reeled across the pasture, shouting about things devilish and unnatural. Jeremy watched this display with interest. When Peppy slowed down, Jeremy wiggled his left ear, eliciting from Peppy a vigorous performance of the passage in Job about the triumphant horse who "saith among the trumpets, Ha, ha." This narrative quieted down too, eventually, and Jeremy wiggled both ears while sliding one forefoot cunningly along the ground, to see what the horse would do about that. A similar scene ensued in which Peppy uttered epic things about horses of wrath and instruction. Jeremy spent the next few hours thus investigating Western tradition since the Middle Ages.

Then, quite suddenly, I saw that things had changed. Jeremy had become Peppy's donkey, and Peppy had become Jeremy's horse. When a donkey really regards a person or a horse as his person or horse, the donkey starts protecting the person or horse.

Jeremy started having opinions about my asking Peppy to do things he didn't want to do. I would take Peppy out and work him in the riding area next to the pasture the two of them lived in. Peppy was a fierce jumper, but slow to appreciate the subtleties of dressage, and would sometimes get a bit grumpy, saying, "Nag, nag, nag. Put your hoof here, put your hoof there, never a moment's peace!" (Peppy came to love dressage in time but always had initial questions about it.) From the other side of the fence would come a terrible braying, and Jeremy would charge up and down, objecting strenuously.

Or perhaps it wasn't protectiveness. It may have been jealousy, Jeremy figuring he was the only one who should get to boss Peppy around.

They have their "far fierce hours and sweet," those two. A kind of rodeo occurs at the change of day, morning or evening, when the breeze and drama of the shift from light to dark to light in the inland Southwest comes up. Ferocious battles ensue, donkey and horse both careening around wildly, making vicious assaults on each other, Jeremy bringing Peppy to his delighted knees. No one gets hurt. "Can they do that and not be laughing?" a friend asked. And Peppy's dressage, curiously, advanced much faster after he and Jeremy began their athletic games in the pasture. Once Peppy started putting passion into his dressage, Jeremy stopped braying and would watch with terrific pride—perhaps the pride of a teacher.

The game obviously began that day, all those years ago, when Peppy first saw this "horse translated into Dutch." It took a donkey to teach the terrible horse of wrath and instruction to laugh at both wrath and instruction, and to do so without losing sight of the meaning of each. This is the sort of thing I think about when I hear of the humility and sweetness of donkeys.

I also used to think about it when I drove any part of the road from Nazareth to Bethlehem. It is not, even now, one of your more straightforward roads. With or without paving, it's the sort of road I'd want a donkey for rather than a horse. The same presence of mind that confounded Peppy is useful in confounding malefactors, too—as I said, some donkeys make good guard animals and will protect you as boldly as the little donkey protected Peppy's peace of mind and dignity against what he perceived as my interference.

Also, if I were pregnant with the Son of God, as human beings are almost exactly half the time, I would want with me a creature who would teach me to laugh with irreverent abandon at my own horses of wrath and instruction. That is a laughter it takes strength to meet. It is the sound of the holiness of donkeys, one of the sounds you may need for spiritual guidance, perhaps on your way to Bethlehem, or through other hazards.

The Heart of an Aristocrat

*R*azzmatazz is a working Golden Retriever, a field trial winner of national standing. In 1980 she was the top-scoring female Derby winner, and her maternal activities made her at one point the top-producing Golden Retriever in the nation. Working Golden Retrievers are special dogs, serious and passionate about their work, and Razzmatazz is a dog in whom the specialness of her breed is written large. She was one of the hottest Goldens going. This says a lot, considering how hot even a relatively laid-back Golden is.

When Razzmatazz gets her first whiff of the taut, crackling air of a field trial, nothing exists in the universe except birds and the landscapes that make birds interesting. In the world that is in touch with the various divinities who oversee such fires of the spirit, Pat Dernardo, Razz's owner, is understood to have been created by God to take care of Razz, to see to her proper training in the hands of Richard Pumphrey. The purpose of the Capitol building in Washington, D.C., is to keep America's birds safe for Razzmatazz. America is a country the Founding Fathers founded in order to provide Razzmatazz with different kinds of terrain in which to find and retrieve birds. The atmosphere is there to support airplanes, the roads are there to support cars, and all of this is dedicated to the greater glory of birds and bird dogs, since the true purpose of cars and airplanes is to transport bird dogs to field trials.

I may be making her sound fanatical and stuck-up, but she isn't. Some Pointers who work field trials do get stuck-up; a Pointer who has tasted field work is a problem around the house because he's always trying to practice gully-leaping and keeps pointing your guests and your cat. Not Razzmatazz, or so Pat Dernardo claims, but not everyone always tells the truth about the great. According to Pat, Razz is kind to guests, careful with the furniture, and cooperative with photographers, cheerfully providing a friendly length of tongue. She is not too proud or too obsessed to talk with people who are ignorant of field trials, and it is only those who are in the know who realize how much class and character she thereby displays.

A female has more trouble than a male collecting enough wins for stardom, because trial rules bar females in season even from the trial grounds, to say nothing of the competitions. This is not because the females behave badly when they are in season, it's because the males do. I have always suspected that women were excluded from London clubs and so on for similar reasons, and reflections of this sort sometimes make me cranky. This kind of thing is hard on an ambitious dog, too, and some female trial dogs become somewhat bitter and, well, *bitchy,* about the unfairness of the situation. But Razz was too much the genuine lady for that, which is probably one of the reasons she was among the top winning dogs in the country; no petty resentments ruined her concentration.

She was a crack personal protection dog, too, not finding it beneath her, the way some of those breed-ring dogs do, to guard her home and family. Fortunately for the history of the world, she was an excellent mother as well, which meant that she passed on her star qualities to offspring in her litters, but more important, that she was diligent about their education, seeming to realize that if she didn't see to it no one else would. One of her sons, Raider, was the cover dog of the July–August 1985 issue of the *Golden Retriever News,* and the general record of her progeny made her one of the top dogs of all breeds and genders in the country.

Scientists and philosophers will give you all sorts of weird-sounding explanations of such dogs as Razzmatazz, but the traditional way of talking about her restraint, courtesy, and dedication in the field is with words like "nobility," and this is the word that keeps suggesting itself to me. I know it sounds anthropomorphic, but it isn't, really. I wish human beings had the gaiety and honesty of a dog like Razzmatazz, but they by and large don't, nor do they have Razz's gentle sense of humor, as well as the courage of her forebears, who gave her the heart to be "steady to wing and shot," the heart of a natural aristocrat, an aristocrat of the field.

Pat Dernardo told me that people think dogs are smarter than they really are, that people don't realize how much training, including corrections for doing it wrong, goes into the preparing of trial dogs. Razzmatazz grinned when she heard that, and in that grin I read volumes. I remembered a story called "Hardhead," about a Pointer. Hardhead pretty much made fools of his trainers, who had to put a strong check cord on him, and the story tells of Hardhead's eventually giving in to them, saying, "Well, you finely cotched me, but I sure give you a time of it!" And the narrator of the tale concludes that the dog's head is so hard because it's "plumb packed tight with brains."

Razz isn't as stubborn as Hardhead was, not because she isn't as smart but because she has a different concept of what goes into making sure trainers are doing their job; even a very hot Retriever, the sort that makes me despair when people speak of Labs and Goldens as "good family dogs," has it in mind to educate the handler if possible, so that the degree of testing that comes from a Pointer's less reverent soul is not in Razzmatazz's concept of things. There is more than one shape and texture and passion and manner of aristocracy.

Scrapper, Who Died
of a Broken Heart

A man I knew only as Tiny, a lion and buffalo trainer, told me about a lion named Scrapper. It seems that at one point Tiny was in Bakersfield, California, with a carnival, doing an act that involved four lions. He had also a fifth, Scrapper, but he didn't know Scrapper very well, hadn't even had him out of his cage. The name, of course, suggested that this wasn't a lion who was going to make history with his gentle and forbearing nature.

Then one of Tiny's other four lions died unexpectedly. Tiny tried to get the carnival manager to accept a diminished version of the act, but the manager was stern: "You contracted for four lions, you give us four lions."

Tiny was, not to put too fine a point on it, scared of Scrapper. But animal trainers can't always indulge such luxuries, so he opened Scrapper's cage.

With the result that the lion was out and Tiny was instantly on the ground—on the sidewalk, in Bakersfield, in high summer—with the lion on top of him. And what Tiny said to me about this was, "So he *injured* me, of course, pretty bad, too, but he didn't *hurt* me, if you see what I mean. That's how you find out if you've got a good lion." I didn't exactly see what he meant, but the remark was impressive.

Scrapper was a pretty good lion, Tiny said, learning all sorts of stunts with astonishing quickness. The only problem was dealing with Scrapper when he got bored. "You could do almost anything with him once, then he started getting opinions," Tiny said. "And then, if you asked him too many times, he got angry. For example, a lot of lions are dumb about hoops. Scrapper wasn't—he got onto it right away. But once he got it, that was as far as his interest went, and you had to respect that when he got bored."

The financial balance of a lion and buffalo trainer is precarious at best, and lions are expensive, and it turned out that Tiny had troubles, so he gave Scrapper to a now defunct wild-animal park in southern California. It should have been paradise for Scrapper, but it seems that it wasn't. He declined, stopped eating, exhibited signs of despair. His nervous troubles didn't, of course, make him any more appealing, any more than a human's nervous troubles do. The veterinarian finally diagnosed heartbreak and said that if the lion was to be saved, Tiny must be sent for. Tiny was sent for, but it was too late, and Scrapper died, virtually in his arms.

Tiny told me that the vet said that the thing is, a lion is different from a dog or a horse. You have a brokenhearted dog or horse, you can turn the situation around at almost any stage. But "once a lion's heart is broke, then that's what you've got. A brokenhearted lion."

Sarah, Who Hated Holidays

A while back I read in *Animal Agenda,* as I recall, a piece that expressed the writer's conflict, as people say in creative writing circles and therapy sessions, over some fire ants who were invading her territory. (I do not use "who" rather than "that" carelessly here. A fire ant who is on your case has a definite personality.) On the one hand, one was supposed to be tolerant of all creatures, but on the other hand . . . well, I ask you, fire ants! I don't remember whether or how the writer solved the problem, but I do remember a man named Warren Estes.

Warren was a herpetologist, and in general a fan of all the wildlife of the Southwest desert, especially the inland southern California desert. I don't remember what brought me to his small house, but I do remember vividly going for a drive with him, along the road toward the Salton Sea, an area of hyperbolic spaces. ("Hyperbolic space" is a mathematical term. When you are on something flat looking toward something—a mountain, say, a most desirable mountain—and you start tramping toward that mountain, and you tramp and tramp and tramp and the mountain stays the same distance away because it is outside your eyes' ability to perform the calculations of perspective, then the space is hyperbolic. If the mountain suddenly looms at your feet, or else at God's feet, or at God's feet if they were tangible and near, you have stepped out of hyperbolic space. I don't know how it's done.)

Warren and I were driving along, and he suddenly stopped the car and leaped out, as lightly as a jackrabbit changing direction, and became tiny as he ran several hundred feet off the road, scooping something up at the end of his run. Or not so much scooping something up as—I saw him do this sort of thing with various creatures more than once—offering his hand for it to scurry into.

This first one proved to be a kangaroo rat of some unusual variety; Warren was excited, and I was too young to know to take notes, or else too lost in the splendor of it all. What splendor? Oh, you know, someone who could see that well, have that degree of responsiveness to the landscape. Nowadays, I am given to understand, kangaroo rats are protected by persons who want housing developments kept free of cats or something like that (animal and environmental protection groups have a curious tendency to exempt cats from their sympathies, in my experience), but this was the good old days, please recall. Perhaps the kangaroo rat had a family—I felt the pull of that possibility—but it is still somewhat difficult to say that Warren was unsporting in his collection methods. Instead of asking for instructions about how to look properly, I tried idiotically to admire the kangaroo rat.

Warren had scientific credentials, so he must have studied and dissected animals at some point, but when I knew him he lived with them. His house was full of snakes, kangaroo rats, insects of all sorts, and Sarah the Scorpion.

Sarah, said Warren, had troubles at holiday times, especially Thanksgiving and Christmas, when relatives were likely to be about the house. Most people can find it in them to produce a sympathetic "hmm" or an admiring gurgle for a kangaroo rat, since they are furry, but Sarah was another matter. The relatives looked and said, "Ugghhh!" and "Ooohhh!!"

Though I had done well with the snakes and so on, I didn't, on the one hand, but on the other hand, quite know what to do when Warren, who had been holding Sarah and petting her, offered her to me, together with sundry instructions about how to pet a scorpion. Do not think I was unwilling; though I may have been too young to know that my memory of an enchanted day would fade, I was up for anything that involved animals, and who could resist this? But Warren gave me a slow, amiably appraising look and said, "If you're afraid of her you shouldn't hold her. She won't like it."

He would speak to her, and she would respond. He talked to me as well, about the various evidences that she was nervous or relaxed. He stroked her poison sac. He admired her for her courage, and for her fine poison sac. And that is all my memory gives me now, at least palpably enough to report—Warren's hand, desert-rat brown, and the scorpion glistening there, with a glisten that started as the glisten of menace, for all my appetite for animals, but became the glisten of something very like consciousness through Warren's talk. He talked with her as some men talk with nervous Thoroughbred fillies, cajoling, admiring, gently admonishing.

Warren Estes was said to have died last time I asked after him. I don't know what became of his animals, though it would have been a simple matter to let them loose, there being little difference between indoors and outdoors in the simple, airy house he lived in. I remember the light on everything, Warren's ordinary voice, neither high nor low.

Of course, Warren would be an offense to virtually all sides of the academic discussion of animals nowadays—I mean the discussion that centers around questions of rights. He would be an offense to some because he captured wild animals—he had a collection. To those who are making careers refuting the animal rights philosophers, he would be an offense for his heavy anthropomorphizing. The knowledge in his hand as he gently held Sarah, just as she liked to be held, he said— there is no room in the animal rights controversies for that knowledge. It does not sponsor or finance any political point of view.

But it is possible that he understood something. After all, he did not get bitten or stung. Gertrude Stein wrote, "Each generation has something different at which they are all looking," and the superficial evidence is that everyone in my literary generation is looking at the animals. But they are not. No one, including me, has any idea how to approach the topic of Warren Estes and Sarah, who became upset during the holidays, needing more than ever, Warren said—and there is no one else left to believe or doubt on the matter—to be held in that confident desert-rat-brown hand.

A Funny Sort of Water Dog

*T*he old-timer stood beside me watching Sam and Barton Eigner perform the graduation exercises for the class in open obedi-ence they had been attending. She turned to me and said, "Boy! I'd sure hate to find myself up against *that* pair in a licensed match!" Sam, you see, is a Pointer, and a serious one, which means that for him fire, speed, precision, and power are the central good of the universe, the rest of which either honors that good or doesn't exist, as far as Sam is concerned. Sam came from the pound but is an aristocrat and knows it, and he has as well the infinite gall of the great artist; he knows he's right, and he knows he's glorious.

I don't mean that he is a snob, though his air of being aware of his worth when he's working could mislead some people. Snobbery is for lesser souls who have to depend on public opinion and institutional records to confirm their worth. So, while his performance in the obe-dience ring is beyond reproach (nobility demands no less), he values the real things in life above mere accolades. In particular he values the swimming pool, into which Barton throws balls for Sam to retrieve. Lately, ball retrieving has become more interesting because all the tennis balls have been perforated. This means that they sink very fast, which means that Sam has to be very, *very* fast if he is to retrieve them before they vanish in the fathomless depths of Barton's pool.

Now, a willing water dog is invaluable to bird hunters who work in territory where the game may fall into the water. There are libraries full of books about how to find and train such dogs, and Clarence Pfaffenberger, who writes about dog psychology, generally with little in the way of fanfare and a lot in the way of scientific detachment, interrupts his book with a suddenly interpolated tale of a dog he took to a trial of some sort without having gotten around to working him in the water, and he tells, with little detachment, of how the dog plunged in like an old pro. If you read and listen to enough of this sort of thing, the phrase "water dog" comes to sound as though it is synonymous with phrases like "a gift from heaven" or "the Holy Grail."

But the trouble with the dog training world is that in it glory and virtue, while they are of course unending and immovable under the aspect of eternity, tend to wobble a bit, waver before the eyes, in the imperfect world we live in, where time and timing don't always cooperate with the Great God of Retrieving.

One day there was a small open obedience match in which Barton had entered Sam. Required exercises in open competition include the dog's leaping out over a significant hurdle and retrieving, on the judge's signal and at the handler's command, a dumbbell that the dog then returns with over the jump. These are substantial competitions, which is why dogs who have performed in them at satisfactory levels receive the title Companion Dog Excellent. This match was in a park, and just outside the roped-off area that marked the trial ring were a portable child's swimming pool, some children, and—alas!—some tennis balls.

The judge gave the signal, Barton gave the command—"Sam, Fetch!"—and Sam leaped out over the hurdle with the swiftness and power that are his trademark. In the air, his eye caught sight of a tennis ball a child had just tossed into the pool. In a dog's heart, the Ultimate Purpose of Things is deeper and more powerful than the American Kennel Club's regulations for licensed trials, so Sam hit the ground and soared at once into the air again, over the rope around the ring. (Sam is not one of your low creatures who would sink to running under the rope when he could leap.) The tennis ball was in Sam's mouth before it hit the water, and then he returned over the jump, stopping to gather up the dumbbell he had been sent for.

This was a perplexing moment for the judge. Did she give Sam zero points for the exercise or double points? I don't remember what she decided, but Sam's performance seems to me an illustration of what T. S. Eliot called "the eternal struggle between art and education." And in Eliot's idea, the great artist is one in whom education and art blend to become one thing. Or, put differently, the true artist—Sam, for example—is the dog who masters the rules of, in this case, formal retrieving so deeply he commands them as things of his own.

Barton tells me that in the Eigner backyard Sam has lately taken to working on his diving technique. Barton is thinking about designing scuba gear for him.

A Distinct Impression of Diamonds

My friend Pat Terry read a book, Isak Dinesen's *Out of Africa*, that had a couple of stories in it about the author's Scottish Deerhound, Dusk. The stories were about how noble, gentle, and wise Deerhounds are, but also about how they have a genuine sense of humor. In one story Dusk devotes all his energies to reminding Dinesen of the time she stupidly almost shot her own cat out of a tree. Every time the two of them go by the tree, the Deerhound gestures toward it with a chuckle. Think about that. Think about spending the rest of your life with a dog who reminds you of your most idiotic moments.

Pat is one of those people who are vulnerable to books, so she went out and got herself a Deerhound, a female, and named her Dusk. Now, getting a dog because of something you read in a book, especially a dog the size of a Deerhound, is a risky business, and makes me wonder about the wisdom of my career, writing books about animals. But in this case it worked out, partly because Pat knows something about dogs, but largely because it is *true* that well-bred Deerhounds are loyal, brave, noble, wise, and whatnot, and have a genuine and subtle sense of humor.

They also have complicated ancestral memories and are closely related to Wolfhounds. Dusk was raised in Connecticut, where for all practical purposes there were no wolves, in the days before the coyotes made a full return to New England. When she and Pat first arrived in California, Dusk discovered coyotes. And knew instantly that she was supposed to *do* something about them. But what? Join them? Hunt them? Teach them knitting? Pat suggested that the best course was a meditative and philosophical one—Dusk should just *understand* coyotes and leave it at that. This she does.

Dusk also has a wrist gene. When Pat arrived at the house of Barbara Birdsall, Dusk's breeder, Lesley, Dusk's mother, took her by the wrist and led her into the house, to the couch, where she dropped the wrist and indicated that Pat should sit down. So Dusk occasionally feels that she is a Wristhound and leads Pat down the hallway by her wrist. She never leads her anywhere in particular, she just leads her.

Dusk is—well, let's put it this way. There is no breed that is as good as a Deerhound is at curling up on a couch. (Deerhounds require couches, some experts will tell you.) You come away every time with the distinct impression that you have seen the dog using a long diamond-studded cigarette holder. You haven't, and when you go back to look at the dog you realize that you haven't, but then you come away from checking with that distinct impression of diamonds. Perhaps because they were originally bred to hunt such elegant animals as deer, they had to develop an answering elegance in order to do their jobs. In any case, when people meet Dusk they often realize that they had not until that moment understood genuine Elegance, the Platonic Form Itself rather than the feeble shadows of it one finds elsewhere.

Deerhounds are not the only breed with a sense of humor, of course, but they possess a rare ability to express it without losing their elegance. Dusk is even capable of using it to express reproach without whining as lesser dogs will.

One hot day Pat had to leave Dusk at home while she took her Cairn Terrier, who had developed a psychosomatic illness as it turned out, to the vet. Dusk is generally noble and patient about being left behind, but being left behind because of a hysterical Cairn Terrier is a bit much, even for a Deerhound. And the one piece of furniture in the house she is not allowed on is the waterbed, and she had never before violated this rule.

Pat returned to find no Deerhound. Dusk was, astoundingly, not there to greet her and not in any of her usual places. A few minutes of panic followed, but Dusk was shortly discovered to be waiting on the waterbed, and to be waiting there to be discovered. Dusk looked at Pat, held the look a few moments to be sure that Pat got the message, nodded to herself when Pat did, and got up off the bed, smiling with the pleasure of the successful moral comedian.

Most times when the world has become too vulgar for her, Dusk simply sleeps with one paw over her eyes.

So I don't recommend Deerhounds to just anyone. Very few people have the psychic stamina required to sustain encounters with Deerhound moral wit.

The Dedication of Tortoises

There is a place in inland southern California called Tortoise Valley because there are so many desert tortoises there. I used to like to ride through and look at them, partly because my childhood in Louisiana was largely an affair of capturing tortoises and giving them names. This I couldn't do in Tortoise Valley, because desert tortoises are a protected species and you have to have a license to keep them.

The tortoises of my childhood weren't, of course, desert tortoises, but there is in my mind a metaphysical identity between them and the desert tortoises Judie Lewellen keeps. Our culture prepares us to some extent for the shock of discovering that no two Deerhounds, or Appaloosas, or whatever, are the same. We are born to allegories that teach us how to deal with the deaths of most animals. The stories about Black Beauty, Lassie, and Rin Tin Tin help us to know what to do or say when our own dogs and horses prove to be mortal. But we have, sadly, no tortoise stories; nothing prepares us to learn that Lettuce Mouth II is not going to be a clone of Lettuce Mouth the Original.

Nonetheless a tortoise is ineluctably an individual tortoise. This means, Judie Lewellen told me, that when a tortoise is doing something, that is what the tortoise is doing. If a tortoise is traveling north by northwest and you interfere, pointing the critter southeast, she or he is so quickly and inexorably going north by northwest again that you have the impression you only thought you'd picked her or him up and turned her or him in another direction. Sort of as though you dreamed you'd deflected the moon from its appointed rounds.

That is as much dedication as you ever get, even in an elephant. Judie has one tortoise named Lucille—a male, as it happens—who has a thing about crawling behind the toilet. It is a primal, visionary thing.

It is what Lucille does, and that's all there is to it. There it is, Lucille wanting to get behind the toilet. The only problem is that Lucille doesn't fit behind the toilet, so Judie sleeps to the comforting sound of scratching. All night long.

Lucille weighs five pounds and is probably between eight and nine years old. He is not Judie's only tortoise. There is Peter, and there is Tank, who earns his name in part by weighing nineteen pounds. (The record captive weight for a California desert tortoise is around twenty-four pounds.) And tortoises have terrible, primeval battles. Like Tweedledum and Tweedledee, they *agree* to have battles, as near as I can make out. Peter, who is very macho, collides with Tank at every opportunity—resounding head-to-head collisions that remind me of the wonderful accounts I read as a child, of Homeric dinosaur battles, horrible and glorious affairs they were, if memory serves and no one lied to me about dinosaurs. Here is the horrible thing about tortoise conflicts: They try to flip each other over, at times successfully, by sliding the edges of their shells under each other and shoving. I knew that human beings, especially young male ones, did this to tortoises, rendering them helpless and physiologically distressed, but I thought that tortoises themselves were deep souls, beyond such tactics. Apparently not. Furthermore, in these battles wit and cool-headedness matter more than strength. Lightweight Lucille has flipped heavyweight Tank.

So why put up with tortoises? Especially when you consider the bother. You can't just let a tortoise hang around the backyard and that's it. Tortoise veterinary medicine is a complicated thing. (Some vets wisely refuse to deal with tortoises.) For example, you can't let a tortoise go to sleep with a cold (chief symptom: runny nose), because when a tortoise hibernates the immune system shuts off. And when the season for it comes, a tortoise really wants to hibernate. A tortoise who wants to hibernate has plenty of resources and is hard to wake up. Their Latin name starts with the word *Gopherus* because burrowing to take a snooze is one of the things they are good at, and a tortoise intent on burrowing and snoozing is as formidable as—well, as a tortoise intent on something. Even in southern California, Judie has troubles keeping Lucille and Peter, who have respiratory infections, awake. A sleepy tortoise is *sleepy.*

Why would anyone bother keeping tortoises? Why bother keeping any animal? Perhaps many people shouldn't, and perhaps even most people shouldn't, but I think that keeping tortoises is plainly part of Adam's task, the one Adam and Eve accepted when God gave them dominion over the beasts of the field and so on, though certain animals are more cooperative than tortoises are at helping one out with this. The way you can tell that it's worthwhile to be a tortoise-keeper is the usual one. When they die, you weep. And the next one won't be the same.

2

$\mathcal{L}$INEAGES

The Airedale

A Case of Genial Fraud

*A*iredale Terriers. Peculiar dogs, really—clowns of dogs, *if* they are dogs at all, a proposition that may improve some if I deny it. They are relatively rare, but that isn't what makes them peculiar. It isn't their striking looks, either. (Striking when groomed, that is. An ungroomed Airedale is just a shaggy dog.)

Airedales have their share of nobility, but they are indeed peculiar, and I don't think their peculiarity has ever been scientifically or philosophically analyzed. One thing that is mentioned about them in print, everywhere and everywhen, is how versatile they are. In *The Book of All Terriers* we find a report of a kennel that advertised in the 1930s that it would supply you with an Airedale trained to just about anything you desired—retrieving ducks, pointing, herding, stock guarding, guide-dog work, police-dog tracking, circus clown, ladies' companion, Rolls-Royce dog, bear dog. It is often said by guileless and enthusiastic fanciers that the Airedale adapts himself to just about any task and does well enough—though never so thoroughly as the specialists, they will sometimes add, in moments of unaccustomed insight and scrupulosity.

From this the unwary conclude that the Airedale has no specialty, but he does, and it is given in these most innocent praises: He is nothing but his versatility and his prance. And his eyebrows and whiskers, which are especially luxuriant on the face, ears, and legs. Thus he is a specialist. His specialty is: being an Airedale.

The truth is perhaps that the Airedale is not in the usual way a dog at all, and that is what is peculiar about him. I don't mean he is human, mind you—the Poodles are the ones for that. The Airedale is a dog mimic, and the better he is at being an Airedale, the more you are likely to suppose that he is in fact a breed of dog, for the better he is at imitating dogs. Wolves too, and coyotes and kittens, if it comes up. If there are no dogs around to imitate, then he will just imitate your best idea of a dog, which is why so many people think Airedales are the best dogs, as did the poet and critic Yvor Winters. But Best Dog is just one of his gigs. He rarely imitates your worst ideas, of dogs or anything else, but may be forced to if nothing of sufficient interest presents itself.

I have a young Airedale named Drummer who has so far shown me that he can be as stalwart as a bulldog, as stick-happy as a Labrador, as quick and deceptive as a wolf, depending on who has come to call. When our cat had kittens and we were admiring how she would lick them and carry them about, Drummer noted our admiration and took to licking kittens and carrying them about, to Cricket's astonishment. When the kittens got old enough to sit up on their hind legs and bat at fingers or balls of paper, Drummer did that too, all seventy-four pounds of him, thus incautiously revealing to me that he had been disingenuous earlier when he claimed that he wasn't built properly for sitting up on his hind legs on command—though come to think of it, he may not have been truly *lying*, since that afternoon he was imitating a German Shepherd who was over for tea. The Shepherd was full of civic duty and nobility, so Drummer was too, but this particular Shepherd was rather wobbly in stifle and hock, so perhaps at the time Drummer wasn't built properly in the hind end to sit up on command.

Since it is generally the play behavior of a dog Drummer imitates, he had a rough time with one Border Collie, a houseguest, who had no play behavior, only the habit, when I was trying to write, of drumming his fingers, pacing, looking at his watch, glaring in disapproval, and staring at the wall. That dog could also herd sheep, but there weren't any sheep in the study. Finally Drummer also lay down and stared away from me, toward the wall, glancing a few times at his watch, but this was hard on him, and he never managed the disapproval part.

Years ago I had in training a comely, flirtatious young Samoyed bitch who loved to warble at you, and she had a clear, sweet way of warbling that charmed everyone, so there was nothing for it but that my old Airedale Gunner should warble also, exactly as the little

Samoyed did, only three registers down and rather gruff. If there is a Poodle around, the Airedale, if well bred, will imitate the Poodle, and since Poodles are almost human, you might get the idea that Airedales are almost human, but they aren't any more human than they are canine.

The Airedale does have his own qualities, unique to him, which he cannot altogether overcome; he must take his place among us in some form or another, and a handsome form it is. Also a cheerful one, which gives him problems with some of his imitations. The prospect of a fight buoys him up rather than angers him, so he has trouble producing a proper imitation of rage (though he fights just as well as if he really were angry). And there is that distinctive prance-dance of his, so some of his imitations of Irish Wolfhounds and the rest of that grand and high-principled lot don't always come off. He is a bit too tall and too straight in his stance to be fully convincing to the stock-dog fancier when he herds, and even the mildest, most courteous and liquid of Airedale eyes, if they don't always have a gleam of mischief in them, tend to look as though they might at any moment, which rather spoils some of his foxhound and coonhound numbers. Also, as I learned while training a Yorkie for a lady, Airedales, even the tidier individuals, are simply too large and rough-boned to draw forth the proper response when they do Lap Dog, and they are not sleek enough or well enough arched over the loins to produce a compelling Whippet or Greyhound.

What does all this playacting accomplish? It brings out confidence in people. They will tell an Airedale almost anything. So is he a con man? Confidence dog? Well, no. You see, it is not that the Airedale is *disguised* as this or that, for he is an honest creature, as honest as the day is long, and it is not his fault that his honest imitations have caused so many to succumb to the idea that this is an instance of *Canis familiaris.* If you doubt me, just ask yourself whether you have ever actually mistaken an Airedale for a Chesapeake Bay Retriever while you were out duck hunting. Well, you haven't, because honesty is the Airedale's middle name; there is nothing spurious about him, only some peculiarities.

They say in the breed books that he is the King of the Terriers, and his full name as inscribed in celestial marble is Airedale (Honest to God) Terrier. I have met many a dog man who complained about the American Kennel Club's classifications—that Dachshunds are properly terriers, not hounds, that Schnauzers are or are not true terriers, I forget which, or else that they are true working-group dogs, that the Nordics belong somewhere apart from the stock dogs, that a Pointer belongs with the hounds—but for all that an Airedale is far too large to go to ground, *à terre,* after anything but a bear or a purse snatcher fleeing into a subway entrance, I have never heard anyone suggest that Airedales be denied their place with the Border Terriers, Scotties, Westies, Cairns, and the like. So they imitate terriers fairly well.

Airedales are a late product, appearing well after the period when the purebred dog was invented, which was the middle decade or so of the nineteenth century. (There were pedigrees before that, family histories for dogs, but there were no purebred Shelties, say, any more than there were purebred raccoons.) But now there *are* purebred dogs in the world—this is a real thing, a *Ding an sich,* just as words and paintings, once produced, are *of themselves* and not of us. Just as in fact the world, once we have made it up, goes its own way, as though composed, as the philosopher has it that God is, of everything we are not. I began by proposing that it be doubted that Airedales are dogs, because I meant to draw attention to the fact that dogs come into things long before writing does, and Airedales came in, not only long after writing itself, but even after dogs were written down in the Kennel Club Stud Book, so they are whelped by wholly literary energies.

Imitations of nature, that is, and such glamorous imitations! Sir Philip Sidney says that the dog trainer, unlike the animal psychologist or the sociologist, presents us with a Golden World, in which things are seen in their true forms, and Airedales, though not perhaps dogs themselves, do something like this too. They are a kind of second inheritance of dogs, as Thoreau said poems are a second inheritance of language. It's not such a bad thing, a second inheritance, especially if the first was entailed. There are things poems can do that speech cannot do, and there are things Airedales can do that dogs cannot do. No dog can clown at ten o'clock, fight a bear at eleven, melt the heart of a stern old lady at noon, herd sheep at one, drive to the city to sniff bombs at two, bring in the cows at five, and change into black tie in time to greet the chancellor at eight—no dog can do all that, but an

Airedale can, for it is his job to present to us as it evolves, spiraling beyond us, each instance of dog in crystal. Not to present it in its best form in *this* world—it is the Bloodhound's job to be the best instance we can know of Bloodhound—but to present each type in close approximation to certain regions of that excellently opportunistic Idea that dogs are reflections of.

And to clown about, therefore, for such a solemn duty must be taken up lightly. If the jester is a serious figure in tragedy, he is even more so in comedy.

The Airedale's Criminal Past

*I*n Germany the Airedale has been an important dog, and one maven of the breed, Christa von Bardelben, opens her book as follows.

> Who knows the war dog? Who knows how an oil dog looks? Now, behind these two designations the Airedale Terrier hides. "War dog" is what many of our fellow citizens still call him, because he proved himself as a messenger and sanitary dog in the different regions where war took place. "Oil dog" is meant to be a joke, because in German the English name of the breed sounds very much like *Erdoel* [*Erd,* "earth"; *Oel,* "oil"].

Behind these two and many other designations the Airedale hides. Dr. Bardelben goes on with talk of the nimble, fearless, loyal, and of course—of course!—versatile Airedale, but what of the truth? What is hiding behind the sundry designations beyond what I have already told you?

The Airedale's most devoted enthusiasts will often say odd things, things you might think would warn you off the breed, and maybe they should. Meiner, for instance, in his 1978 book on Schutzhund, says, "The way to train an Airedale will train scarcely any other dog, and the way to spoil him will spoil scarcely any other dog."

The Airedale—I don't want to dismay anyone, but Truth harasses me this morning—the Airedale is a varmint dog, with a solid fighting history to boot. A. F. Hochwalt, writing in 1928, barely controls his indignation when he refutes the nineteenth-century "authority" Stonehenge, who started a ruckus by saying that Airedales weren't truly game in the pit. In the late 1920s Mr. Brandon, an authority on fighting dogs, asserted that Airedales could hold their own in the pit, and I have known some admirers of fighting dogs who say that the Airedale is about the only dog who has serious staying power besides the pit bull. Others deny this. I have never tested the proposition that the Airedale can stay the rounds in the pit, and never will, but I recall an Airedale I used to have who would sometimes get into unscheduled fights around the house, and who on one memorable occasion was undistracted by some astonishingly creative efforts on the part of six humans to stop combat that could have been mortal for both dogs. He was missing a bit of ear after that one, and the old vet I brought him to, now of sainted memory, regarded him with admiration as I recounted the details. Your younger, improved and reconstructed sort of veterinarian frowns on fighting dogs and in many cases in my ken recommends that they be put down, but there was a time when even respectable middle-class ladies and gentlemen could regard a dog who had shown some gameness fondly, even while frantically thinking of ways to bring the fighting to a halt.

Ah, the Airedale is a respectable dog, and many, I suspect, will consider me at best tasteless and ignorant when I bring up this matter of his fighting history. But if the Airedale wasn't originally regarded as a game dog, one who wouldn't quit on you, one who could survive mortal combat, why does the breed standard require that this dog, like the bull terrier, be virtually without a stop (the indentation between muzzle and forehead) in front of the eyes, and have plenty of bony fill in the front of the skull, its only purpose to protect the eyes in combat and to give good backup to those nice Airedale teeth in case there is need for a hard bite?

To this day otherwise gentle folk brag about the Airedale's fighting prowess, people like my friend in Oxford, Mississippi, who insists that it is an assault on the dignity of man to set dogs on him but writes in his column in *Full Cry,* "I think you would have to keep big attackers away from an Airedale pup until he was close to a year old. After that, I don't think you would have to worry much except for questions of vet bills (I pay my own no matter who started it)."

Everyone is always quick to say that *their* Airedale never starts a fight, only finishes it, which is what James Thurber said about his pit bull Rex. No matter what the breed, the tales of fighting prowess you

hear in genteel circles are nearly always accompanied by tales of forbearance and restraint. (These tales of restraint are often true, by the
way, but they are not always nobly occasioned.) And the good Dr.
Bardelben, aware of the Airedale's pit history, defends him by saying
he wasn't all that good in the pit: "At the time of his development dog-
fights were popular, and he was blamed for not always having an
aligned character at the battle, and even today if someone looks for a
'sharp' dog, he will not be on good terms with the Airedale." She is
writing fairly recently, of course; when Hochwalt wrote, people were a
little more relaxed about these things. Is she right about the Airedale?

Well, yes and no. There are plenty of sharp dogs in any breed,
dogs who are quick to jump other dogs, but this is a wholly different
matter from the gameness that is expressed in such praises as "He
never started a fight and never ran away from one." Of course, I have
encountered some show-bred Airedales who would thoughtlessly and
without any reason jump another dog, but a well-bred Airedale does
not engage in combat for no good reason, any more than a sane and
sober boxing champ does.

I could tell you some stories about Airedales who knew the holy
Law of the Jaw (never let go), and I could also tell you that the best
and holiest fighting dogs are not sharp at all. But let us go on with the
truth of the matter. It is quite true that an Airedale has to have
become pretty fight-crazy actually to jump another dog, and even an
Airedale of mine who had been rolled behind my back, and was pretty
fight-crazy for a while, was not that hard to control and would work
peacefully beside his worst enemy if work there was to be done. However, this does not tell you so much about the forbearance of the
Airedale as it does about his—or her—rhetorical style. For what an
Airedale does is tangle and disturb the peace of mind of another dog,
sometimes just by the way the Airedale sits there panting and grinning
maniacally, often by indescribable indescribables in the way the eyes
roll about, sending off sparks.

For example, I took Drummer, at ten weeks, to a sheep farm in
Virginia, where there were thirty or forty perfectly well-behaved Border Collies. These days an Airedale is something of an affront on a
sheep farm, even though Airedales have been used in the United
States and Ireland and possibly England to keep varmints out of crops
and predators away from stock. (They quite easily and happily learn

that the sheep or the goats or the placid Jerseys are to be protected, not worried.) But many modern Border Collies, especially those who live within commuting distance of Washington, D.C., have had deficient educations and do not know this, and so do not accept the Airedale for the useful varmint dog he is.

I am a finicky obedience trainer, and Drummer took naturally to that whole business, so he was sitting, apparently quietly, at my feet. But he was sending out brain waves. Cocking an ear in an odd way when he caught one dog's eye. Doing funny things with his nose as he stared at another. Not practicing custody of the eyes or the wit. From time to time one of those thrifty Scot Border Collie souls couldn't take it anymore and would snarl and snap or try to jump Drummer. Drummer would giggle happily and look innocent, and the Border Collie's owner would correct the poor Border Collie, who had been driven to distraction by this unseemly presence, and then the owner would apologize abjectly to me, saying, "I don't know what came over her—and your dog is *so* well behaved!"

Drummer was able to excite the minds of some fairly sophisticated Border Collies—at the age of ten weeks.

This is not random maliciousness, at least not in a well-bred individual. First of all, there is no malice in an Airedale, or shouldn't be. Also, an Airedale distinguishes between a sporting situation and one in which lives or principles are at stake, and if the Airedale sometimes perceives as sport a situation we take to be somber, or a situation a Border Collie takes to be somber, we should just recall that it takes all kinds to make a world. Moreover, it is this tendency good-naturedly to tease an opponent that makes the Airedale a dog that can successfully be used on coyotes, as was done in Texas, when a few dogs were apparently brought to the oil camps just after World War II. Coyotes are sneaky—and malicious. In the inland desert areas of southern California you wanted to watch your dog, because one coyote would come and tease and lure the dog away, and then others would jump the dog and finish him off. There is a reason Coyote is the Trickster God of the Indian tales of the Southwest.

That sort of stuff doesn't work as well on Airedales. There are some that are overconfident and get themselves in trouble—only benighted souls like Stonehenge, who is the author of many, many dubious remarks and seems to have gleaned a great deal of his knowl-

edge from *Punch* and the *London Times* letters page, have ever supposed the Airedale wanting in courage—but upon being challenged,
the Airedale will usually respond instinctively by sizing up the opponent, studying his footwork, and his witwork as well, to see what he is
dealing with, being something of an intellectual fighter, a connoisseur
of the game more than a visionary.

Now is perhaps the time for me to say something that will be con-
troversial in certain dog circles, and I hate to say it, but I would hate
even more for an innocent reader of this book to suppose that you can
have a dog as wonderfully and gently maddening as Drummer just by
buying any old Airedale. Also, if you buy an Airedale and "give him his
freedom," you are likely to end up with a dog who roams the neighborhood committing various felonies and misdemeanors, because an
Airedale will find something to do whether or not you educate him in
socially redeeming ways of using his talents. Airedales are rambunctious, and powerful for their size. In police and war work, a well-built
sixty- or sixty-five-pound Airedale can do the same job an eighty-five-
pound Shepherd can do, so this dog is not a joke, no matter how
charming he looks.

At one Schutzhund seminar, I met a man who was a "decoy." That
is, in trials and in practice, he was the one who "agitated" the dogs and
"took the bites" on a padded sleeve. Some persons present were scoff-
ing at my young Airedale, in part because he was very contained and
cautious and well behaved. There they were, strutting around with
their Shepherds and Dobies and Rotties and Belgian Malinois, most
of whom, I am sorry to report, had only hazy concepts of obedience,
though most were quite noble. So to console me the decoy came up
and said, "This is not something I would tell everyone, but I'll tell you
that the only time I was ever genuinely afraid in a trial was when I was
up against an Airedale." And indeed, I recall from my early days in
Texas hearing that the pit bull men were reluctant to match their dogs
against an Airedale because the Airedale would win—but only
because of a size advantage, the pit bull men would quickly add.

If you do right by them and if they are well bred, Airedales are
among the most trustworthy of breeds. Not above making a fool of
you, of course, but that's how so many of them express their affection.
I recall an Airedale named Wimsey, who was heeling along beside her
handler very nicely in an obedience trial, except that every two or

three strides she bounced up and grabbed a glove or a wallet from his jacket pocket. Without losing cadence, of course—these dogs are not petty criminals, they have standards. I had an Airedale I could not teach to pick pockets because he wasn't a thief, so maybe Wimsey would only pick her owner's pockets. She always returned the items.

Airedales are true varmint dogs, and do as well with the two-legged varmints as with lions and bears and such. But they aren't useful if you want a randomly vicious dog. They know far too much about reality for that, and many of them are actually hard to agitate, lacking the suspiciousness of some other breeds. Of course, there exist unreliable, crazy Airedales. You can hear the screws rattling when they walk. They look good, and they have properly set ears and refined heads and level top lines and cheerfully set tails, but they are subject to nightmares, or should I say daymares? In the case of males, neutering does not help and can even make matters worse, since at the heart of what looks like macho meanness is in fact fear—just as in the case of certain politicians. James Thurber's bad-dog story, "Muggs, the Dog Who Bit People," is about an Airedale, and Thurber was not the only one with doubts about the breed. There used to be an expression you don't hear anymore: "Don't be an Airedale." I have discussed with assorted old-timers what this means and have heard many interesting speculations, none of them especially flattering. "Don't be a giggle-head," for instance.

Some twenty years ago I became curious about why the breed history of the Airedale, which used to be called "the Rolls-Royce Dog," is so funny and vague. Then I began speculating about what you might do if the RSPCA or whatever was having one of its periodic fits about vicious dogs and you were devoted to a breed being attacked as vicious, and it came to me. Say you owned bulldogs in the 1830s, when they were taking such a bad rap and constables were clubbing them; you would either breed small and harmless-looking or cross your bulldog (i.e., pit bull) with something rough-coated, so as to produce an agreeably fluffy version that the constables would leave alone.

For a while this was just a notion I had, and then a few weeks back a man who has Jack Russells called me from Scotland, so I put my notion to him and he said it was true and that he had documents to prove it. He added that there is also more Greyhound in the

Airedale than some fanciers want to admit—possibly, I thought, because Greyhound crosses of one sort and another have made such excellent poachers' dogs.

So what an Airedale is, it appears, is a curly-coated underground pit bull who has learned caution, for as Dr. Bardelben says, poaching requires prudence, circumspection, and flexibility, not daredevil antics. Which means that it should be illegal now in Germany to train an Airedale for Schutzhund—literally, "protection dog"—except that Airedales in Germany are one of the seven or eight Noble Breeds, which is at the moment my impudent translation of *Gebrauchshunderassen*. In Germany dogs considered to be fighting dogs are barred from Schutzhund, and dogs of all breeds but the Noble Breeds must first pass a special test, a *Begleithundeprüfung*, to prove themselves "traffic-sound" (reliable in public, around automobiles and pedestrians) before being declared suitable for Schutzhund.

Gebrauchshunderassen can be translated literally as "useful or efficient breeds of dog," not unlike the word "collie," according to some overenthusiastic modern fanciers who claim it originally meant "useful." In Gaelic, of course, so who's to know? The *Oxford English Dictionary* says only that "collie" meant "black," and also cites an instance from Chaucer's "Nun's Priest's Tale" of a dog named Colle. That collies, at least Border Collies, are noble dogs no one has any doubt; I've never heard anyone suggest that a Border Collie be required to pass a test of manners, though the time may come.

It is kennel clubs that decide which dogs are noble enough for Schutzhund and which are so ignoble as to be beyond the pale even if proven traffic-sound. Kennel clubs rather than governments, but their regulations have the force of law, or even something more powerful than law. There are many human and canine tragedies behind the human idiocies that promote such regulations, but I nonetheless find myself forgetting tragedy and feeling only pleasure at the idea of the Airedale, which is not even a German breed, achieving the status of racially pure and noble dog despite his dubious past, flashing his whiskers and prancing at everyone, escaping all the blame.

I would like to know the details of how this came about—how such a scamp achieved so much respectability in a nation that so cherishes respectability, and did it in a century in which his home country, Great Britain, was the enemy of Germany in two major wars. The

German Shepherd did not manage this; there are still a few American laws on the books declaring German Shepherds *prima facie* vicious, despite the accomplishments of Rin Tin Tin, and in England German Shepherds are called "Alsatians" so that admirers of the breed don't have to think too hard about the fact that they were bred by the enemy.

The Airedale is also one of the very few breeds to have survived the class wars of the last century or so, and it gives me a great deal of unworthy satisfaction to think of those old photographs of the impish face of the poacher's dog in the backseat of a chauffeur-driven Rolls. Just as it pleases me every time I hear, as I do frequently, remarks about how saintly a character Drummer is now, at two and a half years. His obedience is gorgeous, and he uses it to shame lesser dogs, working better and more accurately when there are other dogs around than when we are alone, so as to cause their owners to regard them with dismay and him with admiration. And: he has plenty of good bony fill and fighting spirit. And: he is of imported stock. Specifically, stock imported from Germany. And as the good Dr. Bardelben notes, "Never can a fashion [or a war] deprive the Airedale of his [position] as the King of the Terriers."

Whether or not I ever manage to settle these questions about breed history, one thing is clear: The Airedale is the product of poetic, which is to say criminal, genius, and that's why he is so divinely versatile.

"Oyez à Beaumont"

A student of mine called two days ago and asked, "What do the experts do when their dogs die?"

He developed a calcium deposit on his upper spine, did my good Airedale Gunner, and it would hurt him to track, so Gunner and I stopped tracking, stopped retrieving and jumping, not because he wouldn't have gone on if it were up to him. And a while after, he was very ill with cancer, and after a time of that, too much of that, I had him killed. Gallant Gunner, brave Gunner, gay Gunner. Once, late one evening on a beach in Malibu, he took down a man who was attacking me with a knife. The vet had to patch Gunner up some, but he didn't turn tail the way my assailant did. Brave Gunner. Hearken to Gunner. Twenty-four hours later, bandaged, he clowned and told jokes for the kids at Juvenile Hall, performing for the annual Orange Empire Dog Club Christmas party. O rare and dauntless Gunner. Even his hip, broken when a prostate tumor grew right through the bone, did not stop the courage of his gaiety, but I did. My friend Dick Koehler said, "He is lucky to have a good friend like you," to encourage me, you see, to get on with it, kill him, and Dick was right, of course, right, because when there is nothing much left of a dog but his wounds you should bury those decently.

Until he died, he was immortal, and the death of an immortal is an event that changes the world. That is all for now about Gunner, because what it does to you when such a dog dies is not fit to print.

"Der Tod ist gross," writes Rilke. "Death is huge." But various psychologists deny that it is as huge as all that when it is an animal who is mourned. I have read statistically studded reassurances that mourning for a cat lasts at most one month, for a dog three. I have read that when an animal dies there are no regrets, no rehearsal of the wail "If only I had . . . ," and also that the splendid thing about animals, what is said to make them so convenient to our hearts, like antidepressants, is that when we mourn them we are only mourning a personal loss and not "the loss of life and potential," according to *Between Pets and People* by Professors Beck and Katcher, authorities on all of this at the University of Pennsylvania.

That is the way psychological authorities talk—"Eventually an animal can be replaced," they write in their books—but that is not how the experts talk. I realize that psychologists and suchlike are generally understood to be experts, but I have met none who were experts in the various ways my good Gunner's work with scent developed, especially when he started scenting out the human heart. Of course, I am just a dog trainer. My thinking, such as it is, I learned from the animals, for whom happiness is usually a matter of getting the job done. Clear that fence, fetch in those sheep, move those calves, win that race, find that guy, retrieve that bird. The happiness of animals is also ideologically unsound, as often as not, or at least it is frequently wanting in propriety, as when your dog rolls in something awful on his afternoon walk or your cat turns off your answering machine.

In over a quarter of a century of training I have never met an animal who turned out to be replaceable. Dick Koehler says, "Hell, even trees are irreplaceable, but we don't know it, and *that* is our loss." The loss the dog trainer has in mind is the loss of eternity, for as Wittgenstein put it, "Denn lebt er ewig, der in der Gegenwart lebt." "So he lives forever, who lives in the present," wrote the philosopher, and this is how the animals live, in the present, which is why the experts' difficult and apparently harsh advice, advice they occasionally take themselves, is: "Another dog, same breed, as soon as possible." Not because another dog of the same breed will be the same, but because that way you can pick up somewhere near where you left off, say that you have it in you.

In a children's book called *Algonquin: The Story of a Great Dog*, there is a quarrel between two brothers, old men they are, grandfather and great-uncle to the boy who tells the story. Grandsir is angry because Uncle Ovid is going to take on the training of the boy's grand young Pointer, Algonquin; he is angry because he wants no more of the "grief and the rage and the ashes." He shouts at his brother, "Do you know what it does to you? Do you know what it does every time one of them dies?" But Uncle Ovid just says, "Don't tell me. I am an old man and it would not be good for me to know," and he trains that Pointer, who turns out to be something else again at the field trials. Their friend Mr. Washington says, "I think sometimes that he would pity his bracemates, were he not enough of a gentleman to know that they would rather die than be pitied." Algonquin wins and wins and wins, and then he starts to get a lung disease and can't work well, is distressed therefore, because he is losing his work, his happiness, and Uncle Ovid sends him out on his last run and shoots him while he is on point, while there is still something more to him than his wounds.

At the end of the story, when Grandsir suggests that it is time for the boy who has been witness to all this to get another dog, the boy asks, "Irish Setters don't win field trials, do they? I mean, you are not in much danger of getting a great dog?" Grandsir purses his lips and agrees: "Not much." The boy says, "Then an Irish Setter would be nice."

There exist mighty dogs, the dangerous kind who take hold of your heart and do not let go. But avoiding the great ones does not get you out of it. If, like the boy in *Algonquin,* you already know what a great dog is, then the knowledge marks you. If you do not know, then you are still in danger, for if you give her a civilized upbringing, every collie is Lassie *in propria persona,* killing that snake in your heart, driving off the cougar that lurks there, sending for help. This is not because all dogs are great dogs but rather because all dogs are both irreplaceable and immortal and as Rilke says, "Der Tod ist gross."

One day I talked about death with my friend—my teacher and friend, for these are synonyms in the trainer's world—Dick Koehler. I told him about the results obtained at the University of Pennsylvania. "Dick! The news is out! There are no regrets when a dog dies."

Dick said, "Oh, then my several thousand students who tell me, 'If only I had done what you said, Mr. Koehler,' or 'If only I had worked with her more'—they're all hallucinating, right?"

"Must be," I replied, "for it says here that dogs are replaceable and grief for them lasts no more than three months," and right before my eyes Dick Koehler started looking a little funny; he startled me. He was thinking of Duke, dead many years. Hallucinating that Duke had been irreplaceable. Duke was a Great Dane, one of your great dogs, too. Duke was a movie dog; some of you may remember him from *The Swiss Family Robinson.*

"What was so irreplaceable about Duke?" I asked.

"Well, it's not every day you find a Great Dane who thinks a two-hundred-fifty-five-pound tiger is a kittycat. Not every day you find a Great Dane who will hit a sleeve and go through a second-story window, not just once, not just twice, but seven times, and it was as good the last time as the first time."

Soon after Duke died, there was Topper, of *The Ugly Dachshund* and various TV series. "Topper paid the rent for about three years there," said Dick. "I mean, he did all the work on that series." Topper died like this: The great dog and his son were playing, horsing around after a day's work, and his son slammed into him and ruptured his spleen, and Dick realized it too late for the vet to fix things up, and so had him put down. That was over two decades ago, Dick's most recent Great Dane.

Dick talks about Duke and Topper, and the thing starts to happen to me again, the merging of all the elegies, all the great dogs. "There is nothing left but his name . . . but there never was a dog like Algonquin," or "It's all regrets," or "After he got in his car and drove away I dug a grave and lined it with the bright fallen leaves and there I buried all that could die of my good Fox" (George and Helen Papashvily, *Thanks to Noah*), or "He was allus kind to the younguns and he kilt a rattlesnake onct" (Harriet Arnow, *Hunter's Horn*), or one of my favorites, the passage in T. H. White's *The Sword in the Stone.* The great hound (lymer) named Beaumont is on the ground, his back broken by the boar, and the expert, the master of hounds, William Twyti, has been hurt also. Twyti limps over to Beaumont and utters the eternal litany: "Hark to Beaumont. Softly, Beaumont, mon amy. Oyez à Beaumont the valiant. Swef, le douce Beaumont, swef, swef." He nods to Robin Wood and holds the hound's eyes with his own, saying, "Good dog, Beaumont the valiant, sleep now, old friend Beaumont, good old dog," while the huntsman kills the dog for him: "Then Robin's falchion let Beaumont out of this world, to run free with Orion and to roll among the stars."

What next, though? The narrator of *Algonquin* decides to go for an Irish Setter, but that is not what the experts say to do. They say, "Another dog, same breed, right away." It takes courage, courage that

Master Twyti seems to have had, for he rose from beside Beaumont's wounds and "whipped the hounds off the corpse of the boar as he was accustomed to do. He put his horn to his lips and blew the four long notes of the Mort without a quaver." He called the other hounds to him.

Another dog, same breed, right away. Or a pack of them, and not because there were any replacements for Beaumont in that pack. The other hounds were all right, but there were no Beaumonts among them, and there is no point in saying otherwise. I don't mean by that that there are not plenty of great dogs around. "There are a lot of them," says Dick. Yeah. They're a dime a dozen. So are great human hearts; that's not the point. We are by way of being connoisseurs of dogs, some of us, but one falls into that, and a dog is not a collector's item, not for Dick Koehler, anyhow, whom I have seen risk himself in more ways than one, over and over, day in and day out, ever since I met him when I was nineteen and he straightened out Stevie, a German Shepherd cross I had then, who was charging children but was a nice dog after we took care of that, who lived for twelve years after Dick showed me how to train him, who shook the ground just as hard as Beaumont did when he died. My teacher and friend Dick Koehler is a maniac for training dogs instead of killing them. Deaf dogs, three-legged dogs, dogs with chartreuse spots on their heads. He hasn't gotten around to getting another Dane, though there have been other dogs, of course. Of *course.*

But "Master William Twyti startled The Wart, for he seemed to be crying," and this book, *The Sword in the Stone,* is about the education of great hounds and of a great king, King Arthur in fact. Immortal Beaumont, douce, swef, swef. And immortal Arthur—douce, douce, hearken to Arthur, they would say in time about *rex quondam rexque futurus,* the once and future king. Which is to say, this is all of it about the education of any hound and any boy.

"But won't it hurt?" I am asked when I give that advice: Another dog, same breed, as soon as possible. "Won't it hurt?" Oh, it hurts, especially when, as is so often the case, you have a part in the dog's death. Perhaps because you were careless and he got run over, or because, like Master Twyti, you gave the nod to the vet or to the huntsman with his falchion.

There is the falchion, and then sometimes you must speak

abruptly into the face of grief, for grief gives bad advice. Grief will tell you to throw your heart into the grave with the dog's corpse, and this is ecologically unsound. The ants will take care of the corpse in a few weeks, but a discarded heart stinks for quite some time.

Two days ago that student of mine called, a woman in her late thirties. She had gotten a pup for her eight-year-old daughter, and at a few months of age the pup had died because left in her crate with her collar on; the collar got caught on the handle of the crate. "My daughter is so upset, my husband says it would be too bad to get another dog and have something else happen. What do the experts do?"

I said in tones of vibrant command, "Another dog, same breed, right away." Nothing else, for wordiness is not in order when you are discussing, as we so often are, the education of a queen.

A decade went by between the death of Gunner and the purchase of the new Airedale pup. That was as soon as I could get to it, what with one thing and another.

The Thoroughbred Mutt

I was in a gentle state. I mean a gentle state of the Union, one of those south of the Mason-Dixon line, where when you cross the border you are not greeted by those harsh Yankee signs that announce all the things the police and the governor will do to you if you break their laws.

I was on a hill, a hill leading down into a valley, and on the hill was the barn I was in, a barn built to gentle specifications. There was grass, allotted by God and not Man for the hooves of horses. In this state many are privileged to have intimate and daily exchanges with the great, to participate in that conversation, for greatness here is the Thoroughbred. There must be some lowering of the human in the presence of the Thoroughbred, for her hooves must be cleaned daily, trimmed every four to eight weeks, shod, and everyone bends to that task, some more often than others.

In this state I am more often to be found chatting with the grooms than in the dining room up at the big house, and there I was in the breezy, sweet-scented barn at the end of the day. In a tack room, actually. The horses were fed and bedded, and none needed our attention through that long night, not so long as an undergraduate's night, but long enough for people who have to awaken and take care of the horses.

Boozy, too. Not all that boozy by city standards, but boozy enough for that place, there by *those* standards, the ones that held the poles aloft for the horses who were jumpers rather than runners. There are ashtrays in those tack rooms, some of them, for even though horses are much offended by foul odors, as Sir Philip Sidney's friend Gervase Markham averred, in an airy and well-tended barn the smoke is a slight matter and wafts away before anyone can ask what it is, and the horses do not mind.

We were talking about dogs. There were five of us, we were fairly new friends, and it had been a long day with the horses, and now we were in the spring evening in the tack room, so there was little that could be done to improve the occasion. We all had houses and could have gone to one of them, and as we were all middle-aged and better that would have been what we ordinarily did, except that it had been a long day of work but no trouble—and improvement, too, in the manners of the young colt I had taken in hand that afternoon, a nice big bay. Presenting complaint: Strikes and bites the handler. Dangerous. At one o'clock I presented certain considerations to his conscious mind, and by two-thirty, being a feisty and well bred and very fine colt and therefore not in possession of an unconscious mind, he was saying, "Well, why didn't someone just explain it? I can do that," and was standing by nobly and courteously as though bred to it, which he was.

No rough stuff had gone by while we worked with the colt, so it was an airy, easy, young evening and none of us remembered that we had houses to go to, just lingered in the tack room with sandwiches and bourbon as though we were all twenty years younger and had no better sense than to picnic in the barn.

As I say, we were talking about dogs and not horses for a while, for one of the grooms—his name was Francis, and his good wife's name was Judy—was from the Tensas Swamp in Louisiana. We spoke of yellow hounds—what I always called them in Louisiana, though they may have a fancier name—and what one of those hounds could do to addle and shred the mind of an old boar hog. I let drop that I was about to have an Airedale pup shipped in, and Francis said, "Do tell me, have you anytime recently, in the last hundred or so years I mean, seen a *real* Airedale?"

I knew what he meant, not only about Airedales but also about the last hundred or so years, during which we had all grown up to be city slickers, reenacting the Fall. I looked at him over my glasses and said, "Well, this pup has twenty generations of police and search-and-rescue dogs behind him."

"If that's so, I guess your pup could fight a bear if he had to. Whereabouts did you find real Airedales?" Francis asked. I said in Saginaw, Michigan, and he said, "Can you beat that? Michigan!" For

Michigan begins where Eden leaves off, a bit south of Indianapolis, some say. Others say no, Eden, well, Eden quits a few miles north of Baton Rouge.

It was Yankees that ruined Airedales, but we didn't have to say that, knowing well enough without discussion what them Free Staters would gladly do to us and our pups with a bulldozer, given half a chance. I had bull pups, too, pit bulldogs, as one learned to say for the edification of Northerners, so we didn't need to discuss who was going to kill us and who wasn't, so all Francis said was, "Well, Michigan. Can you beat that?"

Francis was, by his own account, a hell of a sheepdog trainer. The only dog he couldn't get to come when called, he said—he wouldn't lie to me about it—that one was truly part timber wolf, and he said that you learned things about breeding if you actually tried to do it with *working* animals; you gotta know your anatomy and your background on that animal, gotta know it all the while knowing that the study of anatomy will make a fool of you, just like any other study will, and the study of pedigree is no exception. Then he asked if I would like to hear a story about pedigree.

Of course I would.

We were stepping here without hesitation into the realm of the sacred. Unlike the realm of human genealogy, the realm of pedigree is the realm of the sacred, not only because, to paraphrase Donald McCaig, no nobleman has ever been as carefully bred as some horses are, but also because a pedigree is a spiritual as much as a biological record, or even more so, a record of moments of genius in some cases. A great breeder is possessed the way a great artist is. But Francis and I figured we could step into that realm as safely as ever happens, having given each other exquisite backup with the bay colt that afternoon, not even having to slew our eyes around to each other to know what to do next to get the colt and his somewhat amateurish owner safely together in the same universe, without the owner's head bashed in. When you find backup like that you don't mind going through the unreliable door at the back of the cupboard again, as you used to do as a child, though perhaps with less understanding than when you do it at forty-four.

Less understanding, and more.

A scholar, according to a book I read recently about Saint Thomas

Aquinas, is someone who knows more than you and I do but isn't always certain why he wants to. (It was a Catholic book, but that may not be the only reason to assign the masculine gender to scholarship as here conceived.) Farriers and grooms are people who know more than you and I do, and know why they want to know, and when this kind of knowledge is combined with the genuine scholarship that a knowledge of pedigree constitutes, a story about it can seem both as soft and as authoritative as an evening breeze on the throat after a day of good work with a young colt.

Francis's story was that Secretariat was a mutt—no big secret, anyone could see it in Bold Ruler's having thrown only that one red colt, but it is a big secret nonetheless, because people could have been hurt, just like in the CIA, knowing about it. (Or maybe not *just* like in the CIA, but there is a lot of money in Thoroughbred racing.) It seems that they had been using a pretty much no-account Trakhener to tease Secretariat's mom, and she really went for him, so he didn't just tease her, he bred her, got in there where Bold Ruler didn't, and that muttly colt as we know made all kinds of history that he couldn't have made had his true ancestry been known, because he wouldn't have been a Thoroughbred and couldn't have run in the Triple Crown.

But I can't tell you this story, for it is too true for print, too subtle for the Jockey Club, too significant for anything but allegory, the allegory of truth in the tack room. People would get hurt if I told this story, even though the roses that graced Secretariat's neck are dust, and so is he, and so will all of us be, one way or another, whether we lie or not, not that I am saying that Secretariat's races were lies.

It is better that he be understood to have been a Thoroughbred, Bold Ruler's colt, for people would not have known what they were looking at on their televisions when the jockey stood up and rode the end of the Belmont Stakes looking back wondering where the pack was. Most people cannot understand who Secretariat was unless they know that he was a Thoroughbred, and the idea that he was a mutt would interfere with the understanding that he was a Thoroughbred, which he was, and I learned all this quite suddenly while breathing that slow, soft air, this truth that would be bitter if I let it out, bitter and uncomfortable, but bitter only if true, if I had not made it all up except for the gentleness.

Or else: It is a kind of truth, but a fleeting one, as fleeting as a colt's awkward adolescence and as uneasily the progenitor of the deepest understanding of the Thoroughbred as a colt's carelessness on excessively hoofy legs is the progenitor of that colt's greatness. Secretariat, mutt or not, was not the guise of an old verity, but *veritas* in person, the truth of the dream of the Thoroughbred.

In any case, listen: If the nameless warmblood had been bred to Secretariat's mom on purpose, it would have been one of those visionary breedings I used to hear some Thoroughbred people call a "nick," the deliberate crossing of two unrelated bloodlines. Only a genius, a visionary, in some of the nobler traditions of chatter about breeding, can get away with this; it's unusual, but not, in the strange world of the Thoroughbred, irregular—what could be irregular in that noble world? There is a tale about the breeding of Eclipse, said by some to have been the greatest racehorse of all time. Unlike Secretariat, Eclipse was prepotent—able to pass on his qualities and abilities to his offspring—but the story of his breeding is entangled with the myths of the Irishman O'Kelly, who was given in his youth to playing "heaven a' harse" in the moonlight, an activity that involved making love while galloping bareback and great faith in one's mount.

In the version of the story I like, O'Kelly was on the lam in England, where he had gone to find the perfect sire and the perfect dam to breed the perfect "harse." Hiding from his English pursuers in a dark stall, he automatically began running his hands over the horse next to him, feeling her lines, and realized that he had found her, the perfect dam, Spileta was her name. In the course of many lies and much intrigue and bloodshed and genius, the breeding was accomplished, and there was a great match race, with the crossbred mutt of an Irishman trembling in his hot, resentful boots for fear he should be made fun of, and Eclipse crossed the line before anyone else entered the stretch, and the famous race result rang out: "Eclipse first, the rest nowhere." And there is the rest of this business—the purest blood, the knowledge of the purest blood, in the hands and hearts of the most crossbred, unsanctioned people, as an old dogfighter told me was almost always the case, except for brief periods when history hiccups. So don't tell me Secretariat wasn't a Thoroughbred, no.

The truth of the Thoroughbred can be as unaccustomed and uncomfortable as any truth, especially when he is doing a high-headed trot, which is why you do not pursue that truth but wait for it as you wait for spring or an answer to a letter, not looking too intently where you want to look, spending an aimless evening in a balmy structure, engaged in balmy gossip. For this, it helps if there is a valley to look out over, unsayable undulations in its rise to the farmhouse.

Beware of the Dog!

$\mathcal{D}$orothy Parker said of Thurber's animals that "it is best to say but little. . . . one goes all weak with sentiment." Dorothy Parker is not the only person to have said something foolish about Thurber, especially about his dogs, but she is perhaps the most interesting person to have done so. The source of her foolishness is, I think, like the sources of the stupidities of lesser commentators, to be found in a peculiarly American terror of being childish or sentimental. But the terror of sentimentality is no less an oppressive and truncating force than any other form of hatred or terror, and results in as much stupidity.

I find myself moved to write about two or three idiotic things that get said about Thurber largely because I keep having the feeling that the world is going to hell in a hand basket, and together with that, a feeling that we need a hero, a champion of the imagination, and at the moment Thurber's books are being reprinted at a satsifying rate, which makes him as good a candidate for champion as I know of. That other tall, thin, forbearing hero, Clint Eastwood, has descended, as American heroes tend to do, into self-parody, which may or may not be intended. Thurber's literary tradition is more or less identical with the tradition that gives us certain cowboy heroes as well as Dirty Harry, namely, the popular adventure story. That is the genre America misunderstood so badly when it elected Ronald Reagan president. (The trouble with Reagan is not, as they used to say in California when he was running for governor, that he is a cowboy. The trouble with Ronald Reagan is that he isn't a cowboy, is not capable of a sustained and intelligent affirmation of the sort we associate with cowboys and other American heroes.)

But Thurber was capable of making a life and an art out of the

American heroic tradition, and, astonishingly, of revising that tradition, long before Leslie Fiedler wrote *Love and Death in the American Novel,* to include women and dogs in it. In fact, I must digress from my main subject, which is Thurber's dogs, to say that Thurber is one of my feminist heroes. His men, unlike Travis McGee, do not get depressed when they discover that women are not necessarily eternally twenty-two years old, suntanned and sinewy and obedient. As Dorothy Parker pointed out, Thurber's men actually love his difficult, bitchy women, none of whom look like making it to the cover of *Cosmopolitan.* A great deal of his art is a celebration, in fact, of the contrary, difficult, stubborn, powerful possibilities of the female in Western tradition. His women, at their best, are virtually never in danger of succumbing to the Cinderella Complex, as recent popular psychology has it, and are not about to let their men settle comfortably into the Peter Pan Syndrome. And what he finds wrong with women and men as twentieth-century America presented them to him is so much like what Simone de Beauvoir found wrong with women and men as twentieth-century America and Europe presented them to her that I could almost suspect the two of them of conspiracy.

Thurber's "misogyny," like Beauvoir's assault on the myth of the gentle and obedient woman, a myth that has killed so many women, has its sources in a vision of human possibility more powerful than the pseudomythologies they both inherited. It took Thurber a while to parlay that knowledge into art, but the point is that he did manage it, as near as one can make out, actually managed grown-up human thought. The famous first-wife-on-the-bookcase cartoon is the product of a mind that knew as much as Tocqueville, Beauvoir, and Virginia Woolf ever did about the lethal forces hidden behind the sweet fairy tale of the tidy suburban marriage.

I will stay with this digression for a while. When I call Thurber a "feminist," I mean that his work comforts, stays, and succors me at moments when new versions of the ideally sweet, supportive, and harmless woman come my way unexpectedly and threaten my peace of mind. Observations such as the following are what I have in mind.

Women writers cooperate with and are grateful to the books of their predecessors. The masculine tradition of relationships among texts is that anxiously suspicious and competitive one so ably and anxiously

described by Harold Bloom; women, by contrast, support and nourish each other's writings. The male tradition of triumphant and antisocial excellence is alien to the feminine literary intelligence.

Although I opened this essay with an unkind and ungrateful remark
about Dorothy Parker, it now amuses me to imagine her response to the
suggestion that she should write cooperatively and gratefully, and for a
moment I wish I had her wittily dismissive gifts, for I find statements
such as the one I have quoted as alarming as I used to find the advice in
the books and magazines of my girlhood, advice that involved quilting,
baby-doll pajamas, and recipes for divinity fudge. My alarm didn't then
have anything to do with divinity fudge per se, it just had to do with my
interests happening to be elsewhere, and with a concomitant terror (I
was only fourteen) that I wasn't really feminine, that I was perhaps
phallic or something. (I also read advanced texts in psychology.) I am
not so terrified these days, thanks in part to Thurber, and also to the
confident impatience that comes with middle age, but I am still
unhealthily aggravated, still afflicted with the impulse to *argue* with certain writers. Fortunately I don't have to, since Thurber himself is to
hand, with his wonderfully combative, aggressive, competitive women. I
just reach onto my bookshelf and open *Thurber's Dogs* at random. I
find the piece "Canines in the Cellar," a tale about one of Thurber's role
models, his mother. The occasion is an impending visit from Aunt Mary,
whom our heroine, Mame Thurber, dislikes and does not nourish. Aunt
Mary in her turn hates the Thurber family's beloved dogs.

> . . . my mother had spent the afternoon gathering up all the dogs of
> the neighbourhood, in advance of Aunt Mary's appearance, and
> putting them in the cellar. I had been allowed to go with her on her
> wonderful forays, and I thought that we were going to keep all the
> sixteen dogs we rounded up. . . .
>
> The big moment finally arrived. My mother, full of smiles and
> insincerity, told Aunt Mary that it would relieve her of a tedious
> chore—and heaven knows, she added, there were a thousand steps
> to take in that old house—if the old lady would be good enough to
> set down a plate of dog food in the kitchen at the head of the cellar
> stairs and call Judge and Sampson to their supper. . . . when the
> door opened and they could see the light of freedom and smell the

odor of food, they gave tongue like a pack of hunting hounds. Aunt Mary got the door halfway open and the bodies of the largest dogs pushed it the rest of the way. There was a snarling, barking, yelping swirl of yellow and white, black and tan, gray and brindle as the dogs tumbled into the kitchen. . . .

When the last one had departed and the upset house had been put back in order, my father said to his wife, "Well, Mame, I hope you're satisfied." She was.

Now, that's a heroine! I identify with her, I emulate her, I want to live up to Mamie Thurber. And where would I be without her? Roughly where American women so often are—gloomily deciding yet once again that if women writers are nice, I must not be a woman, or a writer, or something. In a state of confusion, in short.

Mame's summoning of dogs in the battle against senselessness and oppression is a typical maneuver in Thurber, and one that ought to be taken seriously, as seriously as Thurber ought to be taken when he claims that nothing of any significance happened to him until he moved to Connecticut and began raising Scotties at the age of thirty-three. Sending a Scottie into action, or into the world, is no minor matter, not something to be taken up lightly. Here is the sort of thing Scotties are capable of.

When the colored maid stepped on my glasses the other morning, it was the first time they had been broken since the late Thomas A. Edison's seventy-ninth birthday.

I remember that day well, because I was working for a newspaper then and I had been assigned to go over to West Orange that morning and interview Mr. Edison. I got up early and, in reaching for my glasses under the bed (where I always put them), I found that one of my more sober and reflective Scotch terriers was quietly chewing them. Both tortoiseshell temples (the pieces that go over your ears) had been eaten and Jeannie was toying with the lenses in a sort of jaded way.

This is the opening of the famous piece "The Admiral on the Wheel." The demonic power Thurber is talking about here, in Jeannie, is impressive. Chewing up glasses is a formidable task for a dog, and I have never heard of any but the gamest of terriers taking it on. Lesser dogs go for slippers and books; Scotties, pit bulls, and others typically despise such easy game and go for glasses, can openers, the metal apparatus in your car that moves the seat back and forth, or the foundations of the house. And Jeannie, even more impressively, was accomplishing this quietly and without fanfare, "toying with the lenses in a sort of jaded way." And one must remember that Thurber had only one eye, the other having been destroyed in a boyhood archery accident, and that in the remaining eye he had two-fifths vision without his glasses. And he was an artist! I take leave from a great deal of Thurber that can't be quoted because of length to suppose that when he calls Jeannie "one of my more sober and reflective Scotch terriers," he is not intending the word "reflective" in some simplemindedly ironic fashion at all. This is one of the many places dogs in Thurber figure as emblems of the power of thought, both human and canine.

Dogs and reflectiveness are both to be respected in Thurber. The glasses incident appears again, in "In Defense of Dogs, Even, After a Fashion, Jeannie." He doesn't blame her for the act but says, "Under the bed is no place for glasses. If I had put them on the dresser, Jeannie would not have eaten them, mainly, of course, because she couldn't reach that high, but that is beside the point."

It is beside the point because this story is a parable about what it is to be serious about writing, a version of what you could call "the scene of writing." In this scene, you are blind because that which you have bred and authored and which you love has chewed up your glasses, and you go forth anyway, and you go forth without whining about it, which is exactly what Thurber seems to have done in life. Even in the hands of biographers who seem bent on playing various more or less pseudo-Freudian versions of the game Find the Writer's Blemishes, his gallantry comes through.

Thurber's biographers like to say astounding things such as that the loss of his eye in childhood was what accounted for his genius. For instance, according to Charles S. Holmes in *The Clocks of Columbus,* "The psychological impact of the injury was more significant than the physical. . . . In compensation he cultivated his already crowded fantasy life. . . . Some of the intense competitiveness which marked his character throughout his life obviously derived from this childhood injury and his natural desire to make up for it." Holmes is not the only one who talks this way, and it is a very strange way indeed to talk. It is not unusual, of course, being just a new version of the theory of the writer as human being *manqué*. Or, as in this case, the writer as baseball player *manqué*. I suppose that Thurber's brothers would also have been geniuses if only they had been in some way maimed early on. My suspicion is that if Thurber's eye troubles can be said to account for anything about his life and career, they probably account for the difficulty he had seeing, for his having submitted to five eye operations, and maybe for his habit of writing short pieces, which are less physically (not psychologically) demanding than long pieces are.

Astrology serves as a much better candidate for the Explanation of Thurber than psychology does. Thurber was born under the sign of Sagittarius, which rules, among other things, archery. The placement of the sun is what rules a man's health, so a man born with any afflictions to the sun in Sagittarius is going to be vulnerable to health problems associated with archery. I don't have an ephemeris handy for December 8, 1894, the date of his birth, but I bet there is either an affliction of the sun to Mercury, planet of the eyes and of sense perception in general, or else an affliction from his sun to some planet in Gemini, Pisces, or Virgo. An affliction to Virgo, however, is made fairly unlikely by the enormous intellectual and domestic pleasure Thurber got from dogs—Virgo rules animal training. But Gemini rules dogs, so that lets Gemini as a source of affliction out. It was therefore probably an opposition to Mars in Pisces, which would also account for Thurber's excessive dreaminess and his problems with alcohol, as well as the tenderer and more romantic spheres of experience, as Pisces rules love and all other intoxicants. I would also expect to find Uranus, the planet of the inexplicable and especially the planet of misunderstood geniuses, in the constellation Scorpio, which rules erotic thought, since his brilliant visions of the wars and comedies of the sexes are so persistently misunderstood.

So his life is explained, but his life is not what Thurber left behind for us, and it is too late for me to tell him that the placement of his sun in Sagittarius indicates that he ought to have come to terms with horses. (He never did, as his picture of Quandary makes clear.) I am at a disadvantage in talking about his art because I can't say, as W. H. Auden was able to say in 1940, that "it would be as impertinent as it is unnecessary for me to praise Mr. Thurber's work; everybody knows and loves it." It may still be impertinent to praise Thurber, but it is no longer unnecessary.

In order to praise Thurber's art, I will appeal to a few remarks of his that can be understood as part of his "life" rather than "art"—since they were made in conversation rather than in his writing—and ask the reader to try to believe Thurber, even if you think he was misguided, when he said things such as that he wrote humor "because it might do some good." In one interview, after various comments along the lines that he was serious, he said,

> Some people even think I make jokes about dogs. For God's sake anybody who looks at my drawings with enough observation should be able to see that dogs play the part of intelligence and repose. . . . Typical of the stupidity of our own species was my woman who said, "If I rang the wrong number, why did you answer the phone?" That seems typical of the female intelligence, though I do get intelligent letters from women. Notice the despair and resignation of the dog in that picture. . . . I think we are in a terrible state. . . . I say these things and people just talk about my "charming dogs."

I think that managing to believe Thurber in this and other passages entails understanding that Thurber was as serious about women as he was about art, and maybe even as he was about dogs. The cartoon in question does capture my own sense of the kind of stupidity one is most likely to find in women, for whatever reason, just as so many of his stories and cartoons capture the particular forms of stupidity one is most likely to find in men, for whatever reason. There is a lot of stupidity around; noticing it with such uncanny intelligence and wit is evidence not of a pathology of spirit but of a capacity to care about the mind.

Thurber would complain to find himself at this late date "still taken for a clown," but as I've indicated, readers find him to be cruel, psychoanalyzable, and treasonable (he wrote through the McCarthy era and was duly blacklisted) when they aren't finding him to be a clown. The following are examples of the offensively pious sort of nonsense that irritates me.

> In his later work his repetitions and overextensions are technical counterparts of moral decline and bitterness.

. . . he might have remembered how "comic" books become horror comics in the late forties and fifties. . . . His satire on the exquisite breakdown of communication is undercut. . . . he finds himself without a true position to take.

In the last stage of his career . . . the misogyny is still active. "I like to do what I can," he confesses to *Life,* "to keep the American woman—my great mortal enemy—in excellent condition for the fight."

This, that, and the other turn in his writing is called "a pity" when it is not called something stronger; writers on Thurber seem often to feel that the fact that he wrote great humor made him indebted to the reader's fantasies about what he ought to do with himself. Thurber is not the only American to have incurred enormous moral debts by virtue of having written well. Even so generally civilized a critic as Frank Kermode could doubt Wallace Stevens's sincerity in wanting to make poetry "a human study, fit for all comers," because Stevens declined in his late sixties the offer of a one-year position at Harvard. The grave danger of being a literary critic seems to be the temptation to assume the role of instructor in Creative Writing, Ethics, and Manners 101a, and probably 101b as well.

I mention the critics only as a kind of object lesson, an occasion for suggesting that we ought to learn how to read Thurber, and for examining a short piece called "An Outline of Scientists," which moved one critic to say that Thurber should have stuck to humor and not tried to get involved with "ideas." Of course, these impulses on the part of commentators are understandable; when something like Thurber's writing touches our imaginations, we tend to rush past our gratitude to the greedier position of mindlessly sentimental drunks who just want the musician to "play that tune again" while they forget the musician's ordinary humanity, with all it implies.

"An Outline of Scientists" opens by giving its own occasion, the writer's having been "laid up by a bumblebee." The bumblebee is, of course, the icon of Natural Science, so when Thurber goes on in the opening to say, "It was the first time in my life that anything smaller than a turtle had ever got the best of me, and naturally I don't like to dwell on it," the clear implication is that Science is smaller than a turtle, and also that it has the power to get the best of us.

To amuse himself while laid up by the bumblebee, the writer reads through four impressive volumes called *The Outline of Science: A Plain Story Simply Told,* and describes his perplexities as he tries to follow the simply told explanation of the general theory of relativity. These days relativity is losing its hold on the imagination as an emblem of the perfections of the mysteries of science, but in 1937, the copyright date of *Let Your Mind Alone!,* the volume this piece appears in, both "relativity" and "Einstein" were unsurpassable nouns. The description of perplexity Thurber gives is as fine a description of oppression as any I know of. It reminds me of my attempts at the age of seventeen to follow the arguments in volumes such as Bertrand Russell's *The ABC's of Relativity* without developing dark and impolite theories about the author.

But Thurber does go on to develop dark and impolite theories, after he reads this paragraph in Chapter XXXVI, "The Story of Domesticated Animals."

> There are few dogs which do not inspire affection; many crave it. But there are some which seem to repel us, like the bloodhound. True, man made him what he is. Terrible to look at and terrible to encounter, man has raised him up to hunt his fellow man.

Nearly twenty years later, in "Lo Hear the Gentle Bloodhound!" (which appeared in *Thurber's Dogs*), he gets around to saying, "It pleases me no end that this passage, in its careless use of English, accidentally indicts the human being: 'Terrible to look at and terrible to encounter, man . . .'" I don't know if this fine piece is one of the examples of the decline and fall of Thurber or not. In any case, back in 1937 he went on to say this:

> Accompanying the article was a picture of a dignified and mournful-looking bloodhound, about as terrible to look at as Abraham Lincoln, and as terrible to encounter as Jimmy Durante.
>
> Poor, frightened little scientist! I wondered who he was. . . . Some of the chapters were signed, but this one wasn't, and neither was the one on the Einstein theory. . . . I had the strange feeling that

both of the articles had been written by the same man. I had the strange feeling that *all* scientists are the same man. Could it be possible that I had isolated here, as under a microscope, the true nature of the scientist? It pleased me to think so; it still pleases me to think so. I have never liked or trusted scientists very much, and I think now that I know why: they are afraid of bloodhounds. They must, therefore, be afraid of frogs, jack rabbits, and the larger pussycats. . . . Out of my analysis . . . I have arrived at what I call Thurber's Law, which is that scientists don't really know anything about anything. I doubt everything they have ever discovered. I don't think light has a speed of 7,000,000 miles per second (or whatever the legendary speed is). Scientists just think light is going that fast, because they are afraid of it. It's so terrible to look at. I have always suspected that light just plodded along, and now I am positive of it.

A critic writing in a saner mood than those I have cited says of this piece, "Because scientists do sometimes fail to understand a bloodhound, the reader's heart lifts up. . . . Scientists too can be routed. . . . We can say BOO! It is not much, but it is an action" (Richard C. Tobias, *The Art of James Thurber*). This is right as far as it goes, but Thurber does not say merely that science can fail in this or that particular; rather, he assaults the intellectual foundations of scientific and, in one way and another, almost all modern thought—its claim to "objectivity." It of course follows from the claim of objectivity, the realists' or "god's-eye" view, that a scientist qua scientist is no one in particular, an inference that is identical to Thurber's claim that "all scientists are the same man." This creates a knotty problem indeed— one, I can cheerfully report, that our logicians and philosophers are beavering away at, so I don't have to. What is interesting to me is the rest of the implicit metaphysics of this passage, with its underlying proposition that to be objective, to be no one in particular, is to be too frightened to know anything about anything. (It is incidentally interesting to notice the accuracy of the implied prophesy, in 1937, that something smaller than a turtle would lay us low. There are plenty of turtles much larger than the human brain, and larger, as well, than the business portion of an atom bomb.)

In light of this, it is instructive to recall that although Thurber was blacklisted by Hollywood during the McCarthy era, one of the few times he devoted himself to lengthy and specific arguments was in response to the pious assaults on—I won't say on intellectual freedom, because that isn't quite right, but on, perhaps, coherence, by the intellectual left as well as the political right. He attacks the pieties of the right in various ways, doubting "the virgin birth of U.S. Senators." Of the left he says, speaking of writers like himself,

> It is difficult for such a person to conform to what Ford Madox Ford in his book of recollections has called the sole reason for writing one's memoirs: namely, to paint a picture of one's time. Your short-piece writer's time is not Walter Lippmann's time, or Stuart Chase's time, or Professor Einstein's time. It is his own personal time, circumscribed by the short boundaries of his pain and embarrassment, in which what happens to his digestion, the rear axle of his car, and the confused flow of his relationships with six or eight persons and two or three buildings is of greater importance than what goes on in the nation or in the universe.

Thurber, then, and presumably the Thurber reader, unlike the objective scientist and unlike the collectively loyal servant of either the left or the right, is someone in particular.

Now, this someone in particular is famously, or infamously, nervous and jumpy and given to morbid terrors in the night, at least when faced with scientific and social advances, but he is not frightened of Bloodhounds! Which is to say, on Thurber's own account, not frightened of what may turn out to be demonic: human thought. Remember that he claims that in his work "dogs play the part of intelligence, and repose." And dogs, intelligence and repose are things that people who are anonymous, no one in particular, are frightened of.

Thurber's remark about intelligence and repose applied primarily to his drawings, to "the Thurber hound," the one that made Dorothy Parker go "all weak with sentiment." It is accidentally apt, or maybe just apt by way of serendipity, that Thurber says his hound is partly inspired by the Bloodhound, the dog No One in Particular found "terrible to behold" in his day, but also by the American Bull Terrier, or pit bull, the dog No One in Particular and Everyone in General seems to find terrible to behold and terrible to encounter today.

Thurber was battling, I think, for space in which he, at least, and maybe a few others—Thurber was no evangelist—could be, or recall being, Someone in Particular. This is not the same thing as trying to save the world. It is trying to have an intelligent conversation. And while I thought when I began these remarks that the passage I quoted from the objectionable "feminist" literary critic, like the passage from "Canines in the Cellar," had fallen accidentally to hand, I have revised that view. At least, it happens to be so apt that I will pretend it was no accident that it was the pseudofeminists who offended me and drove me to seek comfort in Thurber.

Thurber was passionate enough about the importance of respecting the individual imagination to lay aside humor and fulminate, in a letter to Malcolm Cowley, then an editor of the *New Republic,* about

> the desire to subject the individual to the political body, to the economic structure, to put the artist in a uniform so like the uniform of the subway conductor that nobody would be able to tell the difference. It is this desire to regiment and discipline art—the art of writing and the art of living—that some of us are afraid of. . . . we need someone to say, listen you sons of bitches, hands off—keep your noses in your economic and political dishes or we'll knock them off! (quoted in Burton Bernstein, *Thurber: A Biography*)

It is intelligence and repose, figured as a Thurber hound, that can say, effectively if temporarily, "Hands off!" to the intruders into our particularities of conducting the art of writing and of living. And here we get, I think, the most important clue to Thurber's refusal to argue, debate, in his prose. (What he did in letters and bars is another matter, and none of our business.) Instead of debating the temperament of the Bloodhound with the scientists on their "own grounds," he closes his piece this way:

> I can understand how that big baby dropped the subject of bloodhounds with those few shuddering sentences, but I propose to scare him and his fellow-scientists a little more about the huge and feral creatures. Bloodhounds are sometimes put on the trail of lost old ladies or little children who have wandered away from home. When a bloodhound finds an old lady or little child, he instantly swallows the old lady or little child whole, clothes and all. This is probably

what happened to Charlie Ross, Judge Carter, Agness Tufverson, and a man named Colonel Appel, who disappeared at the battle of Shiloh. God knows how many people bloodhounds have swallowed, but it is probably twice as many as the Saint Bernards have swallowed. As everybody knows, the Saint Bernards, when they find travellers fainting in the snow, finish them off. Monks have notoriously little to eat and it stands to reason that they couldn't feed a lot of big, full-grown Saint Bernards; hence they sic them on the lost travellers, who would never get anywhere anyway. The brandy in the little kegs the dogs wear around their necks is used by the Saint Bernards in drunken orgies that follow the killings.

I guess that's all I have to say to the scientists right now, except *boo!*

Science, philosophy, Communist-hunters, and the Daughters of the American Revolution have all, to the best of my knowledge, failed to refute Thurber's *boo!* This has to do, I think, with his deep understanding of heroes and with the source of that understanding in his passionate reading of adventure stories. His humor, like all genuine humor, depends, not on his being too smart and sophisticated to believe anything, but rather on his caring so deeply about the heroic possibilities of the human in a certain tradition—our tradition. This is the passion that made the writing of such pieces as "The Secret Life of Walter Mitty" possible. Walter Mitty has been compared to Hamlet, but this seems to me a misguided comparison. Hamlet expires with some lines about warlike noises followed by some lines about silence, and then his silence gives Horatio the chance to say the bit about "Good night, sweet Prince" and flights of angels. At the end of Thurber's story, Mitty's wife may seem to the naive reader to have defeated him by threatening to take his temperature, but Mitty is no more daunted at that point than he has been throughout; the story closes with "Walter Mitty the undefeated, the inscrutable to the last." Whether or not this appears to be existential heroism, agon in the face of complete futility, depends, I suppose, on the reader's evaluation of the imagination, of storytelling. For what it's worth, the biographical evidence suggests that Thurber was committed rather deeply to story-telling.

But it is in the dog stories that the possibilities of the quest, the heroic, are clearest, to me at least. In the piece called "A Snapshot of

Rex," we learn of a Bull Terrier ("an American Bull Terrier—none of your English Bulls"), a dog of the breed nowadays usually called the pit bull. Rex was, on the biographical evidence, the dog for Thurber. Not the only dog he loved passionately, of course, but the One Dog in a Lifetime. Thurber would dream about Rex for decades after his death and wake grieving. Rex was a dignified and powerful dog who seems to have been inspired by any task if it just had sufficient—well, *taskness* to enable Rex to use himself fully, to bring his heart and mind alive. Rex

> never started fights. I don't believe he liked to get into them, despite the fact that he came from a long line of fighters. He never went for another dog's throat but for one of its ears (that teaches a dog a lesson), and he would get his grip, close his eyes, and hold on. He could hold on for hours. His longest fight lasted from dusk until almost pitch-dark, one Sunday. It was fought in East Main Street in Columbus with a large, snarly nondescript that belonged to a big colored man. When Rex finally got his ear grip, the brief whirlwind of snarling turned into screeching. It was frightening to listen to and watch. The Negro boldly picked up the dogs somehow and began swinging them around his head, and finally let them fly like a hammer in a hammer-throw, but although they landed ten feet away with a great plump, Rex still held on.
>
> The two dogs eventually worked their way to the middle of the car tracks, and after a while two or three streetcars were held up by the fight. A motorman tried to pry Rex's jaws open with a switch rod; somebody lighted a fire and made a torch of a stick and held that under Rex's tail, but he paid no attention. In the end, all the residents and shopkeepers in the neighborhood were on hand, shouting this, suggesting that. Rex's joy of battle, when battle was joined, was almost tranquil. He had a pleasant expression during fights, not a vicious one, his eyes closed in what would have seemed to be sleep had it not been for the turmoil of the struggle.

Rex, I think, isn't a bad model of a hero, though someone may be wondering how to distinguish between Rex's valor and the activities of more hysterical types who rattle their nuclear and rhetorical toys as a way of distracting our attention from their vanity and greed. This isn't as hard as it looks, even given the debased and inadequate reporting these days of national and international situations. Rex did not draft armies and direct them from air-conditioned conference rooms; he put no one's life but his own on the line, and he never started fights. His last and bravest battle, in Thurber's account, was the one with death, a battle he fought for the sake of love. His story ends like this:

> One of his three masters was not home. He did not get home for an hour. During that hour the bull terrier fought against death as he had fought against the cold, strong current of Alum Creek, as he had fought to climb twelve-foot walls. When the person he was waiting for did come through the gate whistling, ceasing to whistle, Rex walked a few wobbly paces toward him, touched his hand with his muzzle, and fell down again. This time he didn't get up.

It should by now be easy enough to see why the author of this piece would be aggravated when people called his dogs "charming." Malory might feel the same about readers who called Launcelot or King Arthur "charming." And should a misguided fan of Dorothy Parker's want to invoke some handy term of dismissal for the story of Rex, by calling it a "tearjerker" or saying something about going "all weak with sentiment," then I find myself reminded of Wallace Sevens, who said that "sentimentality is the failure of feeling." If there are any authenticated instances of a failure of either feeling or intelligence on Thurber's part that can't be attributed to such causes as general anesthesia, I haven't been able to find them, though of course I have been able to find quotations such as the one above about the "moral decline" in Thurber's joyously intelligent later work, from people who suppose him to have failed. This is not unusual; seeing in intelligence, especially joyous intelligence, evidence of moral decline is a persistently if not an exclusively American tradition.

That is the tradition too many of us inherit, but we don't need to. We could inherit Thurber instead, and through him alternatives to the junk-food versions of heroism, intelligence, and political thought that are littering the landscape these days. But to inherit Thurber is to inherit him whole—dogs, women, and all, and with them the need to understand that his canine heroes, like his women and like his men, are more often ridiculous than they are heroic, because to understand the hero is to understand the failure of the heroic and manage to love it anyway.

For me it is of particularly urgent moral and intellectual concern that his women should be fully inherited. His women are often dangerous, ridiculous, stupid, relentlessly difficult, his "mortal enemies." And as we have seen, dogs in Thurber are dangerous, ridiculous, once in a while stupid, relentlessly difficult, and sometimes his mortal enemies, as in "Muggs, the Dog Who Bit People." This story, like the story of Walter Mitty, is a meditation on the part of a devoted student of heroism about what happens when the heroic story goes just a little bit askew. Muggs was an Airedale; a "big, burly, choleric dog, he acted as if he thought I wasn't one of the family. There was a slight advantage in being one of the family, for he didn't bite the family as often as he bit strangers." To try to get the best of Muggs was as hopeless as we know it is for the husband in *Men, Women and Dogs* to try to get the best of the implacably obnoxious wife to whom he is saying, "I assume that you regard yourself as omniscient. If I am wrong, correct me!" Muggs's story, though, is meaningful against the possibility of the stories of Davy Crockett, Wild Bill Hickok, the flying aces of World War I, and Lad of Sunnybank Farm. And the stories of the dangerous and unpleasant women in Thurber are meaningful only against the possibility of an undefeatable heroine. His mother, Mame Thurber, provided him with one of my favorite examples.

Thurber was pretty explicit about this from time to time. In *Alarms and Diversions,* which is dedicated to his wife, Helen Thurber, he opens with a piece called "The Ladies of Orlon." It is an appeal to the muse—well, maybe to the comic muse—for the gift of heroic women, and it is not a despairing appeal; it is made in grateful awareness of the opportunities opened to the world by suffragettes and feminists. He says, for example,

I no longer see the faces of men and women at the parties I attend, or in the streets I walk along, or the hotel lobbies I sit in, but I hear their voices more clearly than ever. The voices of the women, it seems to me, have taken a new and quiet quality—a secret conspiratorial tone, the hopeful and reassuring note of a sex firmly dedicated to the principle of not being blown into fragments. For centuries Woman has been quietly working at achieving her present identity. Not many years ago the *Encyclopedia Britannica* listed nothing under "Woman," but merely said, "See Man." The latest

Oxford English Dictionary, however, gives woman twelve columns to man's fifteen. The development of her name . . . is fascinating to trace. . . . Most writers, glibly discussing the origin of the word over their brandy, contend that it derives from the derogatory phrase "with man" or the physiological "wombman." They don't know what they are talking about. Earlier male writers, equally mistaken, declared the word derived from "woe to man" or "wee man." Some of them were serious, others merely kidding, in the immemorial manner of the superior male.

He goes on to cite emblems of female power of the sort that most feminists in my ken despise as examples of male chauvinistic sexual pathologies—the scorpion whose ritual ends in the disappearance of the male, a species of fish that "has reduced the male to the status of a mere accessory." The piece ends with a request that the women in the audience "please keep their seats until the men have left the auditorium. They need, God knows, a head start." How we read this depends on a lot of other beliefs, of course, just as the reader's interpretation of my comparison of women to dogs depends on a lot of other beliefs. I suppose that my fondness for such comparisons leaves me open to the charge of the sexist version of "Uncle Tomism," but I am a dog trainer and I think *that* complaint leaves the complainer open to the charge of speciesism. So there. *Boo!*

Muggs, like Mamie Thurber, could and would get to you whether or not you were reading him as a sweet doggie who only wanted to please. Thurber's women get to his men, and to the reader, as Thurber himself does, whether or not we think it's safe to pat him or them on the head and go all weak with sentiment. So I think I would like to end by revealing that when Muggs died, there was written "in indelible pencil" over his grave a single line, *"Cave Canem."* This line is usually translated into English as "Beware of the dog," and certain authorities tell me that its meaning may be ambiguous, that it may carry the connotation "Take care of the dog" or "Be careful with the dog." It quite pleases me to believe this.

The last line of Thurber's story of Muggs tells us that his heroine, Mame Thurber, was also "quite pleased with the simple, classic dignity of the old Latin epitaph."

What Is His Name?

$\mathcal{I}$ have for many years thought off and on—as who has not?—about the naming of dogs. There are books on the subject, not only general books about what to name the puppy, but also more specific books that give both traditional and contemporary names for, say, Irish Wolfhounds. And I have had more than one occasion to labor over the question of whether to name a new dog in a traditional fashion or to give the dog the generally ill-advised name the devil suggests and someone usually talks me out of.

However, I never realized that there was an ethical problem about names, and following hard on the heels of the ethical problem, a philosophical conundrum, until a couple of years ago, when I read a column by the well-known city slicker William Safire, on the subject of the names of dogs. He there yearned for the good old days when dogs were given *dog* names—Rover, Spot, Troubador, I don't recall which ones were acceptable—and lamented the degenerate modern practice, a practice he associated with people who know nought of dogs, of giving dogs human names. He then went on to show that he knew nought of dogs by complaining about the snapping cur in *The Accidental Tourist*. That dog's name is Edward, but the main point is that he is no cur, but a true and proper Welsh Cardigan Corgi (as opposed to the true and proper and more commonly encountered Welsh Pembroke Corgi). Edward is a herding dog, a cattle dog, one with a deep sense of what is and is not honorable; his snappishness in the novel is the good herding dog's morally outraged response to the human incoherence around him, the disorganized herd on the point always of a stampede.

Also, Edward is a perfectly reasonable name for a Welsh dog.

John Hollander, a dear friend, a poet, and not only that but a poet with tenure, who therefore should know how to advise me, suggested that I write a friendly chiding letter to Safire, but oh, I thought, what's the point of trying to educate city slickers? Because say I explained to Safire that Edward is a Corgi (Welsh Cardigan, not Welsh Pembroke). Would he then want to know what passions stir the stout and stern heart of a stock dog when faced with such characters as Anne Tyler faced Edward with? Would Safire travel to Virginia with me, to a sheepdog training clinic, or even to my friend Diana Cooper's place in Bethany, Connecticut, which is practically Manhattan as farms go, perfectly safe for city slickers, to meet Gaddis, Diana's very well-behaved because well-occupied Corgi (Welsh Cardigan, not Welsh Pembroke), who would then alert William Safire and me that the chitchat had gone on too long and there were farm chores to see to? Gaddis does this every single time I visit, by herding me as my friend and I sit with coffee, his way of trying by sheer force of character to still our mouths so that his mistress will go out to see to the horses and the goats and especially the cows, since it is now Gaddis's resolute and joyful duty to escort the cows up the hill each evening. His mistress is more attentive than I am to these things, but she is also an impeccable hostess, and Gaddis knows *everything*, blast him, which is why it is me he herds and not her.

No. Safire would not come to be herded into silence by a Corgi, whether Cardigan or Pembroke. What use is a letter to the editor?

But about the names of dogs. I have a hound named Lucy Belle, a Plott Hound. Her voice is not so beautiful as a bell, but she is a belle, hence the name, a good traditional name. And there are Annie, Mike and Rosie, pit bulls—all three names frowned upon by city slicker Safire because they are "human" names, but traditional for these dogs nonetheless. Pit bulls are often given sort of home-cooked "human" names—Pete the Pup, the pit bull on the old *Our Gang* series, or Bud, the pit bull who sang for FDR at the White House in 1940. For pit bulls there are also Tina, Susie, Buster, Rex, and so on. They all mean "My Old Pal."

Other breeds have traditions too. The other day I was chatting on the sidewalk with my friend Jim Ponet, rabbi to Yale. Beside us was my Drummer, a fine young Airedale. Jim the rabbi said that I must not have named Drummer, that it wasn't a "Hearne" name, and he was right—it's an Airedale name. Airedales are: Rusty, Gunner, Rags, Joker, Blackjack, Crackle, Popper, Kelly, Jeep, P.J., Tiger, Lion (in Faulkner's *The Bear*, for example), Saucy. Airedales imported from Germany may be named Ignatz, Frei, Veto.

Sheepdogs (I mean Border Collies) may have long registered names for American Kennel Club purposes, such as Windwillow's Dreamy Blossom, but not for the International Sheep Dog Society, which will not register a dog under the name Penny Jumped over the Moon, say. For true sheepmen there is a limited stock of one-syllable names that are acceptable. Pip, Gael, Tess, Bess, Scot, Spot, Maid, Hope, Kep, Sweep, Mirk, Cap—that about does it. An American with respect for this tradition would have to have a potential trial dog she really thought the world of before she would honor the dog with the name Spot. Names such as Harry and Gypsy, because two-syllabled, are eccentric, avant-garde, verging on degenerate. (Windwillow's Dreamy Blossom, or Sally Jumped Freddy in the Outhouse—these are beyond degenerate.) The true names are treasured in the culture and handled with Scot economy. You would perhaps not name a dog Pip if your neighbor's dog was named Pip, but if a dog named Pip lived over the next hill, that would be far enough away, given the requirements of thrift.

Hounds are another thing. The names of hounds, especially but not exclusively foxhounds! Liberty, Trevor, Beaumont, Bugle Anne, Trumpet, Seeker, Finder, Valiant.

In the heedless city, by which I mean the place where traditions are lost in the not always painful vibrations by means of which the distinction between the literal and the metaphorical comes into conscious question—prompting us to doubt not only that Santa Claus is literal but also that gifts are, prompting us even to doubt whether manhood and womanhood are literal, prompting therefore the displacement of tradition with wit, with living by one's wits, with sophistication—dogs may be named almost anything, but traditions do arise even among those who fail to read the *New York Times Sunday Magazine.* This phenomenon has received some press attention, for the names are: Satan, Hitler, Killer, and so on. The appeal to what we see as vicious but what may in the ghetto be seen only as vigorous political and theological powers is as natural to the yearning inner-city imagination as the name Bugle Anne is to the rural houndsman. You name your dog Bugle when you think she might have a voice to get you into the woods and safely out again; you do the same thing in Spanish Harlem; and on occasion, if you do more than name the dog, if you walk with her as well, take heed to what happens when you call.

When you call Bugle or Hitler to your side, in the hills or in the city, your voice becomes invocative, transuming what threatens otherwise to consume you. Still, if you call your old pal Hitler to your side, you are in danger of invoking the vicious rather than authentically vigorous powers that lie behind that name; it is possible half-wittedly to invoke the Holocaust. Indeed, half-wittedly is possibly the way the Holocaust is always invoked. You may think it makes no difference to a dog what his name invokes for the owner, that "Hitler" might just as well be "Fido" as far as the dog is concerned. And so it is, but if and only if "Hitler" means "Fido" to the owner; a dog whose owner's consciousness stirs to viciousness when the dog's name is called is hearing and responding to viciousness, which is on occasion why some dogs, like some people, become afraid or else aggressive when addressed.

Did I say any of this to my friend Reb Jim? No. So how is the poor city slicker to learn? However beloved the city slicker may be, he does not learn unless I teach, but I didn't just then know how to explain. Not knowing the true explanation, I gave another one. I said, "Well, watch his front feet," and heeled Drummer up and down the street, making drumming motions with my hands as I did so, and the Reb saw it, or said he did, that precise Airedale prance. . . .

But any Airedale worth a name at all can prance; it is their birthright. You don't name a dog after his breed, or not exactly. So I lied. To a rabbi! To lie to a rabbi is to betray scholarship if the reb in question is given to thinking about what is said to him, as this one is.

The name Drummer, besides being traditional, invokes precision and music, therefore art and performance, and this is a dog for whom I have show-ring ambitions. I want him to work, not only precisely but in time with joy. I want precision to become his inventions, the way a flush becomes the cheek of a young girl. I am a poet; precision—measure—means something to me, so I wanted to be able to call upon the ground of music. The beat. The soft, crystal-clear beat, the steady, fragile ground of thought that is the only one upon which the muse will stand. The careful, devout beat, meter, rhythm, the only one she will stand still for. But you can't name an Airedale Iamb, for crying out loud, even if there weren't already a dog food called Iams, and Trochee is no better, except perhaps for people who do not know what it means—it does have a sprightly sound to it. Nonetheless, Iamb and Trochee would be too literal, and even Spondee shortened to Spunk for daily purposes would offend the muse; one cannot call upon her at will. So: Drummer.

But all that is wrong, too. Here is the real reason I named him Drummer. I once had a great Airedale named Gunner. He had belonged to some people who named him that because he was half-brother to a much-mourned and grand Airedale named Drummer. So that's why, in honor of their mourning and of the original Drummer, whom I never met.

When I told John Hollander the new pup's name he said, "A different Drummer, right?" A low, coarse bit of humor, that, but why not? He is a different Drummer, different from the first Drummer in this story, so yes, that's why.

And when I told Dick Koehler he laughed and said, "That's good. That way he won't get upset when you call him Gunner." So that's why.

How do we learn traditions? I bought and named Annie, my good lady, named her, actually, Ruffian Annie, before I saw her pedigree or had any (conscious) knowledge of AmStaff/Pit Bull lines. (Red brindle she is, once a color that even the most foolish could recognize as breathtakingly beautiful, now one that only the wisest can see for what it is, for red brindle is the color that the media selected in its 1987 celebration of "vicious" dogs. In her case brindle is the mantle of a true and kindly heart, Annie's heart, in which nowadays serenity is a robust accomplishment.) Upon getting her pedigree and examining it, lo and behold, I found that half the dogs in it were Ruffian Something-or-another, and there were a few Annies here and there too.

I have heard and read and forgotten far more than anyone has a right to about dogs. What did I know at that point, when I looked at the young puppy and wondered, "What is her name?" Only that it was: Annie. I knew this but for a day or so refused to admit it, because before I brought her home I had brought home a littermate of hers and after a few days brought her back; she was too shy and poor in the hind end, it was painful, but I later learned she was put down at six or so months because the hind end just did not develop, the pup in too much distress. Anyway, for those two or three days I had called that pup Annie, so I thought the name had been used up.

My husband is a philosopher, so he mostly leaves the naming of the animals to me, which is foolish of him because he is far better at names than I am. (When I try to write fiction, the names of my characters are so insipid even I can't tell them apart. For me, fiction is not an invocation.) But in this case, gently impatient, my husband said, "Well, yes, you *called* that pup Annie, but this one *is* Annie." And so she is. So you need the philosopher or at least the theoretician for naming, not despite but because of the philosopher's habit of peering unmannerly up the muse's robes. If he thereby forgets that the robes are as literal as what he set them aside to peer at, and if he imagines that any old fold of her gown reveals her heart rather than a chance piece of anatomy, if he does not know that he is as a blind man identifying an elephant in his refusal to stand back and take in with rapt admiration the surface of her gown, if he forgets everything in his haste to disrobe her, well, that is forgivable in a philosopher, as excessive voice is forgivable in a foxhound even though in a lurcher it is a capital offense, fatal for the owner, who has the lurcher with him in the greeny woods in the first place because he has designs on the king's deer. (Excessive voice is not, by the way, forgivable in a poet.)

Annie, "accidentally" named in such a fashion that I might have been studying her pedigree for months. What was I thinking? Consciously, I was thinking that I was more of a ruffian than I had liked to think earlier, that my more fastidious friends were right in their dismay at my coarseness, and perhaps I wanted (weakly) to transume their dismay, so: Ruffian. But I was feeling a bit lost in the woods, too, and may have been remembering Nana, the dog in *Peter Pan*, the nanny dog who couldn't do much, but a Ruffian Nanny could do plenty.

And so she does. A nanny she is. You never saw such a dog for minding the children, keeping them out of scrapes, and gentle with it all. Troubled people who like dogs need only sit next to her in the back seat of the jeep on a longish drive to discover that she is all made of comfort and protection.

But what do we know when we go about naming animals, or each other? You know how annoying it is when someone refuses to know your name, perhaps by calling you, however lovingly, by a nickname you object to. (I learned slowly that there are nicknames for Drummer, or moods of nickname, that Drummer does not care for.) And what about naming in the first place? Wittgenstein objects to the philosopher's habit of being fascinated by the occult power of names; he pooh-poohs the idea that in staring earnestly at a name, whether a proper name or an improper one, whether an uppercase name such as "Wittgenstein" or a lowercase one such as "rose" or "cat" or "mat," the philosopher is thereby going to get any closer to what is being invoked. "A rose by any other name smells as sweet," as one Wittgensteinian friend of mine has it, so moving the word "rose" around in a logical proof is not going to tell you what roses are.

Wittgenstein's grandfather, Hermann Christian Wittgenstein, son of Moses Maier, adopted a new name (even a new middle name, Christian) in an attempt to have the family reclassified as non-Jews. This worked so well that a tradition of anti-Semitism became part of the family heritage, until the Third Reich, with its more scientific bureaucracy, got onto the situation. Hence Wittgenstein, having as it were inherited a name not his own and having still managed truly to be Wittgenstein—*the* Wittgenstein—may have been in a position to pooh-pooh with some rights in the matter, unlike, I submit, William Safire on the topic of Edward the (Welsh Cardigan) Corgi.

What goes on when you call a dog? Well, to take the simplest case, the dog comes, so you call the dog both through and over something, particularities of the world, and also away from particularities—you call him off of deer, or you call her while she is in hot pursuit of a bunny. You cannot control the world, and in some parts of it the dog, in his haste to respond, may step on a wide-awake rattlesnake. In any event, you call the dog *from* something, sometimes from (or so the dog sees it) the whole wide wonderful world, into the house, into the kennel, boring! You call the dog to you, or so you promise when you say the name. In the simplest case, that is. A sheepman may use a dog's name plus a command or whistle to redirect his work, and I may use the name plus a command to send the dog to retrieve or on a Go Out, into the world and away from me. In a way I go with the dog as he works, of course, prepared to stop him if I see trouble; I follow him with my eyes and thoughts, but really the dog goes alone when I send him on a Go Out. I summon the move by saying his name, but he goes it alone.

In the best case there is a balance, fluid and temporal, between word and world, creature and creature, a point of integrity brought into being, like the integrity that sends cathedrals vaulting over the greed of cardinals, as though greed did not exist. Yes, it happens this way.

That is, it can happen this way when something happens, but unless something happens a name is no name at all, just a label or a noise the owner makes. Something must happen, something in the world must move to your voice when you call the dog's name, or it is not a name! If the world is inert, and for all I know it may be, then this is an occult power, beyond the world.

Even words that are not, or are not yet, names have this much power: they are unique. Improperly so, most of the time—I am not here talking about proper names, just true names. Take the word "red." You'd think there was no reason we couldn't mean the same thing by the word "blrummmph," or so a roomful of philosophers told me earnestly one time. But when we say a word and it is truly a word, then we mean to be saying the word, and it has the power to mean to be saying us as well—that is, we can find ourselves altered by the words we say even if we didn't start out meaning to be so altered. In either case, when we say a word, something is meant, intended, brought into the world. I did not try to say that to the philosophers (we were reading Wittgenstein aloud on vigorous Saturday afternoons). What I said was that there is no such thing as a paraphrase, no such thing as saying "the same thing in other words," and they pooh-poohed this idea, so I pulled out of my meager bag of tricks the following lines—

Never blew the rose so red
As where some valiant hero bled

—and pointed out that here "red" rhymes with "bled" and thereby ties itself through the "bl" to "blew," and also through the "r" to "rose"; furthermore, the short "e" of "red" echoes "where" and the first syllable of "never." "Hah!" I cried. "I dare you to say the same thing in other words."

Or to call me by some other name, or Annie, and see if she comes as sweetly. Oh, she would learn to do it in time, but her pedigree and therefore her history would rearrange themselves in the process, and I am not so eager to revise her pedigree just now, for all that there are troubles in it, witness the pup I called "Annie" who didn't turn out to be up to responding to the name, not like my Annie, who with her name has now outlived that other pup a good eight or nine years. Names, like poets, cannot be so productive without longevity of one sort or another.

The philosophers were cross with me about that rose blowing so inarguably *red*—or at least blowing so for the moment beyond argumentativeness—and with good reason, I suppose. One solution that attracted one philosopher in the room was to deny that poetry is part of the language because it is . . . you know, too metaphorical and . . . well, weird. Perhaps there is something to this. The philosopher was far too civil to have said, "Go away," to the poet, but he thought of it, as had Socrates before him, and Stalin.

It is considered bad luck to rename a horse. I have done so, renamed a mare whose papers, as I recall, said her name was Fabulous Swell. Bleccchhh! Not a flaw or hitch in that gal's movement, so I called her Drummer Girl, but perhaps it was bad luck, for the horse never came truly to be mine. Names may or may not have occult powers, but they do have powers, the power of history anyhow, as when the ghetto dweller, calling his pal Hitler, inadvertently calls up something else. Let us say that the powers of names are not our powers, and corporations and revolutions might do well to think that through, to think what powers they are meddling with, powers not their own, when they rename or inspire the renaming of streets, or families, for what if the family we call the Wittgensteins had never been troubled about its name? Well, then there would have been no such family, and so no philosopher as Ludwig Wittgenstein.

Poets, like dog and cat owners and parents and corporations, are namers, but even then the power of the name does not belong to the poet, the poet only sometimes invokes that power. The skillful poet does so without making a mess, the unskillful one leaves blotches large and small on the landscape of language. The politician or the corporation, skillful or not, is best advised to leave names alone, or at least to show some humility in the face of them. Use your own name—it is humble and ready to hand—as Henry Ford did, and as the owner of the corner grocery store does, or if not your own name then the town's. I don't mean to imply that there is a "should" in names, an "ought," only that if a name is a name, then things will happen when you use it, so see to it that you proceed with honesty and good taste.

Cats do not come when called, or at least not the way dogs do, so when we use their names, language can feel suddenly vitiated to us if we are expecting a human or canine response. This may be why T. S. Eliot privileged the naming of cats as a case of central poetic action. Eliot was a modern, a contemporary of W. H. Auden, who wrote that poetry "makes nothing happen / It is a way of happening"; hence a name that makes nothing happen, a cat's name often enough, might have seemed to him to be like poetry, or anyhow like modern poetry, which tends to pretend that it cannot invoke gods and that it is not in any other way literal. But I think that Eliot had lost, in his passage across the Atlantic, perhaps, or somewhere on the streets of London, the realization that the world responds to names, that something is supposed to happen when a genuine name is genuinely called.

Dogs respond to their names, which may be why they trouble some cat people. Cat people of a certain sort may disguise their anxiety with a barrage of insults thrown at dogs for so nobly and gallantly coming when called, but secretly they would rather be, if not free from language, then required to deal with it only at teatime, when it is on its best manners and not rudely calling things into being.

I have become increasingly unhappy with the habit people have—complete strangers—of coming up to me out of nowhere and asking my dog's name, since I know that they are going to use the name to try to call my dog to them, a risky annoyance at any time, but especially when the dog is working. (I have seen guide dogs with large signs on their harnesses begging passersby to leave the dogs to their work.) It is heartwarming that the sight of a dog disarms shyness, just as it is heartwarming that feminine beauty prompts affectionate impulses, but being warmed by the sight of a dog or a person is not sufficient reason to address them, touch them, or feed them. Strangers coming up and wanting to call my dog bring out the worst in me.

The other morning Drummer was on the sidewalk on a Stay while I rummaged through the car for sundry items. A voice behind me said, "What's his name?" in jovial fashion. I glanced around to find a man fondling Drummer, who was doing his best to hold his Stay. I said, "Don't pet him, please, he's working"—though why the hell one needs a special reason for telling strangers not to pet one's dog I am at a loss to say. The man said, "I just asked what his name is. What's wrong with that?" What's wrong is that there are too many people who have no concept, none, of etiquette around a dog.

Sometimes when people ask my dog's name I lie; other times I tell the truth and add rapidly and despairingly, "But don't call him!" They do it anyway, maybe they can't help it. I give the dog an extra Stay command, though I am often tempted to give an Okay, in part because it is hard for a dog to hold a Stay while being importuned, and in part because I hope, perhaps a touch bitterly, that people will learn something from finding themselves with, say, fifty-four or seventy-two pounds of exuberant evidence of the power of names leaping into their arms, for my dogs learn not only *to* respond to their names but also *how* to do so, and when I cry out carelessly, "Drummer!" he is free to leave his precisions and give me a celebratory body slam.

Drummer has become more aloof with age, but when he was younger, being a vigorously gentlemanly dog and realizing that strangers didn't have the full right to call him by name, he was given to somewhat rowdy off-duty humor. So it would sometimes come about that someone who had no right would insist on calling his name after being asked not to, because the hunger for fluff is powerful, and sometimes I would say, "Okay!" If it was my friend the rabbi saying in respectful wonder, "Drummer, Drummer," then Drummer did not body-slam him, for he is a creature of judgment and discrimination, and there was no wanton calling of the name or the dog here. If it was a young tough or a journalist and I was feeling experimental, the illicit use of the name might lead to a near-tumble, whereupon Drummer would depart to mark a tree if there was one, like a disgruntled but amiable cop shaking off the mild aggravation of a false alarm.

Wittgenstein noted that the color green would cease to exist for us if we had no word (language game) for it. We would perhaps know bluish yellow instead, as Goethe before him noted. So Wittgenstein betrayed himself, for he can't have it both ways: either names have occult powers or they don't! In *Remarks on Color* he shows how a name can bring a color into existence; in the *Investigations* he shows how names and rules and such bring mathematics into existence, right there in the world of fact, too (a point missed by Kripke). A name cannot bring the whole of a creature into existence, or even the whole of mathematics, but the creature without a name, the number without a name, properly and sinuously used, does not have whole existence— just see what happens when you get into unpronounceable names of numbers, such as $\sqrt{-1}$. Don't tell *me* you can pronounce that! How do you spell it? (My husband the philosopher and mathematician says mulishly that it is spelled "*i*," same way it's pronounced. I doubt the concepts here of both pronunciation and spelling, suspect we are getting into something like aural ideographic rather than orthographical territory, but will let it stand.)

There are no Airedales, so far as I am concerned, without the word "Airedale," and there is no Airedale named Drummer unless I call him so and he answers. What I call him for, when and how, and how he answers, will determine, in invisible interaction with the invisible world of things as they are, what kind of dog he is.

If that interaction and that actuality are beyond our ken—witness the accident of Annie's having a name to fit her ancestry, an accident of *das Ding an sich* and no thanks to me—then how do we know what a proper, if not the proper, name for a dog is? If the dog fails to come when called, is it because we are using the wrong name or using the name wrongly or calling the wrong dog? The predicament does not stop there, because while a name may come entirely from the materials of yourself, your dreams, your mistakes, your psychohistory, even so, once it is said, it becomes part of the world, and so *das Ding an sich* and nothing to do with your feeble powers of observation and analysis.

Dog names present us with a conundrum about *das Wort an sich* sooner than people names do, because while a dog answers to his name, he doesn't answer quite so plainly, unless to a subtle listener. A dog answers to a name, but does the dog know his name? There seems to be a much larger intersection between my knowledge of my name and your knowledge of it than there is between Drummer's knowledge of his name and mine. For one thing, I respond, usually with a groan, when I see my name written down, but Drummer has no response at all to his registration papers.

Indeed, I am beginning to suspect that that is the major difference between a dog's relationship to his name and mine: for the dog, the name can never become a label, so even for a dog named Hitler there are certain confusions that cannot resonate in his own name, even though a dog can, in response to another sort of resonance, come to hate or love his name as much as you or I can. Dogs can't read or write, cannot follow us that far into certain realms of the literal, so their names cannot become labels. Thus, in a way, there is no danger of a dog's name becoming a human name. A dog named Hearne cannot perform genealogical research in an attempt to discover which of the disputants in the family are right—those who claim "Hearne" is straight off the playing fields of Eton, or those who say no, it is Irish, a shortened and Anglicized version of an old Gaelic name that means "descendant of the owner of many fine horses."

Two rather different philosophers, separately so far as I know, have come to the same conclusion in trying to make sense of the fact that plainly dogs have names but they are dog names, have the grammar of dog names and not the grammar of human names. Jacques Derrida playfully wondered why Ryle used "Fido" when giving an example of a name, and Pierre whispered to him that it was so the example would remain docile, the general idea being that dogs answer to their names but do not answer back. Stanley Cavell, a great philosopher whose work is hampered by the fact that he has cats but no dogs, also believes that animals do not talk back.

Well, dogs do talk back, all the time. The (almost entirely forgotten) goal of obedience training is to rectify the tilt in exchange, relationship, language, so as to make answering back, talking back as well as answering, a given, but the language that arises between people and dogs is not fully cultural in the way a language that arises between creatures with the capacity for writing is, in that it cannot so readily be recorded in the memory of the tribe, so each instance of the language is at least a dialect. Therefore it is difficult to overhear a conversation between a person and a dog, and difficult to report it. Some people have learned to answer and to read the answers and back talk of so many dogs that they can do a fair job of overhearing exchanges between handlers and dogs they have not spoken to themselves, in somewhat the same way someone who knows many Indo-European languages can pick up a fair amount listening to a new dialect, but with grief-stricken regret I must report that neither Cavell nor Derrida shows evidence of such delicate philological studies. They are, of course, head and shoulders above the rest in realizing that dogs answer to their names, an observation closed to most philosophers, who appear to be as dog-blind as some people are philosophy-blind.

In any case, one of the things language does is to create an overlapping awareness between two speakers, or a writer and a reader. This can be highly deceptive; quite often it turns out if you inquire too closely that your friend's sense of what the conversation was about is entirely other than your sense, and even when that is not so, it is impossible to convey a wonderful conversation to someone else. And even in cases where language goes wholly awry and the Holocaust is half-wittedly seen into the world again, sired by the written and thus perhaps sired by the city, or by the irrigated cornfield that is the city's precursor, you had to be there. You can see how this might be if you reflect either on your own lost loves or your own lost prejudices—you are no longer there, in the area of overlap between your awareness and the other person's, the overlap that constituted the love or the hatred (unless like a madman or certain novelists you are determined to live in your own past), and so you don't know what the conversation was about, or even if there was one! So you diagnose the lost love or hatred, analyze it instead of speaking it, and there you are: science is born again. The overlap in awareness is language itself, and is all of our joy and worthy of worship, but its powers to do good are not infinite, which is why so much care must be taken with language, why constant repairs are needed, why there are editors, why there are poets, why there are even healing silences as well as Auden's healing fountains.

I do not know how many philosophers own dogs, nor how wise it makes them, since I encounter philosophers primarily in buildings that have No Dogs Allowed signs on them. I do know that many are as dog-blind as an ex-lover can be blind to the present actuality of the formerly beloved. Cavell and Derrida are not dog-blind, for they know that dogs have names, but they do not know what to say next. There have been other philosophers who have noted that dogs exist but have not known what to say next, because so often for us the true grammar of the dog's name is hidden by the labels we paste over the name. As I mentioned earlier, the ISDS does a better job of acknowledging this than others, by refusing to allow the "call name" to be different from the registered name; and yet they not only say but write the names of dogs, in the third person, and on the registration papers the dog's name always appears with the name of the owner underneath, and in conversation people speak of "Templeton's Roy" to distinguish him from "Wilson's Roy," and we are right back to labels, pasted all over the landscape, obscuring our view of the name.

Indeed, now that it is evident that the senses with which we observe names or the world are equally unreliable, someone may suggest that it is best to leave off discussing the matter. But I opened by saying that Safire's column had made me aware that there is a problem about names, and I have come at the problem elusively because it seems so silly when put bluntly. Bluntly: There are dog names and there are people names, and I have a dog named Annie, so is "Annie" a people name or a dog name? (I use the term "people" rather than "human" as it more clearly indicates the arrangement of creatures at a kennel—no Humans there, because a kennel is not an allegory or a scientific treatise, and no Canines either, just some people and some dogs possessed of various kinds of mind.) Or: If there are two dogs named Pip, to which dog does the name Pip belong? And what does the word mean—that is, which dog does the name Pip mean? It depends, plainly, on who is calling the name and to whom.

It is our condition that we do not always know what to say when asked, "What is his name?" even when the problem is not one of immediate safety for the questioner, as when I am tempted to allow my Airedale to answer fully to his name with a grand jeté and entrechat. For one thing, the dog who has only one name is rare: "We named her McGrugg, but we call her Mikki, except when she tries to get on the furniture," or "It's Zooey, except that Charlie calls her Aurora because she's red, like the dawn." I don't mean, exactly, that when you ask what a dog's name is, *some* sort of name doesn't pop out fairly freely, but that you should be wary of supposing that when you know one name for a dog or a person, you thereby know the Proper Name, or that anyone knows what the Proper Name truly is. There may be more than one unpronounceable name.

But all this is to wander from the first question, the one raised by my irritation with Safire's glib claim that dogs shouldn't have people's names, that it is traditional for dogs to have different names from people. In *Gaelic Names for Celtic Dogs* one finds much lore, not only on human names for dogs, but also on dog names for humans; indeed, one discovers that the great Irish hero Cuchulain himself is named for—no, named himself for—a dog.

When masculine names for dogs are considered, the first which comes to mind is that of Cuchulain (or Cu Cullan), the legendary hero who derived the prefix of his name, "Cu," meaning Hound, from a youthful adventure. [Irish is the only form of English that is noble enough to sustain the capitalization of the word "Hound."] Originally Cuchulain's name was Setanta. One day, as he approached the home of a blacksmith named Cullan, Setanta thought, in error, that he was being attacked by the hound of the house, which he quickly killed. In remorse, Setanta said to Cullan, "I shall henceforth be your Hound, O Cullan." And from then on he was known as Cu Cullan, or Cuchulain, the Hound of Cullan.

The author, John A. K. Donovan, then goes on to tell us that the word "Cu" is associated with many Gaelic first names and surnames, giving as an example McNamara (MacCumara, or MacCunamara: Hound of the Sea).

I once heard a story that went like this: A linguist was attempting to elicit from a Serb peasant the nominative "cow" by asking questions such as "What do you call that animal?" Instead, he kept getting the vocative "Bossy." At one point the linguist tried, "What would you call your neighbor's cow?" The reply was, "I don't understand. Why should I call my neighbor's cow?" (Or so I am told. Since the conversation did not take place in English, there are certain obscure questions that arise here.)

My question for Mr. Safire is this: If (as actually happens) someone were to name an Irish Wolfhound after the Hound of Cullan, would he be giving his dog a "human" name? Oh wot ye not, ye city slickers who were born yesterday in the rubble of the literal and the metaphorical, whereof ye speak when ye invoke the names of dogs. That much we can know, and when we can know so little in this vast world of words and powers, it is best to speak softly and to inquire not at all into the name of the great Hound, unless it is your devotion and purpose to call Him to you.

3

$\mathcal{A}$DVICE

About Josephine Trainer

*J*osephine Trainer, whose advice columns occupy this section of *Animal Happiness,* may take a little explaining. She is quite elderly and a little cranky. She keeps saying, "What do I *tell* these people?" as though she weren't an old hand at it. (It is said that many of the columns Harold Ross refused to allow Thurber to run in the *New Yorker*'s Pet Department were suggested to him by Josephine Trainer.)

In many cases she repeats the same old piece of advice, like those pet columnists who always end with "See your veterinarian." This advice is: "Train your dog. Learn thereby to take responsibility for the critter, and to be responsible to her," but people don't want to hear that over and over again, so she has developed odd ways of trying to get her point across. What she doesn't tell you is that there are dog trainers and dog trainers.

She is a true cynic—that is, she sees situations as a knowledgeable dog would see them. I have therefore decided to reprint a selection of her columns here, because despite her oracular impatience, there is this and that about what she says that is epiphanal.

As I mentioned, some of these columns are rejects from the Pet Department. Others were originally published in the newsletter of the National Pit Bull Terrier Defense Association and Literary Society.

Columns by Josephine Trainer

DEAR JOSEPHINE TRAINER: When you meet a dog, how should you pet him? I love dogs, but I don't want to get bitten.   —A Dog Lover

DEAR DOG LOVER: Pet him just as you would pet the Queen of England or a Secret Service man.

DEAR JOSEPHINE TRAINER: I have a Dachshund who chews everything and will not come when called. This was all right before I had my knee surgery, but now hunting her through the house and under the bed and so on when I need her for something is taking up more time than I have to spare. I asked Vicki Hearne for a suggestion, and she said that I should train my dog, but I had another dog that I took to obedience class, and after that he wasn't a pet anymore, he seemed to have things in mind that I didn't understand. And anyway, I hadn't asked her about training, I had just asked for a suggestion! What kind of person is she?   — Sincere in Kansas City

DEAR SINCERE: You have hit the nail on the head about the difference between a pet and a trained dog. Pets chew on the furniture and won't come when called, and trained dogs have things in mind. I have no idea what kind of person Vicki Hearne is; she is my editor and I am therefore even more confused than you are.

But I do have a suggestion, unlike Vicki. "Dachshund" means "badger dog." Badgers can be somewhat tricky animals to raise if you are, as you say, a bit creaky on your pins. Also, badger baiting is probably illegal in Kansas. Dachshunds, however, are often quite enthusiastic about rabbits, so there is hope.

Many species of pet rabbit don't move very fast, so you could raise rabbits and bring one out on a string whenever you wanted your Dachshund for something. There are, so far as I know, no laws against rabbit baiting in Kansas.

A Dachshund will also come for the mail carrier—Ms. Cooper suggests that possibly something about the uniform is badgerlike. Check local ordinances about mail-carrier baiting; they vary a great deal.

DEAR JOSEPHINE TRAINER: The Dogcatcher says I have to do something about my dog because he chases joggers and bicycles and once bit a little boy. I can't keep him tied up because he is an Airedale. Will a change of diet help? He is in the pound right now, and they don't feed him properly.
                                        —Tearful in Amherst

DEAR TEARFUL: If only people would use spay-and-neuter clinics, these things wouldn't happen, because there wouldn't be any Airedales. But we have to accept gracefully what we cannot change. Airedales are fit to be tied if you use that tree in front of the den window, the one that has all the blue flowers on it in the spring. Make sure you use a color-coordinated collar. Or take up jogging.

DEAR JOSEPHINE TRAINER: My best friend has Labradors and a Wales Cattle Dog, so I was just wondering how, or at what age, an Airedale starts taking the cosmic perspective, learns to settle down and meditate on oneness with the slow earth's diurnal course, and so on, like my friend's dogs. The other day he brought a bag of popcorn into the study and drove me nuts, taking it out kernel by kernel, dropping each kernel to the floor individually, and then hunting it down and killing it before eating it.

—Not Exactly Dissatisfied

DEAR NOT EXACTLY: Be patient. Airedales are slow maturers, but frequently by twelve or thirteen or fourteen, arthritis or some other ~~problem~~ maturity sets in, and the Airedale thinks for upwards of a second or two before bouncing his ball in the living room or tap-dancing on the jeep. In some individuals, this is very like wisdom, aye, very like, and if you wanted the cosmic perspective you should have gotten a Black-and-Tan Coonhound. Besides, Annie is wise enough for two.

P.S. It is possible to take popcorn away from an Airedale. Consult your local obedience dealer about the details—don't try it on your own. Airedales are very sensitive.

DEAR JOSEPHINE TRAINER: My West Highland White Terrier, Cream Tart, chases cats, and Vicki says to make him stop that, but isn't it natural for a dog to chase cats? He seems tremendously happy when he is doing it, and what is the point of life if it isn't happiness?   —Natural in Connecticut

DEAR NATURAL: Perhaps Vicki has in mind a greater happiness—living to fight another day, or other game. I know of no reputable trainer who encourages cat chasing, especially in terriers. In the immortal words of Geoffrey Sparrow, M.C., T.D., F.R.C.S., author of *The Terrier's Vocation,* "A dog should never be allowed to chase cats; for if he kills one— which he will, sooner or later—the resultant reaction will be 'alarm and despondancy': a vast number of proprietors or part owners will turn up, as if by magic, and all in full cry: while the man and his dog will have to beat a hasty retreat and maintain the maximum morale consistent with such an undignified manoeuvre."

So, cat chasing leads to alarm and despondency, and I know of no authors on the subject of happiness who do not find alarm and despondency to be inconsistent with any happy state, whether that state is realized through luck, achievement, or divine grace.

Some terriers are cheerful when chasing sticks and balls, and my information-gathering services tell me that the ecology organizations have yet to concern themselves with the fate of sticks, especially the ones you find lying on the ground, as opposed to sticks deliberately cut or broken off trees to provide the terrier with an outlet for his bloodthirstiness. The other day Drummer crunched a stick down to dust and splinters, in just two great crunches, and it made him quite happy and also saved someone's having to haul the stick away for kindling.

The stick fell to the ground and rapidly became one with earth's slow diurnal course, with the rocks and stones and trees, which is about as ideologically sound as you can get. Also, encounters with sticks, unlike encounters with cats, raccoons, skunks, coyotes, and the like, do not entail conversations with representatives of the Department of Agriculture, or Fish and Game, or the Division of Wildlife, who are concerned about rabies.

DEAR JOSEPHINE TRAINER: I have this dog who keeps biting everyone, and I found out how to prevent her from doing that, and now she trembles and is afraid that she doesn't get to bite me. I feel so sorry for her. Could you fax your reply?   —Dedicated in Lourdes

DEAR LOURDES: Well, as you say, she is afraid that she doesn't get to bite you. With a frightened dog the first step is to begin building the dog's confidence. In this case, you can dissolve her fears by making her confident, absolutely certain rather than merely afraid, that she doesn't get to bite you. This will throw her back on her own resources, and she will discover, come in touch with, her inner strengths.

I do not have a fax machine. Will you please tell this to the gentleman from the Vatican who keeps calling me for the Answer, and also that the Answer has more dimensions than will fit in a fax machine?

DEAR JOSEPHINE TRAINER: I have six dogs, and although it's the big Samoyed and the Husky who really fight, it starts when the little Samoyed grumbles at the Poodle. That gets the two Cockers running around, and one of them always jumps over the big Samoyed, who then bites the Husky—but the Husky wins; it's the Samoyed who is in the vet hospital right now. Which dog should I have you train?

—Told You Can Help

DEAR TOLD: Is this a religious question? I am not sure you should train any of them—they are obviously leading full, rich lives, working things out for themselves, and as for the Samoyed being in the hospital, why, that's Nature, too.

Otherwise, walk softly and carry a big stick. This is a situation, not a training problem.

DEAR JOSEPHINE TRAINER: A psychic explained to my dog that fighting with other dogs is inappropriate behavior, and yet he still does it. The psychic said that Brutus misses his first home too much for us to whomp him.   —Concerned in Cincinnati

DEAR CONCERNED: You cannot embarrass dogs into changing their behavior, but you can whomp them, which is why we say that dogs are noble.

You do not specify Brutus's breed or say how large he is in relationship to his enemies. If he is, as I suspect, a Standard Schnauzer, then he thinks mostly by way of going at sudden angles to himself, and most dogs will appear at sudden angles to a Schnauzer. If he is larger than the other dogs, bribe the dog warden.

You could try a leash and collar. You could also try training him, but be careful, because we have not so long ago been promised a Kinder America. Needles, not leashes.

DEAR JOSEPHINE TRAINER: I am afraid that I am a humaniac. I have two kittens, and I cannot bring myself to discipline them. I am too kind to them.
            —Trying in Tuscaloosa

DEAR TRYING: What kind of kittens? If they are Siamese, then you should get professional help. If they are Himalayans, not to worry. No one can discipline a Himalayan kitten.

Humania is to be suspected only if you have violent fantasies when you contemplate your kittens or the seal act at the circus. Melting with pleasure at the sight of a kitten and being unable to firm yourself up again is a response that *can* be artificially manipulated to trigger and eventually be replaced by violence, because the human brain has so much RAM (Random Access Memory) that a human can learn to bypass reality altogether and learn by rote instead. Human consciousness is not a possibility I am refuting here, just brooding about.

Cats are too dumb to learn by rote.

DEAR JOSEPHINE TRAINER: Is being in favor of the environment the same thing as being in favor of Nature? Because if it is I don't know how to vote. My conscience tells me, of course, that I should ratify the environment, but if the environment is the same as Nature I don't think I can, because I suspect that Nature is out to get me. And that I am not as high up in the food chain as I thought.

Also, yesterday my kitty Cricket got hit by a car, I think. In any case, she was dragging one hind leg, so the vet said watch her. She and her sister Kettle have been at odds with each other ever since the kittens came, and her sister is much stronger than she is, so while Robert and I napped (we both have horrendous colds), Kettle drove Cricket off the electric blanket and Cricket dove through the hole in the kitchen floor into the crawl space under the house, whence she was unable to reemerge, because of her leg, so I had to unblock the crawl space and fetch her out and put her in Lucy Belle's crate and feed her Starkist Chunk Light Tuna, and that's where she wants to stay, in Lucy Belle's crate with the Starkist. And I know Starkist isn't Nature, but that is what Cricket wants.

I noticed, not for the first time—I am always the one who goes into the crawl space, because Robert is too large to fit into it conveniently, and doesn't fit any of the warm winter booties made by L. L. Bean either (which means that civilization is a little like Nature for Robert, who also, he would like me to add, does not fit in the subways and on top of that is left-handed)—that nobody seems to want to live under the house, not even rats or spiders.

Is any of this Nature? Should I let Cricket and Kettle sort it out? Cricket says no, but I am not sure she is thinking of the Future; Kettle's chances of surviving if we die of our colds are a lot better than Cricket's.

Also: taking Cricket to the veterinarian—is that an action for or against the environment?
—Concerned About the Law in Connecticut

DEAR CONNECTICUT LAW: "Nature" is not repeat not the same thing as "the environment"—these are different kinds of nouns. Nature is just there, an intransitive noun, not something you can do anything about. Nature serves God.

The environment is different from Nature in that it does not exist. There are, however, environments. For instance, while Cricket was stuck under the house, that was her environment, or the environs of Cricket. "Environment" is always a transitive noun; it has to have something or someone to be the environment of. Subways, for instance, are nothing in particular until they become Robert's environment.

Environments and Nature are both tricky bastards, which is why there exists medicine. Also animal husbandry—just ask Cricket.

DEAR JOSEPHINE TRAINER: I have a ten-year-old German Shepherd named Fido, and can no longer keep him because I am moving to a place that has a swimming pool and an exercise spa and does not allow dogs. He is a true gentleman and healthy, so I don't quite know what to do with him. This is very hard on me. Is it kinder to take him to the vet to be put down, or to the pound?

—Wanting to Do the Best Thing in New York

DEAR BEST THING: Don't take him to the vet. Veterinary offices tend to have people working in them who have failed to develop sufficient distance about putting dog owners out of their misery, which is a pity since they have the supplies right at hand. But we must sympathize with human beings as well as with dogs, and if you take Fido to the vet some shortsighted veterinary assistant will fall for him, feed him, and spend money on shots and such. The food won't be so expensive right at first, because an older Shepherd whose owners have left him off like that doesn't have much appetite to begin with, but that doesn't last forever.

Nature's way is better. Turn him loose on the highway.

DEAR JOSEPHINE TRAINER: I took my bull terrier to obedience class, and he did well at that. The only problem is that I take him riding, and when I am first mounted on my horse he jumps up on the horse and dances around. I thought of having him hold a Sit-stay while I mount and before we set off—he is fine once we set off—but when I am mounted I can't lean down far enough to give him the cookie reward for his Sit-stay.

—Happy Otherwise in New Mexico

DEAR OTHERWISE: Either find a method of training that does not involve food rewards, or else get an Irish Wolfhound who is tall enough that you can reach his mouth from the saddle.

DEAR JOSEPHINE TRAINER: I am in a puzzlement about my dogs and a book I am trying to write. Whenever I sit down to work, they vacuum-clean the area, and then they set to casting elaborately offhand glances out the window or gazing vehemently into space whilst drumming their fingers on the floor and tapping their feet. They also pace, and glare.

Yes, my dogs are crate-trained, and I could put them in their crates in another room, but they cannot read or knit. Consequently I find that every day I am going with them on longer and more circuitous walks. Today, my puppy did her first retrieve in water over her head; the older dog came to heel when called well into his pursuit of a bunny.

The problem is that my dogs and I pay too much attention to each other. My old dog no longer has this problem; she mostly prefers solitary meditations on bygone rabbits. When I had just her and her son I got all kinds of work done. When I am in Switzerland I do not miss my dogs. However, I cannot afford to live in Switzerland indefinitely.

—Distracted

P.S. Whilst I was writing this letter, the puppy brought in a sheepskin slipper and lay down near me and put her nose *in the slipper* and stared at me. Any hints you can offer about your success in this area will be received gratefully.

DEAR DISTRACTED: Notice that you continue to perform simple tasks of husbandry, such as distinguishing between "the puppy," "the older dog," and "the old dog." Also, I am worried about the slipper episode; the puppy still registers you as a sentient being. This means that she is not yet benefiting as a well-bred dog can from a literary upbringing.

If you stay with the book, your dogs will learn a great deal. A literary upbringing encourages ingenuity in dogs. Of course, Sophie is liable to get pregnant, but she and her puppies will know how to open refrigerators, answer telephones, and raise the blinds so that some light gets in in the daytime. And make their own beds, if you don't watch what Rosie is up to when Robert goes to the city five days in a row. Dogs make beds much the way the little birdies do, by collecting bits of fluff. They generally find the fluff inside of things, such as the cushion on Robert's favorite chair.

DEAR JOSEPHINE TRAINER: My neighbor's dog is cruelly confined during the day—tied to a chain! I go over and comfort her, but lately she has begun nipping me. When my neighbor comes home from work, he takes her in the house, and then they both bark at me when I try to help.

—Too Kindhearted in New Jersey

DEAR KINDHEARTED: Stop attack-training your neighbor's dog and seek counseling for your aggressive tendencies.

DEAR JOSEPHINE TRAINER: I have a pit bull puppy named Fiddle. She is eight weeks old and bites my husband and my son. What should I do about this? She doesn't bite me because I don't let her, but my husband says discipline is not good. He plays the oboe, and my son is in college.

—Puzzled in a Big City

DEAR PUZZLED: Well, it could be worse. He could be a string player, violin or something—they're the ones who really rely on their fingers. Still, don't let your husband play with the puppy anymore; he will get an Oedipus Complex, which can be a strain on a marriage.

If you write to my secretary, she will supply you with forms I devised some years ago, for your husband and son to sign. They are release forms. The husband or son or parent signs, accepting all responsibility. Then you can sue your husband if Fiddle bites him and destroys his musical career together with your marriage.

DEAR JOSEPHINE TRAINER: I have a Welsh Terrier dog who tends to bite people, especially those wearing expensive clothes, though he doesn't always. I read in the newspaper about the Jekyll-Hyde syndrome, where dogs are one way sometimes and then suddenly another way, and I would like more information about this, which seems like a funny thing, and I don't understand about who causes dogs to be this way. My dog is just like in the paper, he isn't always the same, though I thought he was okay before, when I had him around some dog trainers. Are the Welsh like this? Who does the Jekyll-Hyde syndrome? Where did the syndrome come from?
                        —At Wit's End in Washington, D.C.

DEAR END: You are confused because Stevenson was not a comic writer. To save you (and himself) the trouble of understanding this, he has Dr. Jekyll kill Mr. Hyde and not the other way around, so that's who does it. People wearing expensive clothes, that is, cause the syndrome, a fact the dog trainers may have made your dog aware of. If you read dogs on the comic page instead of in the news section, you run across a better class of K-9.

Welsh Terriers sometimes fall for Italian Spumones, and the resulting grammatical confusion looks like murder, but is only a lover's quarrel. I mention this in case your dog one day suddenly comes into the other part of his heritage and becomes ambitious or amorous in relationship to well-dressed dogs as well as well-dressed people.

DEAR JOSEPHINE TRAINER: Which kinds of animals are most interested in helping people?

—Interested in Helping in Kentucky

DEAR HELPING: Animals, unlike people, have no general sense of altruism, so it depends on local conditions. In Kentucky, there are a lot of Thoroughbreds who help people, but their motives are impure. They act like they want to help their trainers and fans, but they are just doing it for the glory.

DEAR JOSEPHINE TRAINER: I am afraid of dogs. What should I do about this? Also, what is Animal Psychology?   —A Sabra in Jerusalem

DEAR SABRA: Christians are not afraid of dogs. There are some very fine churches in your neighborhood, and you may there find a statue of Christ holding a little lamb. If you stop and think about the lamb, you can imagine the nice Border Collies herding the little lamb, and then you will feel better.

If you think about the little lamb for too long, you will begin to wonder why Jesus is holding the lamb, and you might get into what some kindly folk nowadays call exploitative and dominionistic territory, so just get your thoughts to the nice Border Collies (who, unlike Christ, will not grip a lamb no matter what) and stop there.

Border Collies, unlike human shepherds, work for the sheer love of it and not with ulterior motives.

Animal Psychology is Psychology, one of the subdivisions of the Special Effects department of the academic show. Special Effects crew members often must be specially trained. They are the ones that create the monsters at Universal Studios.

DEAR JOSEPHINE TRAINER: I want to have another dog—we already have an Adirondacks Mountain Hound—but my wife says that is too many. I say that we need two dogs because just having one dog is Unnatural. We have three cats.

—Anxious in a City

DEAR CITY SLICKER: Josephine Trainer has difficulty with both viewpoints. First: One dog is not many dogs—one is one thing, many is another thing. Your wife may have meant to say "too much" rather than "too many," in which case she is on the right track, because one dog or even just the thought of a dog, especially if it is a Glen of Imaal Terrier, can be much, or too much.

Only in Nature do you get the One and the Many in one package. But a dog is always either one or else one of many, and not both at once. Thus a dog can't understand the Modern State, in which everyone is at once One and One of Many.

One of Many is different from Many, except in political theory. Kings and bureaucrats are at once One and Many, so they are Nature—coming at you from everywhere and nowhere, like locusts or AIDS—but dogs are not Nature, even on camping trips.

So don't get another dog.

The cats are okay. Cats are neither here nor there in a discussion of Nature.

DEAR JOSEPHINE TRAINER: I want my dog back? I asked the goats and he wasn't there.
                              —Stupid ~~Quester~~ Questioner

DEAR ~~QUESTER~~ QUESTIONER: Now you're talking. But what the hell do I know. The other morning I called Bandit by the name of an Airedale of insufficiently sainted memory, thus showing my failure to master the problem of the One and the Many. Or it may be that dog trainers are not always helped by the consolations of philosophy.

DEAR JOSEPHINE TRAINER: Now my husband is putting vodka in the dog's water bowl. The dog staggers around in circles, walks into walls, then falls into a corner and goes to sleep. I've thought of calling the Humane Society, but I'm afraid they'll come and take my dog away.   —Teetotaler

DEAR TEETOTALER: You are right about the Humane Society. They might come and take your husband away too, especially if you live in a developed Metropolitan Statistical Area.

You do not say what the dog's breed is, or yours. If the dog is Irish, as it sounds from your description, then he can't hold his liquor and needs help learning how. If you prefer a more patriotic approach, try your local police department, the K-9 unit. They may be willing to teach you their poison-proofing techniques, which do not involve the use of Antabuse. Antabuse does not work on dogs, as it depends on an appeal to the subconscious mind and dogs do not have subconscious minds, which is why they do not become abusive under the influence. That is also why AA and Al-Anon, which are branches of the Humane Society, do not help dogs, despite what Ann Landers told you.

DEAR JOSEPHINE TRAINER: I am a professional dog trainer. I have dogs in the kennel, but none that follow me about, because that kind of dog is a lot of responsibility. My friend Vicki Hearne says that is wrong, a dog is not too much responsibility, and that I should get a dog to get in my way.

—Dogged in Ontario, California

DEAR DOGGED: There is no clear question here. Vicki is wrong, of course—such a dog is a *lot* of responsibility, far too much if ever you stop to think about it, and clearly she hasn't and you have, and once that happens there is no going back, on the one hand, but on the other hand, if you don't have a dog getting in your way you are not in fact Dogged. This is not a case where getting a cat is the solution, because cats do not help with the kind of identity problem this situation has created—that is, are you Dogged or aren't you?

Also, has a cat ever bugged you about being taken for a ride in the car? *Think* about it.

You are the only one who can answer this question.

DEAR JOSEPHINE TRAINER: When I was little we always had dogs, and that was understandable, but I met a Borzoi breeder the other day, and that was different. Do you genuflect when a Borzoi walks by?

Also, if I may ask a second question, my father had a breeding stallion, and when I was four and a half I had a ride on him with my father, and he bucked and spooked and jumped, and I have never really felt that I understood horses. Is it my gender?

—Asking for Knowledge

DEAR ASKING: No, it is not your gender, but it sounds as though the horse may have had gender—

that is, may have been just as rambunctious as tradition has it intact males are. In any case, gender theory is irrelevant to the central problems here, which are: *Who* bucked and spooked? *What* did your father have in mind?

Seek professional help immediately. Your failure to mention your having become terrified of your father is worrisome, and suggests a possible character disorder.

Unless the horse was a Morgan of the classical, ultracivilized variety, in which case your father couldn't have known, and you are probably in your right mind, as these things go.

There is no need to genuflect when Borzois pass by if you are the incense bearer.

DEAR JOSEPHINE TRAINER: My wife says our Norwegian Elkhound bit her, but do I *know* that he bit her? I say it's because of the female Elkhound; she growls at him when she wants him to go away, and he growls at us when he wants us to go away, so it is natural, but my wife says it is a serious problem, and I don't want to call that dog trainer because I really love this dog. I am a police officer.

—On Night Duty in Orange

DEAR NIGHT DUTY: Well, it's because of *some* female Elkhound or another. In any case, yes, you know that he bit her, or at least mentioned the possibility vigorously. This is not like rape, there is no need to impeach your witness. Go ahead and call the dog trainer; training has no effect on anyone's love for a Nordic nerd, but it can cause your wife to stop saying things, female Elkhound or no female Elkhound.

DEAR JOSEPHINE TRAINER: Sometimes I get so angry about people breeding too many dogs and cats that I could just murder someone. What should I do?
—An Animal Lover

DEAR ANIMAL LOVER: When you are feeling violent, remember that you can go down to your local humane society or animal shelter and adopt a kitten or a puppy and do whatever you want to with that animal.

The only thing you will have trouble doing is training the puppy. Many people object to training, which is why there exist humane societies and animal shelters. In this culture it is cruel to teach a puppy to behave, but not to kill the puppy for misbehaving, because the Constitution, which mentions the individual but not the Public or Society, has recently been revealed to be an old-fashioned document that does not properly acknowledge the fact that while death is not healthy for the individual dog or person, it is healthy for Society as a whole.

The next best thing to death is spaying and neutering. Since these operations frequently cause behavior problems, or make existing ones worse, they can lead to euthanasia quite quickly, but they don't do so reliably. Nonetheless, they prevent puppies of all descriptions, both wanted and unwanted. After all the dogs and cats are spayed and neutered, and have died peacefully, you will have to find another outlet for your aggressions—and if you are young, this might happen in your lifetime.

DEAR JOSEPHINE TRAINER: I may be the only member of the Riders of the White Rhinoceros Club.
—Love Ya in California

DEAR LOVE: My goodness. Do tell more.

DEAR JOSEPHINE: It's hard to explain without dropping names. The thing is that my parents were, and are, antisocial types, and so they went first to Mexico and then to Africa, looking for a place that didn't have a government, I mean, not in the sense that the United States does.

Mexico didn't work out, so it came about that we were staying with these people in the Serengeti, and there would come to the lawn outside their house from time to time a white rhinoceros. He was an amiable type, and I was fifteen, and the servants had a vigorous sense of humor, so one morning at dawn I was out with my camera, getting pictures— this was what one did—and one of the servants, laughing like hell, you know, popped me up on the back of the rhino.

The rhino wasn't alarmed, but he had, I think, a slightly uneasy feeling. Wanted to get back to the herd, so headed back there, not charging, you understand, but definitely in motion.

The gait of a white rhino is very comfortable, sort of floating, but rhinos are subject to uncomfortable opinions, it turns out.

I was only fifteen, and so it wasn't hard to sit on him at all, but there was the herd looking interested, so I just sort of let myself go limp.

The camera wasn't damaged and the pictures came out okay.

Did I tell you what mongeese are like?

—Love Ya in California

DEAR LOVE: No, you didn't tell me what mongeese are like, though of course I read about Rikki Tikki Tavi.

Are they actually white? The white rhinos, I mean.

DEAR JOSEPHINE: White rhinos are paler than black rhinos, but the name is a corruption of the Afrikaans word for "wide"—they're called that because their mouths are so wide. Really wide.

Mongeese are really sweet, and they like to cuddle, but they have moods. The moods only last about five-eighths of a second, counting the part where you get on the mongoose's bad side, the part where he acts on that, and the part where you're back to normal, so it's not that big a deal, though their teeth are sharp.

We had a German Shepherd, a nice big dog, male, you understand. He was out on the lawn sleeping, all laid out on his side. A mongoose came and crawled between his hind legs, to cuddle up and get warm for a nap. The Shepherd's eyes had been closed.

Then they opened very, very wide, but nothing else moved on that dog. And the mongoose napped for about half an hour, and all that time the Shepherd was motionless, but with his eyes very, very wide, so as not to disturb the mongoose's nap, you see.

The Shepherd was a big, tough dog, and the mongoose would have been history in a sustained battle, but there he was, napping sweetly between the Shepherd's legs, his hind legs, you see, and there wasn't any reason to disturb his nap just to prove a point, is the way the Shepherd figured it.

Our new Rottweiler puppy is having trouble adjusting. I wish we still lived in Africa.

—Love Ya in California

DEAR LOVE: All right, but I am going to send you, privately, the name of a dog trainer who has never gotten accustomed to the ways of African wildlife, only the ways of California Animal Control, and you and that Rottweiler puppy are going to get together with the trainer, okay? *Autres temps, autres moeurs.*

DEAR JOSEPHINE TRAINER: In circuses, people ride white rhinos all the time—it's just what is done. What's with this Love Ya person, with the bit about being the only member of the Riders of the White Rhinoceros Club? —Just Back from a Research Trip

DEAR JUST: Of course, I knew that. But Love Ya was talking about the Serengeti, okay?

DEAR JOSEPHINE TRAINER: I wrote a book about Bandit, and that was all right, except that it took me a while to write the book, which is not the sort of book a person like me normally writes, if you see what I mean, so while I was writing it all of my friends had time to write their own versions of the book, and now their versions and mine are completely different, and they say I was not accurate enough. In particular, there is nothing in the book about the time the kennel manager cuddled with Bandit and got knocked to the floor, like this: *Thwomph!!!* And my lawyer doesn't say anything warm or friendly when I mention justice to him.

Should I have tried to be more accurate?
—Conscientiously Yours

DEAR CONSCIENTIOUS: No. There is nothing like accuracy in a book, especially a dog book, to destroy friendships, which is why Franz Kafka, the greatest journalist and animal writer of his age, never published anything if he could help it, which he couldn't always.

Since your friends only wrote their versions but did not write them *down,* they can afford the luxury of accuracy; yours is the Authorized (i.e., written-down) Version, and was presumably published—you don't say who your publisher is, by the way—so it is best to avoid putting in anything accurate or anything that might be of interest to anyone.

My information is that lawyers, like poets, are on their own so far as justice is concerned, which is why lawyers are traditionally so reticent, but you are not asking for justice anyhow, but mercy, so justice is irrelevant to your case, as your lawyer could tell you if you would only ask. Just get everyone one of those ties with Scottish Deerhounds embroidered all over, and a box of imported chocolates, and perhaps they will forgive you. Except for Bandit; chocolate isn't good for him, and he prefers black tie.

DEAR JOSEPHINE TRAINER: I trained my Dalmatian with Vicki Hearne, who is a great fan of yours, and she said that one of the reasons my Dalmatian—his name is Spot, because like Vicki I believe in traditional names—bit everyone all the time was because of his red ball. I mean, he was really a maniac about that red ball, and she says that "ball-happy" dogs can't concentrate properly on their duties, and become bite-happy, and then she told a really gruesome story about a police dog who was made ball-happy and choked to death on a ball—not a red one, like on the cover, a green tennis ball, but still, a ball. So what are that red ball and that Dalmatian doing on the cover of this book, subverting all of Vicki's good training work?

—Not Meaning to Complain, but Fond of Vicki

DEAR FOND: I heard from Vicki about this one, too. Josephine Trainer sympathizes with both of you, but facts are facts. The expressions she uses are after all "ball-*happy*" and "bite-*happy*," and the book is called *Animal Happiness*.

If you read a bit more in this book you will discover Vicki in the act of praising happiness for being subversive of everything that is upright and righteous, and that includes animal training, maintaining the public peace, and so on. Since making a dog ball-happy can be dangerous and subversive of the public peace, I don't really think that you and Vicki are on such firm ground here, much as I sympathize.

Happily, your question and the cover both demonstrate the problem about happiness that Vicki quite happily ignores in the parts of the book she has shown me. The word "happiness" is related to "perhaps," which means "by chance." It's just a matter of chance that your Dalmatian was so ball-happy that he became bite-happy. Yet Vicki writes a book celebrating happiness—once in a while distinguishing, but rather perfunctorily, especially toward the end, between giddy thoughtlessness and something more fulfilling—and implicitly celebrates Spot's superior leap and catch and grab as well as the superior leaping gear of the dog on the cover, without once dealing with the fact that not all Dalmatians are physically or mentally sound enough for the project and when is someone going to do something about this, and so on.

She could at least have mentioned Augustine, who calls God the Giver of Felicity.

Also, the cover made Vicki's editor very happy.

4
POSSIBILITIES

Wittgenstein's Lion

*I*mmanuel Kant proposed a distinction between human beings and animals at the opening of a longish essay on education. He said that baby animals, unlike baby humans, don't cry, because if they did, some wolf or wild animal would get them. But they do cry, of course, and quite often a wolf or even a wild animal does get them, and I do not bring this up to be disrespectful of the mighty dead, but to suggest that most of the time when a philosopher starts a discussion by distinguishing between people and animals, it is prudent to skip that part.

A philosopher's mistakes about animals are like anyone's mistakes about animals, of no real significance unless something follows from them, but when something does follow from them it is wise to watch carefully, because mistakes with things following from them can be tricky guides.

But there are mistakes and mistakes, some worthier than others. Wittgenstein, for example, made the most interesting mistake about animals I have ever come across. At the end of the *Philosophical Investigations,* he said that if a lion could talk, we wouldn't be able to understand him. There is a minor mistake of fact here—since lions do talk to some people, and are understood—married to another mistake that is probably a consequence of the seductions of the first-person plural, in addition to the ordinary mistaken tendency bookish types have to mystify animals (not, perhaps, in Wittgenstein's case but in other cases), as if they were, like lovers and like gold, more precious when uninterpretable.

The scholar Richard Maxwell has pointed out to me one aspect of the "we" of Wittgenstein's remark: The only instances of talking animals that virtually any set of literate Americans and Europeans all have experience of are the talking animals of children's books—a power of communication that can be controlled, turned on and off like electricity (you take a drug or eat a magic cookie, or Merlin waves his wand). These books vary enormously in their sophistication about what communication means. Some, such as *The Sword in the Stone,* are of an uncanny loveliness, and not only because T. H. White actually knew something about training. His is not an easy fantasy; The Wart has to earn his knowledge of animals. But most talking animals in the usual run of story spring from arrangements that erase the need to earn, work at, learn understanding.

Wittgenstein wanted to dispel a fantasy about language—a reasonable desire, but also one of heroic proportions that took him inevitably to a lion that daunted reason. That wasn't his mistake (if so fastidious and powerful an image can ever be put in the category of mere slippages in the gears and fears that mistakes are). But what I want to say just now is that in philosophy and in literature there are lions and lions. I can easily imagine some lion trainers I have known reading Wittgenstein's remark and saying something along the lines of, "What does he mean? That if my lion Sudan started talking we would stop being able to understand each other?" And a lion trainer who said that would be in his or her turn mistaking Wittgenstein, whose remark, mistaken properly, is of course powerful support for such claims as that Lion Trainers Are Almost Human—They Practically Speak!

It is easy to say, "There are more things in heaven and earth than are dreamt of in your philosophy," but much, much harder to say, as Wittgenstein does, with stunning precision in the course of an almost miraculously exacting mistake, that there are more things in heaven and earth than are dreamt of in one's own philosophy—locating them by dreaming, in this case, of lions, even as he mistakes lions for himself.

My friend Diana Cooper has suggested that when Hamlet says that bit about heaven and earth and philosophy to Horatio, he is perhaps not being harsh, as we generally suppose, but polite. Or, to put it another way, he is wimping out. Her point is valid, because it would have been unkind and/or reckless of Hamlet to say, "Look, fathead, there's been murder done!" The line should be spoken, then, as one would say, distractedly and with no particular confrontational intention, "Well, uh, there's quite a lot going on right now."

There is often a lot going on if there is a lion around, even though the lion is assuredly a noble beast, or else most emphatically because the lion is a noble beast. For example, when you put "noble beast" together with "Hollywood," interesting situations arise. Say a scene calls for a lion to be, sadly, run over by a truck. A large truck, of course, because a large truck is required if the lion is to look pathetic. (Alas for the Voice from the Whirlwind, who praised his servants the animals for being ever beyond human capacities to subdue, we have learned to make lions look pathetic, without the use of weapons. Our imaginations are no better than Nietzsche's psychologists, mucking about in the souls of men as if in a swamp.)

Anyway, if the scene calls for the lion to be run over by a truck, the lion must hold a Sit-stay in the road while a semi bears down on him, as fast and as close as negotiations and arguments between the lion trainer and the director and producer will allow. So the lion trainer is riding on the front bumper of the truck, the camera cunningly placed so as to show lion and truck but not lion trainer. The trainer is saying, "Stay, Sudan. Stay!" The truck bears down, then screeches to a halt. Too far away and at too slow a pace to please the director, who wants a retake. The lion trainer, Hubert Wells, is of course an agile person who enjoys demands on his ingenuity, but there are risks and risks, and a lion, as I was saying, is noble, therefore Hubert wants to get this scene safely shot before the lion's nobility is awakened in the form of distrust of the trainer's judgment.

The lovely thing about Wittgenstein's lion is that Wittgenstein does not leap to say that his lion is languageless, only that he is not talking. Wittgenstein's remark here, like other remarks of his that I have had occasion to question, is nonetheless of a profundity rarely achieved, because of all it leaves room for. The silence of Wittgenstein's lion is like many of Wittgenstein's own silences: there is something there. Or it is like the silence of God, called in the landscape of Kabbalah *zimzum*. According to Harold Bloom in *Kabbalah and Criticism*, *zimzum* originally meant a holding-in-of-the-breath, but there was a visionary named Luria who transformed *zimzum* into an idea of limitation, Bloom says, "God's hiding of Himself, or rather entering in Himself," a contraction that creates space for creation.

However that may be, consider the possibility that the lion does not talk to us because he knows we could not understand him. And the vast self-containment of this lion! Which is particularly impressive to me, since it is sometimes my wont to prattle the most when conditions, or my condition, are such that understanding just isn't in the cards.

I am not saying that Wittgenstein had these thoughts about his lion and didn't mention them because he wanted silence, only that the reticence of this lion is not the reticence of absence, absence of consciousness, say, or knowledge, but rather of tremendous presence, the presence of the king of beasts, after all, and so the reticence of all consciousness that is beyond ours, in some accounts of Creation.

Reticent, but not languageless, or not necessarily. We are creatures who can read and write, and even our talk, even the talk of someone who doesn't happen to know how to read and write, is the talk of creatures whose awareness is mediated by the peculiar ways writing organizes consciousness. Hence it is bootless to ask how many "vocabulary words" a lion has, since the very idea of a word is by and large a written idea; the trainer's command—"Sudan, Stay!"—is a particle that appears to translate into human language, and can even be written down easily. Further, whether it is in Lionese or Sanskrit or English, the command has the same reference for the lion as for the trainer and the philosopher or psychologist or movie director. The "object" in this case is a posture in relationship to a complex of other objects and postures, but it is not indeterminate in the way, say, Quine imagines indeterminacy of translation. It is not indeterminate in that the lion and the trainer both know exactly what they are talking about, and since what they are talking about, the lion's Stay, is in a language that overlaps English, I can know what they are talking about—that posture.

A posture as an object: it can be known that the posture is what is meant by "Stay!" just as one can hang out with people who speak no English and learn something of which objects are meant by which words. What is much harder to know, what you have to be deeply, genuinely bilingual to know, is what the object or posture itself means. I may know that *shlumah-ney* means what I call "candle," but not whether candles are sacred to my "informants," and not such things as whether to ask permission to use the candle to read in bed at night.

The difference between "Sudan, Stay!" as part of a complex of exchanges between the lion and the trainer and "Sudan, Stay!" as overheard by a non-trainer cannot be captured by any epistemology in my ken, for the thing about lions is that they do not talk, that no bit of their consciousness is informed by the bustle and mediations of the written, the symbolic. Indeed, the commands are there largely for the trainers, or so I am sometimes tempted to think, for the human mind is nervous without its writing, feels emptiness without writing—and most of human language is writing, narration, even when it is inscribed by means of the mouth and throat. This may not be true for tiny children, but it is for adults. So when we imagine the inner or outer life of a creature without that bustle, we imagine what we would be like without it—that is, we imagine ourselves emptied of understanding.

The lion trainer, in interaction with the lion, is engaged in exchanges that create overlap between his consciousness and the lion's, which does not mean that the trainer loses himself, becomes emptied, but rather that he is for a while inside the fullness of lionhood.

In an earlier book, *Bandit,* I considered some of the implications of the fact that dogs can recognize, "read," many human social forms and many human intentions better than we do, but not uniforms, memoranda, and the like. It is all this that Wittgenstein's lion is reticent about, all this that would interfere with our understanding him. But not every single one of us, for there are lion trainers. Lion training is a world, and some people want to live in that world; for some people, the life of richness and peace looks like a small house in the Serengeti where one can live with one's lions and without hassle—many of the hassles in question being those of writing, words broken off from the Word.

There is a tendency nowadays to suppose that without the hassles of civilization we would live in something called "Nature," but in animal work, as I have said before and have to keep saying, there is the strong sense of something else being recovered, not innocence, but knowledge that is unmediated and therefore not so nervous. It is sometimes suggested that the erotic is what is thus recovered, and that human sexuality has something to do with the exchanges between trainers and animals, which may also be why images of death and brutality so often accompany fashionable discussions of training, in which diagnosis of the trainer replaces genuine analysis of the work, in somewhat the way diagnosis of the poet replaces criticism of the poem in the writing of bad critics. But it is something else that happens when one transcends writing for a few moments, or perhaps even for days in the case of a great poet, for poetry is, among other things, transcendence of the noise of writing (the extraordinary freedom of certain prose texts from mere noise is what prompts some to say that those texts are "poems," though they are rarely completely free of psychological noise); eros is noisy in most of its regions (not all).

I am tempted to call the region one inhabits when one's consciousness overlaps a lion's richly (though not fully) timelessness, for time, like writing, pursues us with relentless discreteness of moment and disjunction, pursues us to days, to the false awakenings of our days—but that is not it either. It is more the images and shapes of days and hours, and for that matter words, that one says an effortless farewell to, and one is therefore left in the richest of worlds, worlds of days themselves rather than their images. "And," writes Wallace Stevens,

> therefore, aquiline pedants find
> The philosopher's hat to be part of the mind,
> The Swedish cart to be part of the heart.

Please do not suppose that I am here recommending solipsism; a lion is reticent, but he is no solipsist, which is why there can be exchanges between lions and trainers. And it is also the case that while the commands are, as I said, more instructive to the trainer in some ways than they are to the animals, the animals do learn what we call words, do participate in that form of understanding in which those discrete units exist. (Though I watched one trainer who always spoke to his animals in sentences and even paragraphs. He would come onto a location or a set with a cat, for example, and turn to the cat and say, "Would you mind waiting over there by that blue chair for a moment?") But language is altered by such an exchange as by any overlap of consciousness; that is what language is—that which is altered by overlapping consciousness as it alters consciousness.

Hubert Wells's lions are not anything like so reticent as Wittgenstein's. Their otherness is not so absolutely unalterable. They have personalities, temperaments, moods, and they can be voluble about all this, sometimes chatty, sometimes (when they are working) radiating a more focused informativeness. Nor are the exchanges and the work in question suffering-free. In particular, they are not free of the suffering that accompanies failures of understanding, refusals and denials of the sort that characterize many human relationships.

Nor is this a realm of love, a Christian realm. It is a realm, rather, of Respect. Lions are dangerous, for one thing, and for another they are mortal, subject to mortal moods, and so are trainers. What interests me here is simply that something happens in lion training that is in part possible because of the trainer's literacy, his capacity for mediated knowledge, but is nonetheless a transcendence of the noise and skepticism that are the inevitable accompaniments of mediated awareness. This is a world without symbols and shapes of days but only the day itself—a world that has gone beyond words (by means, in part, of words). Auden wrote that time worships language and forgives all those by whom it lives. A word for someone by whom language lives is "poet," and I am here saying that the noise of language (one traditional word for which is "sin") is not what time, perpetual time, worships, and that Auden's remark was not all that cheerful. The glory of language is often silent.

Or at least reticent, like Wittgenstein's lion, who in his restraint remains there to remind us that knowledge—at least the knowledge given by those aspects of language that live as writing, as discrete words, even when not written down—comes sometimes to an abrupt end, not vaguely "somewhere," like explanations, but immediately. His lion, regarded with proper respect and awe, gives us unmediated knowledge of our ignorance. Whether we choose to be terrified, chatty, or cautious in response has no effect on the lion.

This lion of Wittgenstein's, by the way, has received a lot of attention, as though really something has to be done about him. In *Consciousness Explained*, Daniel C. Dennet quotes the famous remark and then says, "I think, on the contrary, that if a lion could talk that lion would have a mind so different from the general run of lion minds, that although we could understand him just fine, we would learn little about ordinary lions from him." But lions do talk, as I said, if largely not in words, and I am not the first to discover that exchanges—that is, second-person grammars—are an important mode of knowledge. And a mode that fails continually, so often indeed that its successes have an arcane and dubious look. What Dennet is evading is what Stanley Cavell calls tragedy, a process that includes denying in various ways the consciousness of the other. Dennet does not deny animals consciousness, but he does deny them language. There are enormous problems in attributing language to animals, of course, even greater than the problems involved in talking to them, but what I hear in Dennet and in the triumphant announcements that the ape-language experiments failed is an enormous sigh of relief. The lion is silent, not because he has nothing to say to us in our present mode of being, but because he couldn't have anything to say, to us or to anyone, so we needn't worry about it. It is not the limits of knowledge that we face here after all, especially knowledge of consciousness. The philosophical problems have been solved; cognitive science can proceed on its merry way.

There is one more thing to say about Wittgenstein's lion. Living still in that uncanny moment of achievement in prose, he is almost intolerably beautiful. When I say that, I am not making a claim to superior understanding of the lion by virtue of my report that he is beautiful there in his great and eternal moment; what I am getting at is that Wittgenstein has said that he exists, that he has something that could lead someone to say, "If he could talk . . . ," and that he is outside our understanding, except perhaps aesthetic. Hubert Wells has something more than aesthetic understanding of lions, and so knows them better than Wittgenstein or I do. Dennet says the lion would be such a peculiar lion if he could talk that we could learn nothing from him—about the ordinary run of lions! He has other proposals for learning about lions, as if this lion who could talk would not and should not compel attention. Hubert Wells has lions with whom he talks, and indeed, this compels no one's serious attention, including that of animal rights philosophers, who have even less interest in finding out what the lion and Wells might be saying to each other than the ordinary run of philosophers, and are even more hostile to reports of those conversations that filter through the brush of the canyon in southern California where reside Sudan and Asali and others.

Wittgenstein has a lion of towering beauty who is not talking to us. I think that we court more than one kind of tragedy when we dismiss either the volubility of Wells's lions or the tremendous silence of the lion of the *Investigations*.

The Case of the
Disobedient Orangutans

Those masterful images because complete
Grew in pure mind, but out of what began?

—YEATS, "THE CIRCUS ANIMALS' DESERTION"

*B*obby Berosini is an animal trainer. When I first met him, in 1990, he had an act in Las Vegas, where he performed live, twice a night, with five orangutans, all working at liberty in front of an audience—close enough to share their champagne. Like a fair number of significant trainers, he lives in exile, having come to this country at the age of twelve with his parents, who owned the hundred-fifty-year-old Circus Medrano until the Soviet invasion of Czechoslovakia in 1968.

Berosini was accused of animal abuse, not in court, but rather on television and by people picketing his act. There were telephone threats against his life, his wife's life, and his animals' lives, and harassment severe enough to prompt the hiring of round-the-clock armed guards, continuous closed-circuit television surveillance of his property, and so on.

Berosini sued People for the Ethical Treatment of Animals. After a trial that lasted six weeks, during which he brought his orangutans into court—to show the jury that they did not cower, urinate, and defecate when he approached, and also, I suspect, so that they could use some of their coarse humor against opposing counsel—he was awarded $4.2 million in damages, which PETA was ordered to pay for "reckless disregard of the truth," among other things.

I spent a week not only watching Berosini's act but backstage as well, listening to Berosini and looking at what was going on with the eye of a particular sort of trainer, one who is interested in what is phony and what isn't. I listened in Las Vegas, in the midst, you might say, of all that is tawdry, though the lights at night are wonderful if one is in a certain mood. On the way to the stage each day, I passed by the gamblers, intrigued by the gray faces there, reminiscent of the gray faces one sees at racetracks.

W. H. Auden says that poetry survives in places "where executives would never want to tamper." The knowledge of animals survives in places where academics would never want to tamper, and don't, even now that some academics have added their voices, sometimes unwittingly and sometimes witlessly, to the babble that obscures the reality of animals. The knowledge lives in the circus, so eerily revealed by Mark Twain as a place where truth is guarded by scams, by what most would consider tawdry but what Huckleberry Finn enthusiastically embraces as "gaudy." It lives in YMCAs or the shabbier parts of parks where training classes go on. It lives at the racetrack, where the beauty of the horses, who glow as though each were the darling of the infinite god of detail, is in sharp contrast to the grayness of the faces of the gamblers, and where the reality of the risks the horses and jockeys dwell in, the glory of those risks, is parodied into grayness by the false risks and glories that constitute gambling for most people.

But Berosini's face is not gray, and the faces of his animals are not gray. They are to be sure masters of all that is gaudy, and masters of something else as well—a miracle! The miracle that was unavailable to Job, the miracle of generative cooperation between a man and some wild animals.

Berosini is not a phony trainer. Indeed, he struck me as very gifted, not only as a trainer but as a comedian. In the week I spent watching Berosini with his animals, onstage and off, I saw no abuse, no nose thumps, and I am therefore going to seize the opportunity to talk about what can be glimpsed when the bogus issue of nose thumps is tabled. The issue of nose thumps is philosophically and poetically (though not scientifically) bogus because it prevents attention to and speculation about the wondrous phenomenon of five orangutan comedians.

Berosini says, explaining what motivates his orangs to work, "We are comedians. *We* are comedians. Do you understand me?"

Comedians? Orangutans? This is not a reasonable remark from the point of view of either popular or institutionally sanctioned wisdom. On the view that animals are capable of feeling and suffering, but not of elaborate intentions and creative thought, a view prevalent in much animal rights literature, it is certain that Berosini's orangs must be beaten into submission, since food rewards are not powerful enough to motivate their complex actions, and since they cannot possibly know the mood or muse of comedy. This view is supported by academic psychology and philosophy, which by and large deny that animals have the conceptual apparatus required to make jokes.

When Berosini tells me, between shows, in a coffee shop in the Stardust, that his orangutans are comedians, I nod my head vigorously; the enchantment of the act has not worn off. But what *would* it mean to say of an animal that he or she is a comedian? This question leads one right back onstage, to the act itself, to the question Berosini and his orangs toss about, invert and capsize and rescue only to turn on its head, time and time again.

The running theme of Berosini's act is "How I Train Them." Berosini keeps saying, "People ask me how I get them to do things," or "People ask me how I train them," and then he supplies different answers. At one point the answer is, "You have to show them who is boss." He brings Rusty out to show him who is boss, and Rusty not only refuses to jump onto the stool provided for the purpose but tricks Berosini into doing so by pretending incomprehension until Berosini finally shows him how, jumping onto the stool himself. Once Berosini has dutifully jumped, the orang invites the audience to clap for him.

Berosini mocks much scientific and popular wisdom about operant conditioning by demonstrating how he doesn't need to train them because "I have magic orang cookies." A fast and lively slapstick round results from his failed attempts to get Bo to eat a cookie; the cookie is juggled, spit into the audience, hidden, fed to Berosini, but never eaten by the orang.

Then it comes again, this slapstick leitmotif: "People ask me how I train them. The truth is, I do not have to train them, because I just mesmerize them." Bo is then asked to come forward and be a hypnotic subject. There is much crooning of "You are getting very, very sleepy." Bo drops her shoulders, stands stiller and stiller, and—wonder of wonders—closes her eyes. Satisfied with the trance, the "trainer" whispers, "Are you asleep?" Bo grins outrageously, nodding her head vigorously, and then droops immediately back into her "mesmerized" posture. The joke, again, is on Berosini, or rather on the Berosini character, who in this case stands for the audience, which is to say, for humanity, or at least for that human tradition that tends to come up with overblown ideas about our superior intelligence and ability to control nature, especially animals, with animals passively responding to our active will.

"How I Train Them" is a problem whose depths are not understood until you understand something of why Berosini's orangs are so rare in the world of performing animals.

First, on Berosini's account, the way he trains is not "traditional," in that he does not teach his animals what he calls "tricks" but rather teaches them through the flow of their intelligence and his. "I do not train them to do what I know how to do," he says, "because you just cannot do that. It doesn't work!" According to Berosini, it is hardest to teach tricks to orangs, of all of the apes, because they are so self-contained, so mentally poised. The same idea is expressed in literature on orangs with reference to their marked lack of social interaction in the wild. You can say that they are not dependent on social support and approval, and if you admire this in them, that an orang is irredeemably his own person, "the most poetic of the apes," researcher Lynn Miles told me once in an unguarded moment. What she had in mind was the difference between orangs and chimps in the way they carry on their discourse with the world.

Chimps are much admired for their tool use and for their problem-solving relationship with things as they find them. A chimp looks inferential, ingenious, and ever so active while taking the various IQ tests that science presents him with—a hexagonal peg, say, and several holes of several shapes, only one of them hexagonal. In such a situation, and properly motivated, the chimp shows his tremendous initiative right away, holding the peg this way and that, trying out this, that, and the other hole, this, that, and the other angle; he *experiments*, he is filled with the inventor's work ethic, he tries, essays, tests, probes, he is full of the integrity of logic, or if not logic, then at least something very American: he is so enterprising, so resourceful.

Also, your basic chimp is inarguably a stunning athlete. Once, Bill Koehler told me, he was working dogs on a film that involved chimps.

During a break the chimps were playing with the trees on the set (this was the old days, when a lot more work was done in studios than on location), trees that were fifteen, twenty and more feet high. Three of the chimps were taking turns at a game: one chimp would climb a tree and leap off, landing on his *head*, and then jump up full of the divine hilarity of it and climb up and do it again, not only unharmed, but positively cheered by the exercise, so a chimp is *formidable*, eh? You can have him do many tricks, you can have him swing around the top of a set doing acrobatics so ebullient and rich with energy that they will express whatever triumph or stress or adventure or climax the sound track suggests.

Not your basic orang. An orang may have some acrobatic ability, but not all that much, by which I do not mean that he cannot kill you as easily as a chimp can, only that the orang is, let us say, not so replete with enterprise. Give your orangutan the hexagonal peg and the several shapes of hole, and then hide behind the two-way mirror and watch how he engages the problem.

And watch and watch and watch—because he does not engage the problem. He uses the peg to scratch his back, has a look-see at his right wrist, makes a halfhearted and soon abandoned attempt to use his fur for a macramé project, stares dreamily out the window if there is one and at nothing in particular if not, and the sun begins to set. (The sun will also set if you are observing a chimp, but the chimp is more amusing, so you are less likely to mark the moment in your notes. An orang observer has plenty of time to be a student of the varieties of sunset.)

You watch, and the orang dreams, and your notes perhaps consist of nothing more than memoranda on the behavior of the clock, when casually and as if thinking of something else, the orang slips the hexagonal peg into the hexagonal hole. And continues staring off dreamily.

Professor Miles says that such behavior contradicts the traditional finding that orangs are dumber than chimps. It is, she says, more like this: Chimps are problem-oriented, orangs are insight-oriented, the dreamers and visionaries of the world of the great apes—which is all well and good, but how do you entertain five hundred people for half an hour every night, twice a night, six nights a week for seven years, with animals whose forte is meditation, animals who do not do tricks? It would be like entertaining a Las Vegas audience with five perform-

ing poets. I am aware that there are some acrobatic poets—Allen
Ginsberg, for example. But please note that like Berosini's orangs, he
requires a straight man. He is his own straight man much of the time,
but that does not affect Professor Miles's fundamental insight, which,
put harshly, is this: You can't *do* much with an orang.

In the wild, too, orangs have not given ethologists the glamorous
behaviors that Jane Goodall's chimps have supplied her with. I found
no reports of orangs doing anything like the equivalent of fashioning
special sticks to fish out termites, for instance. Orang observers report
such vigorous phenomena as the "fruit stare," which some people say
is a function of the difficulty orangutans have foraging for food in the
wild. The trees are coy about when, where, and how much they fruit,
and the fruit is often hidden in the canopy of leaves. The fruit stare is
an expression of reverie, but it is a reverie directed outward rather
than inward, says writer Sy Montgomery, "like thinking with your
eyes." Orangs need to develop the fruit stare because the fruit is so
hard to find—"that's why they are so spaced out."

Montgomery says she has seen the fruit stare on orangs, on the
face of Birute Galdikas, an orang researcher, and on the face of a
painter friend who deliberately unfocuses her eyes, doing something
with her mind so that she can see the true outlines of things. In the
orangs' case, perhaps, they learn to detect the peculiar expression that
comes over the face or outline or figure of a canopy of leaves that is
concealing fruit.

Again, this is fascinating, but it continues to explain why there are
not so very many orangutan acts in the world, and not how Bobby
Berosini manages to have an orang act night after night.

What Berosini says, passionately, is: "We are comedians. Do you
understand me? Do you realize what I am telling you? *We* are comedians, my orangs and I." His voice is urgent now, but not frantic the
way it is when he discusses PETA or the charges of abuse brought
against him. He glitters with the knowledge he has of his animals, and
you can understand, not only listening to him but watching his act,
why some poets and philosophers have said that knowledge is an
activity. In this case the activity is training; the training is Berosini's
intimate knowledge of his orangs, just as dance is knowledge of the
dance and the dancer.

It is clear enough that Berosini is a comedian. I find the act screamingly funny, not only because the timing is so good but because the content is so intelligent. For example, there are many sardonic jokes about "monkeys" and "monkey business." These are jokes about the audience, about humanity as an ignorant audience for orangutans, because of course orangs are not monkeys. They are apes. But this is the sort of detail people consistently get wrong. One witness in another performing-ape controversy told me a story about a zookeeper and an animal he identified as "some sort of monkey." I pressed to discover what sort, and he said, "It doesn't matter. They are all monkeys, aren't they?"

Well, no, they are not, and it does matter, especially when you are claiming to speak with any authority about the animals in question. Yale anthropologist Daniel Povinelli speaks with energy about the importance of understanding the differences, not only between monkeys and apes, but also between different species of ape and different species of monkey. He says that there are pronounced morphological differences between apes and monkeys, and also pronounced psychological differences. The great apes—chimps, orangs, gorillas, and humans—"form an exclusive grouping. Orangs are just a bit older than humans, probably about twelve million years, and are the great apes most distantly related to humans. But this is still in a completely different arena from the monkeys, who evolved about twenty-five million years ago."

Great apes are much, much larger than monkeys—sometimes twice as large—and no ape has a tail, while most monkeys do, but the deepest differences are psychological, Povinelli suspects, having to do with stance and attitude toward the world. "These animals are clearly doing something different," he says. It is hard to explain just what they are doing different, since monkeys and apes both spend a lot of time looking for food; but for a student of these animals it is particularly hard to explain because it is so obvious, just as it is hard to explain the psychological differences between dogs and cats, or between elephants and lions, or between quiet, modest human temperaments and bold, rambunctious ones. Most studies have focused on cognitive differences, on what we call intelligence, the studies of signing apes being the research that has received the most attention in general publications.

For Povinelli, it is almost as radical a mistake to confuse monkeys with apes as it would be to confuse elephants with pigs, or wolves with Golden Retrievers. And to put someone who is bemusedly indifferent to the differences between animals in charge of their welfare makes about as much sense as putting a person who can't tell which of two dogs is the Saint Bernard, which the Chihuahua, in charge of a dog show. This is not only because to call orangs "monkeys" is to show insufficient respect for orangs and other great apes, but also because it is to show insufficient respect for, attentiveness to, monkeys and other "lower" species. "Evolution would be impossible without difference; there can hardly be anything more fundamental than recognizing, studying, and appreciating the enormous differences, especially the psychological differences, among different animals."

As you listen to Povinelli, whose work has been concerned with cognitive abilities in chimps, you begin to have the impression that it is not just academically but ethically unconscionable to confuse monkeys with apes. Further, the notion of intelligence does not capture the richness of the subject, since a researcher might be as awed by the abilities of a certain species of spider or wild sheep as by the more striking intellectual splendors of the great apes. That is, for Povinelli, or for an animal trainer, it is as much an insult to monkeys as it is to apes to be indifferent to the differences, since it is variety and difference itself, the many wondrous shapes and textures of mind there are in the world, that compel his respect and admiration. It is not that he would blame anyone who just didn't happen to know, but that for him caring about animals at all means being concerned to look at similarities and differences with all the rigor at your command rather than greeting information about variety with "What does it matter? They're all monkeys aren't they?"

Povinelli and Berosini are very different people, with very different relationships to animals, but what they have in common is a passionate belief that the details about an animal, whether these are psychological or morphological, are not mere pedantic decorations and should compel our respect. Berosini is a performer, Povinelli a scientist, so they would probably disagree about exactly what counts as a violation of this intellectual code, but they meet in insisting that there is a code and that it matters. Indeed, when I told Povinelli that in his act Berosini calls his animals "monkeys" and makes no attempt to correct the misimpression, he was somewhat shocked, and not entirely reassured by my explanation of the dark comic irony of the uses of the term "monkey" in the act.

As a scientist, Povinelli lives within the university world, which for all its failings is a world where knowledge is honored as highly as an institution constructed by mere mortals can manage. Things go wrong with a university, but at its best it is a place where you have to earn the right to assault someone else's claim to knowledge. Good traditional circuses are the closest the animal trainer comes to such a world, but Berosini lost his circus when he was twelve and now must live in a world, or worlds, in which there is very little acknowledgment of the depth of knowledge and commitment required to do what he does. Trainers do not even command the modicum of confused respect scientists have traditionally been paid by society at large.

I once surveyed philosophers and academic psychologists on their attitudes toward trainers, curious as to why no attempt was made to incorporate the knowledge of trainers into formal studies of animal intelligence. I found that the most frequent idea held in the academy about trainers was that "they spend so much time with the animals they become sentimental about them, and so do not understand how they achieve the effects they achieve," together with the related charge that because trainers love their animals they lack objectivity. This is an odd way to accuse someone of ignorance, since most of us would prefer to have our cars worked on by people who love engines, and our bodies worked on by people who love medicine. The trainer's experience of this sort of charge is constant, which is not only why trainers generally stay away from universities, but also why many of them experience forms of soul muddle often expressed as bitterness, and a kind of insanity.

Berosini is not, however, one who is muddled. He is very canny indeed, and it means something when he monkeys around. When Bo nods her head vigorously or applauds his "wit" when he makes a "monkey" joke, the effect is not unlike what the effect might be of seeing a Kenyan and a Jamaican comedian onstage cavorting around and inducing the audience to laugh as they call themselves "niggers." There is also a sophisticated edge here, as if Einstein were to joke around, blurring the difference between an atom and a molecule.

You have to know a great deal more than the bulk of the audience knows, about animals and the politics of animals, in order to hear the sardonic references in the reiteration of the idea of "just monkeys." These darker comments ride on the back of traditional slapstick, but the jokes are, as perhaps true slapstick always is, both constructed from and about our intellectual ineptitude and hubris; every time one of the orangs makes a "monkey" out of Berosini, the joke is on us, who in some moods, or at least in some cases, would call them "just monkeys." If you do not happen to know that orangs are apes rather than monkeys, and great apes at that, then all you know is that the human being is trying to show off and isn't getting very far, and that is funny enough. If you do know that orangs are great apes, and that for some-one who cares about them it is a shocking carelessness or lapse or even an insult to call them monkeys, and if you have, as I have, met in various parts of the country supporters of PETA and other enemies of training who are indifferent to the distinction in somewhat the way a racist is indifferent to the distinctions among "niggers," then the gags reiterating the theme "They are just monkeys, and all they (and we) are doing is monkeying around" acquire a rough edge in which you feel for a nearly painful moment that our brutality and our intellectual incompetence are one.

Berosini enacts that incompetence with gag after gag in which the "trainer" character is unable to get the demanded response by domi-nating, bribing, hypnotizing, or tricking the orang. The efforts fail, time after time, and the audience laughs, seeing that it is in fact a van-ity, an egomania, to imagine that an orang can be dominated or bribed or tricked, seeing intellectual carelessness ("They are just monkeys") and ethical carelessness ("I just have to show them who's boss") col-lapsed into one form of doomed arrogance.

But the act is comedy, true comedy, and not merely a collection of dark and sardonic jokes. The orangs and the audience and humanity itself, represented by the character Berosini portrays, are redeemed, in part by the sheer quicksilver beauty of the timing. When the audi-ence laughs with glee, and at some points with true joy, a joy free of malice, it is after all humanity that is celebrated, even humanity's ethi-cal and intellectual competence that is celebrated, because the ability to laugh without malice at one's own failings, and to see in those fail-ings one's connection with everyone else in the room, a connection made through laughter, is no mean ethical ability. The show is, as the narrator says of a comic revue in a Margery Allingham book, "a recognized intellectual leveller and [provides] one of those blessed Alsatias wherein the eyes of the moron and the highbrow meet and wink." It is this power that prompted George Meredith to celebrate comedy as the most humanizing of forms, and as the form that flourishes best in cultures in which intelligence can, momentarily at least, be freed to a rich accuracy of diction.

But the topic of our poor vocabulary is secondary to the main topic, which is training—obedience—itself. "Obedience" comes from an old French word that means "to hear" or "to heed," "to pay attention to." The great trainers of every kind of animal, from parakeet to dog to elephant, have said for millennia now that you cannot get an animal to heed you unless you heed the animal; obedience is a symmetrical relation. In a given case it may start with the human, who perhaps says to the dog, "Joe, Sit!" Soon, however, the dog will take the term and turn it, use it to respond, to say something back, and it is at this moment that true training with any species either begins or fails. If the human being obeys, hears, heeds, responds to what the animal says, then training begins. If the human being "drops" the animal at this point, not realizing that the task has only begun, then the dog or orang (or for that matter, monkey) will not listen where there is nothing to heed.

Animals, like people, are motivated in many ways. Berosini's orangs are motivated offstage in the way they seem to be motivated onstage: when they make a gesture, they get a response. The intelligent responsiveness of animals is one of the most deeply attractive things about them for us, not only because we are a lonesome and threatened tribe but because intelligent responsiveness is a central good. The intelligent responsiveness of trainers, which some of them say is respect, is what makes trainers attractive to animals, and may be the whole of the secret of "having a way with animals."

Hence, in the mismatch between the Berosini character's ideas about the orangs and the nature of the orangs themselves as they triumph continually over the would-be lordly "trainer," our fond hopes are mocked, but not cruelly. The world, which is to say, the human project, is in trouble, but within the smaller world of Berosini's act a way is found, even if it is a stumbling, awkward way, to true response. Even the audience gets a response, as when Rusty invites us to applaud Berosini, or when Tiga gives an audience member one of her "magic orang cookies," and does so gently enough, even if without subservience.

In mocking ideas of animals that are both rigid and careless, and are dangerous to both human and animal welfare, as Berosini knows as well as anyone can, he is working in what is for him a natural artistic tradition. There is the tradition of circus, of course, and of the disobedient-animal act, but there is also another tradition. Milan Kundera is only one of the best known of the Czech writers and artists who employ a cunning form of humor that only occasionally turns directly on its objects or occasions, most of the time seeming to consist in self-mockery.

The intelligence of the orangs is repeatedly mocked as well—Tiga's onstage character has a drinking problem and loose morals—but the "How I Train Them" series of gags is the most intellectually satisfying. Interestingly, Bo's sudden and startling moment of cunning awareness while she is being "mesmerized"—the moment when she grins and shakes her head mischievously, showing that she was just going along with the fiction of the hypnotic trance—is an artistic replica of Lynn Miles's account of the way orangs frustrate received ideas of what intelligence looks like. There is the dreaminess, the trance that frames the unpredictable moment of alert intelligence; Bo's eyes are closed, but otherwise she seems to imitate the fruit stare or a related trance in the same way that a dressage horse imitates, with some variations, the postures (and therefore thoughts, meanings) of "nature."

The radical claim here is that the animals are "referring to" or at least imitating the gestures deliberately, with some sense of the meaning of what they are doing. Berosini says that Bo is fully aware of the joke, and that it is her interest in thus monkeying around that makes it possible for him to work with her. This is highly speculative, but it is a more parsimonious explanation than an appeal to conditioning would be. Talk of conditioned responses is helpful in understanding some of a trained animal's development, just as it is helpful in understanding some of a dancer's or a poet's or an actor's development, but the performances of the greatest animals make much more sense if they are understood as rudimentary progressions of at least one primeval artistic impulse, the impulse to play with meaning.

Bo's grin is wonderfully timed, a case of high slapstick if there is such a thing, but it is also, for me at least, an eerie instant of revelation, when I see something fairly exact in Berosini's claim that his orangs are comedians. The joke is not the same for Bo as for the audience, or not exactly, but it is a joke about who is in control. My knowledge of other animals leads me to suspect that the important "payoff" for Bo is Berosini's response rather than the audience's; one energy driving this partnership is the continual pleasure of having one's partner, night after night, appreciate one's gestures and even jokes.

But Berosini himself does not perform as the intelligent audience for his orangs. His act is an intricate display of human foolishness, and a loving display of the orangs as knowing watchers of that foolishness who are not taken in by it. The onstage Berosini character is continually tripped up by his foolish assumptions about how simple and ignoble orangs are. When he is showing Rusty "who is boss," attempting to get him to jump up onto a sequined stool, Rusty triumphs by tricking Berosini into doing the jumping. Having seen numerous dogs in real life trick their handlers into going out and fetching the dumbbell for them, I find this and many other such jokes to be deeply expressive of one continual truth of animal intelligence.

That is, the act gives the orang's point of view and intelligence pride of place. In this it belongs to an ancient tradition of humor, the tradition that starts with the Greeks, in which the *eiron,* or apparently lowly character, triumphs over the apparently nobler character through wit, awareness, quickness of perception. The word *eiron* gives us our word "irony." In circus and movie tradition, the most familiar form of the comedy of the *eiron* is the disobedient-dog act, in which the trainer character attempts to induce the dogs to display loyalty, nobility, and willing service, and instead they trip the trainer, disgrace Rin Tin Tin by stealing a purse from an audience member, "bite" the trainer, and so on. Like Berosini's orangs, the dogs in a well-done disobedience routine mock our importance and our state, but Western audiences are more likely to be finely sensitive to the jokes in such an act, because more likely to know also the serious literary tradition against which the disobedient dog lifts his leg.

It is not Lassie and Rin Tin Tin themselves who are mocked by the disobedient-dog act, but rather our self-serving ideas of the selflessness of dogs, such as the pious idea that dogs "want to please," and work "for love of the handler." This is an idea I encounter frequently, not only in my work teaching people to train their dogs, but also in my studies of the Western tradition of philosophical and ethical thought. The idea that dogs want to please us leaves us free to believe that our pleasure is worth working for, and that dogs are far too deeply in the grip of adoration ever to have a critical thought about our intellectual or physical failures of grace. We call dogs who are not particularly impressed by our posturing "stubborn" or "dominant" instead of considering the possibility that dogs' disobedience, which is far more common than their obedience, is an expression of their opinion of our intelligence and authority. There is a tradition of dog writing, such as Terhune's collie stories, in which the central character's right to command is never doubted, but there is another tradition, with comic versions in books as well as in circuses and onstage, in which disobedience shows that a healthy dog can find our grandiose ideas quite funny and yet, miraculously, remain fond of us.

In the case of Berosini's orangs, there is no Western cultural equivalent of Rin Tin Tin in the background, no rich version of the noble orang to play with. So Berosini's orangs do not trick Berosini by appearing to go along with his foolish ideas of how noble they are, but rather by appearing to go along with his foolish ideas of how stupid and debased they are. Westerners have had some grand conceptions of the horse and the dog, and even on occasion of the lion and the elephant, but very little in the way of grand conceptions of apes, so an ape who is duping a human being has less material to work with. Berosini's orangs work with the material wonderfully, performing their intelligence against the backdrop of our ideas of their debasement.

I suppose that the next artistic step would be for some literary genius, some modern Dickens, to become as entranced with the European circus tradition of which Berosini's act is so brilliant an example as Dickens himself was with the dogs that frequently appeared onstage in his beloved pantomime, an entrancement that gave us the first instances in serious literature of the dog as citizen. One of my favorites is Merrylegs, the dog in *Hard Times*, who represents fancy or imagination, the grace that saves us from our overly solemn moral moods. Merrylegs is the moral center of that novel and its long, hard, dark, bleak narrative of what life is like without Merrylegs, who is a circus dog. At the end of *Hard Times*, the world is redeemed through dogs.

Berosini's act is only half an hour long, and that is not enough time for the redemptive vision of a Dickens to be fully elaborated, but the basic structures are there, in the development, for instance, of the orangs' relationship to Berosini. At the beginning of the act, he gets the finger frequently and vigorously in one way and another; by the end the orangs are still displaying amusement at his efforts to control them, but it has become affectionate amusement, as when Tiga from time to time gives him a big smacking kiss and makes bedroom eyes. Human arrogance and ineptitude are redeemed as all friendships are redeemed, in part through the sheer persistence of the parties involved—they keep coming back for more, negotiating friendship.

Therefore, if anyone can give us the ape equivalent of Merrylegs, it is Bobby Berosini, not only because he is a splendid trainer, but also because he is a gifted comedian. If his comedy is somewhat dark and sharp-edged when you begin to take a close look, that may be in part because of the tradition of comedy he inherits as a Czech, a tradition that has had to learn, over and over again, how to institute the survival of intelligence and social criticism in forms that escape the more violent scrutiny of various states and regimes. Berosini's orangs enact, among other things, the comic courage by means of which sanity survives in social and political darkness. Humor, especially Berosini's humor, is too quick and active to be a weapon against the state, but humor is sometimes a shield for the mind in that it deflects the kind of overwhelming questions that destroy the mind. It seems from Berosini's act that this is so also for orangs, that they use their humor to shield themselves from the onslaughts of human ignorance and pride. I mean nothing apocalyptic by this, only those thousands of forms of benign amusement at our vaunted ideas of control familiar to any dog or cat owner who pays a little attention to what the animal means by it when he or she emphatically refuses to do a "trick" for guests. Orangs and dogs and cats are moved to "make monkeys" of people for the same reason schoolchildren or citizens of any bureaucracy are.

A major question arises. Is Berosini's act all a cunning illusion, Czech literary tradition or no Czech literary tradition? If the allegories in the routines, which are allegories of orang humor, mischief, and mental poise, reflect something real, then the act should move us to stand up and take our hats off to the orangs rather than pity them.

One of Berosini's most famous monkey jokes occurred in court; during my stay in Las Vegas it was repeated to me at least two dozen times. At one point PETA's lawyer asked Berosini to tell the audience how he taught Bo to give the finger. He replied, "I would be glad to demonstrate the finger for learned counsel." This is just the way his orangs perform in his act, ragging him around. In the act, Berosini plays the role of a trainer. The trainer he portrays is named Bobby Berosini and is continually foiled by the orangs' impudence, back talk, irreverence, impiety. And they give him the finger. In one way and another animals do give trainers the finger, and animals vary in the extent to which they enjoy and elaborate on their forms of humor. Of course, a great deal of animal humor is a bit coarse, to put it mildly. I have long suspected that the real reason it was for so long heresy, an excommunicable offense, to say that animals have souls is that if you say they have souls then you have to attend to their jokes and comments, and no bureaucratic or ecclesiastical or philanthropical dignity can survive animal vaudeville.

In offering to give a demonstration of the finger to defense counsel, Berosini was in one sense answering the question asked, because one way orangs learn is by "aping," mimicking; the reason the verb "ape" means "mimic," the reason we have the expression "Monkey see, monkey do," is precisely that apes do love to mimic people. But of course in offering to give counsel the finger he was also refusing the question, changing its meaning, deflecting its meaning, and the dislocation or refusal of meaning is the heart of all humor, from the lowest slapstick to the highest wit of the Elizabethans.

Joan Berosini, Bobby's wife, reports that one juror, who asked to remain anonymous, said after the case was over, "It would be abuse to take the orangs away from Bobby." If there is something to this, something that can be understood without elevating Berosini to the status Patron Saint of Orangs—a status that would destroy his comic art—what is there to it? Or rather, what is there about this whole enterprise that makes the improbable idea that the flow and liveliness and energy of the orangs' performances is achieved through beatings more popular than the far more likely idea that the orangs, even if they do not mean their antics the way the audience interprets them, nonetheless mean something by them, and are motivated to stay onstage working with Berosini rather than running loose in the audience, not by terror—which is a poor motivator—but by an interest in what they are doing?

Some people tell me that it is nonsense to suppose that there can be any higher meaning to the training of any of the great apes, because they are not and never will be domestic animals. One such person, a gentleman at dinner who had previously asserted that domestic animals are by definition perverted and debased forms of their wild cousins (an opinion I dared him to express while face to face with my husband's witty, sardonic Plott Hound, Lucy Belle), also ranted somewhat messily (I had to have my blouse dry-cleaned afterward) about that brutal Las Vegas chimpanzee trainer, Borkanini. I wondered if he had Berosini confused with Reagan's luckless Supreme Court nominee. In any case, one charge against Berosini and circus trainers and zookeepers adds up to the following: It does not matter whether or not the animals are physically abused, since it is unnatural (or sometimes "ethologically inappropriate") to keep these animals in any relationship to humans at all. What I hear in this, and in much of what is touted as a new concern for animals and for the environment, is despair at the possibility of the hearth, of what is secure, domestic, of what you might call a cozy rationality.

Berosini's orangs live with him, but to live with orangs is definitely not to live as one does with dogs or horses. They are too mischievous for that, and too alien, too dangerous. Of course, dogs, cats, and horses often refuse the terms of our domestic pieties, especially the one about their wanting nothing more than to please us, but there is a difference in kind as well as degree in the care and trouble and study and effort involved in working with orangs. The demands of keeping these animals and working with them are such that an orang trainer pretty much gives up most of what goes under the heading "the hearth." For a wild animal-trainer, home is work.

The shepherd and his dogs share their work, and at the end of the day they also share without much trouble agreements about what counts as resting around the house. Furthermore, in an area where dog laws are not too strict, dogs can be residents not only of a house but of a neighborhood or community. Not so orangs; their worlds and ours are too different. The orang trainer cannot, say, go visiting with his animals the way I can with my dogs; the arrangements involved in going anywhere with an orang are cumbersome, elaborate, costly. An orang trainer, like a monk or a nun, gives up the usual solaces of the world for the sake of his or her animals. A dog and a trainer, or a horse and a trainer, do not have to "meet each other halfway"; they are already in the same social space. An orangutan and a trainer must travel some conceptual distance to meet each other and work together. That this is possible, what it means that it is possible, what implications it has for the possibilities of mutual respect—this begins to strike me as a matter of the utmost importance.

One way to express my disappointment with the various manifestations of the humane movement—which is a disappointment at the possibility of impersonal kindness, or in any case kindness at a distance, kindness in the absence of a relationship—is to say that I am astonished that people who care about great apes, or say they do, are not flocking to Las Vegas or Animal Actors, making sacrifices in order to learn more about the rich, intricate options there revealed, especially in light of the rapid disappearance of wild habitats. It looks as though we no longer have the option of simply leaving nature alone, looks as though something more radical is necessary in the way of a transformed relationship with nature than has yet been suggested. Wild-animal training is certainly not a solution to all problems, but the knowledge trainers have may contain clues to imaginative and enlightened ways to take up the burden of responsibility toward animals.

There was a Shar Pei named Charlotte whose owner drove six hours to take lessons from me because no other trainer would work with Charlotte; she bit too fast and too hard. The owner loved the dog, and so was willing to do the work involved. Most of such work is subtle, the language is subtle, the way genuine teaching of anything worthwhile is subtle, but we did have to bop Charlotte on the nose for trying to bite. Charlotte now wags her tail when approached by strangers, instead of attacking them. She enjoys playing with her owner's nephews and is interested in explanations. She is one of the important success stories, not because training her was harder than training many dogs, but because the change was so obvious and dramatic.

I told the story of Charlotte's transformation from a frightened, snarling mess into a sane, happy dog to a young Nietzsche scholar of my acquaintance and asked him the question I was asking anyone who was unwise enough to come within hearing distance: "Why is no one interested in the fact that Charlotte is wagging her tail?" He said, "Because no one is interested in language." On the face of it a curious remark, since he is a late-twentieth-century philosopher, and twentieth-century philosophy has apparently been obsessed with language. So what did he mean by that—or rather, what am I choosing to learn from his remark, whatever he meant?

What comes to my mind is the question that grounded an earlier book of mine, *Adam's Task:* Why do great animal trainers talk the way they do? Why do they talk in parables and stories, and why does it seem that one can't get a straight answer to a question about how some piece of animal work is accomplished?

And how do trainers teach and think in the odd language they teach and think in? Jack Knox, for example, will say to a student, as an explanation for a dog's failure with a particular herding problem, "You've asked your dog, and you've gotten the answer, but you're no listening to the answer." Or people will ask him if they should talk to their dogs, and his reply is, "Oh, aye—but talk sense!"

It does no good to say that this is "anthropomorphic" and therefore fallacious, though it might begin to do some good if we began to wonder what an accurate characterization of "asking" and "getting an answer" and "no listening to the answer" would be like. It wouldn't be wrong to call this language metaphorical, but it wouldn't be exactly right either, for there is no literal account. The language is invocative; it exists before the divorce between the literal and the metaphorical. There is no point in taking out cameras and computers and analyzing the movements that are characterized as "asking" and "listening to the answer," since that project will not tell you what people learn from Jack Knox's sometimes oracular ways of thinking and speaking. Or, to put it another way: Knox's language does not need to be cured of anything. His dogs and students are successful. It is the philosophers and others who accuse him of confusion and error who cannot teach a dog or a person to herd sheep. His is a wonder-working language, and even a wonder-working philosophy.

In some corners philosophy and other disciplines are becoming obsessed with animal issues. Yet there has been no useful writing, none at all, that addresses the wonders of animal-human work of various sorts. The philosophers whose books come my way still imagine that they can "refute" a writer such as Konrad Lorenz by triumphantly pointing out that he made anthropomorphic remarks. This is in the worst sense childish, since the family of tropes damned as "anthropomorphic" points us to the places where the greatest secrets of animal thinking, and thinking in general, begin to be revealed.

The language that needs curing is the language of those who want to "cure" Jack Knox or Bobby Berosini of their ways of talking, or at least laugh them out of court, but if you want to know something of what orangutans are like, you have to listen to Berosini, listen to his words rather than analyze them. Anthropomorphism is not truth, any more than metaphor is poetry; anthropomorphisms are language and therefore the bane as well as the glory of the human enterprise. The bane because they are language, which is for us the principal vehicle of the unreal, of confusion. The glory because they are language, and when some turn in language opens reality to us, divinity becomes a possibility.

There is something here, something to be heard in anthropomorphisms that make certain philosophers and linguists and psychologists sneer in triumphant disgust. But I am not listening to those people just now, I am listening to Bobby Berosini.

What he says does not put him on anyone's "side" in the animal rights argument as it is presented in public discourse at any level. The philosophers of animal rights and consciousness do not have the intellectual and imaginative tools needed to understand what he is saying. It is possible that a rabbi for whom the Book of Job resonates like a prayer or a god could understand him, especially in light of the fact that orangutans are wild animals, the ones Job cannot, as the Voice from the Whirlwind keeps pointing out, compel cooperation from. The wild goat and the unicorn and the ostrich and the war horse are beyond Job—but the orangutan is not beyond Bobby Berosini, and it behooves us to understand this, to know that there is something to understand and that the contemplation of nose thumps will not open understanding here.

While I find the idea that Berosini's orangutans are "enslaved" to be self-serving and irresponsibly sentimental, the expression of a thrill-seeking emotional/political impulse, I do not find the idea that they live in a kind of exile to be so nonsensical. Not because they can yearn for a Malaysia they have never seen, but because they are not, as some thinkers have said post-technological humanity is not, living in the environment in which they evolved. In effect, I agree with PETA and others who say that they are displaced persons.

Exile is difficult, but whether it is necessarily and always evil is not clear. In any event, I think of Berosini and his orangs as both living in exile. Berosini's exile from his homeland is literal: when he was twelve, his parents fled in the face of the Soviet invasion of Czechoslovakia. His exile from the circus—that is, from a culture that would give both him and his orangs fuller psychological and intellectual room—is equally literal, though harder to see unless you follow him around for a few days and learn something of the disciplines of his life. Like his orangs, he lives apart from his own kind. Thus he shares their refugee status. We may all be refugees, from Eden or from the possibilities of speech, but the Czech orangutan trainer cannot help but know this about himself.

And if Berosini is not deluded or lying when he says, "We are comedians. Do you understand me? *We* are comedians!" then he and his orangutans share another kind of exile, the exile of the artist who must in effect leave home for the sake of art even if he or she remains physically in the house. For the artist, truth itself is a kind of exile. (As it is for any human being; we are confronted with confusions and must do something about them, and we do, with varying degrees of success.)

Within exile, there is home on the road, a mini-culture with its own rules. These are not as severe as the rules of the jungle. In Sumatra and Borneo, failure to obey the rules of the jungle means death, sometimes a quite horrible death, just as in Czechoslovakia in 1968 the failure to please and obey the conquerors meant terror and death. In exile, or in, let us say, the temporary refuge from confusion that the life of art is, a failure on Berosini's part to obey the nature of his orangutans (rather than the rules of civilian or domestic life) can mean that he gets injured. For his orangutans, a failure to obey the rules of decorum in such a life can mean that they are thumped on the nose—not fatally, not even with the result of physical injury. Obedience to the rules of the artistic or performing life, for both man and orangutans, means new forms of life, new discoveries of what it means to be: human, orangutan, at home or in exile. When Bo gives the stage version of Berosini the finger, or when Rusty induces him to jump up on the stool, or when Bo breaks the trance of superstitions about our influence over animals by grinning with cheerfulness and glee, nodding her head vigorously, a window is opened into possible realms of animal-human relations. And the moral question here is not the one raised in court or in the press about abuse. The question is the one a friend of mine asked many years ago when we were at a performance of the Preservation Hall Jazz Band. The question is, "Should they be allowed to have that much fun?"

James Thurber, who defended the intelligence of animals and animal wit as vigorously as anyone ever has, once wrote, about human wit, "The perfect tribute to perfection in comedy is not immediate laughter, but a curious and instantaneous tendency of the eyes to fill." This, I keep thinking, this and not weepy displays of ignorant outrage and pity, is the tribute owed to Berosini's orangs. But be careful your vision does not mist too much. Bo and Rusty and Tiga and Nick and Benny are quite clear-eyed. Trainers speak often of how uncannily good animals are at "reading" people, and of training as a humbling activity because when you train an animal you give yourself and the animal a "vocabulary"—if not a language—by means of which the animal can tell you more than you wanted to know about what he or she sees in looking at you. If there is a moral to the act that the orangs are in on, it is this: Be sure that when Tiga looks into your eyes she finds a clarity and amused intellgence fit to answer her own, lest she turn from you, leaving you in the foolish darkness yet again.

Why Dogs Bark at Mailmen

A *Theory of Language*

*O*ne of my projects these days is to rescue the topic of rights from its current disgraceful state, both in and out of the academy. But first I have a story to tell. The story is about two Airedales, a breed of dog I have already discussed at some length in Part 2 of this book. Here I will simply repeat that words such as "choreography" and "wit" are what come to people's minds when they are trying to explain Airedales. Their origins, as even the earliest writers readily say, are clouded in mystery, probably because they were originally poachers' dogs, which is no doubt why they are so versatile, since a poacher's dog has to be able both to hunt boldly and nobly and to respond fast in case the game warden is chatting up his master when he returns with the game. Airedales, therefore, are the product of a particular kind of criminal, which is to say poetic, genius.

One evening I was working on scent discrimination with Drummer, who was two years old at the time and has always been fairly solemn for an Airedale. The exercise required him to go to a group of visually identical articles laid out on the ground, pick the one that had the designated scent on it, and bring it back. Until that evening he had been performing this exercise rather perfunctorily, with a bored and even slightly disgruntled air, as if he were saying, "Well, it's a living." Then, suddenly, he was nailing that sucker every time, and coming back with zest and animation, and celebrating with high (though always dignified) glee.

Drummer's performance may have had something to do with the presence of Texas, who is the first dog of mine Drummer has really disapproved of, and who was watching Drummer work with both dismay and intent interest from about twenty feet away. There is nothing like a lively, ambitious young male dog in the house to motivate another male dog, I have discovered.

Having finished with Drummer, I put him and the equipment in my jeep. One scent article—the one with my scent on it—I put in the passenger well, along with his collar and enough in the way of other scent articles, dumbbells, collars, leashes, Utility gloves, and the rest of it to stock a small store. Then I got Texas, who, as I say, had been watching the whole scent-article routine with great concern. I worked him for perhaps half an hour, and he was so brilliant on his Finish—a movement that is at once a kind of grace note on the general melody of novice and advanced obedience work and also has the practical effect of returning the dog to one's side, at the "ready" position—that my· friend George was moved to say that Texas had excelled just because George was watching, so that George would think he isn't as dumb as he looks. (George calls Texas "El Wacko.") I commented sadly that I seemed to be the only one who liked Texas, and George, who is an ex-cop, said yes, it's always that way with the hard-core criminals—their mamas talk about what good boys they always were.

Anyway, I took Texas to the jeep, to drive home. Texas rides in a crate because he doesn't yet grasp certain social realities. There, very neatly placed next to Texas's crate, in the back of the jeep, were the collar I had been working Drummer on and the scent article. There they were, side by side, those three objects. A message? A passionately thought-out message. How should I read it? (How respond, that is?)

What I did was to look at the objects in bemusement, and then at Drummer, who was solemnly watching for my response rather than wagging and bragging. I nodded at him and began to wonder as I (thoughtlessly? carelessly? indifferently?) returned the items to the passenger well before telling Texas to kennel up.

Drummer, I believe, is too much the gentleman to resort to physical violence in order to make a point, and would not resort to mockery, either. If the dogs were of some other breed, a less pleasant sort of resentment might appear, but they are classic Airedales, not above a fight, but always keeping an eye out for the stylish way to manage any situation.

Now a riot of interpretation begins. Soon after this event I happened to be conversing with an acquaintance who has Huskies and studies pack behavior, and she was quite clear about what it all meant.

The message was for Texas only, not for me, and went something like this: "Okay, youngster, you can go out there and do your twinkle-toes thing and get praise from Miss Vicki and that's well and good, but when you're in here you remember your place, and you remember who I am!"

Well, I couldn't deny that there was something of that in it, especially as this is a very strenuous friend, but I found myself thinking that Drummer and Texas are not Huskies, they are Airedales, and that there are different kinds of social relations. In Airedales, pack hierarchy is not a visionary affair that covers as much as it might in the Nordics. For one thing, Airedales don't "pack" as well as the Nordic breeds do, which is natural enough—Huskies, bred to pull sleds, are bred for a work that is a virtual map of a pack. Airedales, bred for police work, guide-dog work, and big-game hunting, are bred for something that includes the idea of partnership more strongly than it does the idea of pack, and the politics of an animal born to the idea of partner—as when a cop explains an action by saying, "She's my partner!"—are different from the politics of an animal bred to the social relations of a pack. A Husky might well explain an action by saying, "That's the way the pack order is," but pack order is not meaningful to the terriers, which is why you don't hear much about "packs" of Airedales but you do hear of packs of foxhounds or Huskies, dogs bred to work as packs. I am willing to give Konrad Lorenz, to whom we owe most current talk of "pack order," a lot of credit, but not everything, especially not everything about Airedales, can be explained this way.

There is a further problem for—for which branch of the intellect? Linguistics? Semiotics? For consider the incredible specificity of the pile: the exact two articles I had just been using to work Drummer, plus Texas's crate, and the articles *not* blocking the door to the crate but, more interestingly, lined up beside it, in such a way that my hand would have to pass over them in order to open the crate for young Tex. A lesser dog, with a lesser education, might just have peed on the crate, perhaps—but this dog did not.

I am tempted to use the expression "symbol." I have already called what Drummer did a "message," which I spent time trying to "decode" or "read"—who was the message for, me or Texas or both?— and so on. I have said elsewhere that dogs cannot read or write, and I meant it, and I will say it energetically again, but Drummer's action forces me to realize that I am not sure what I am saying when I say that. I cannot but believe that Drummer consciously created a "message" for me to "read," and yet a message is very like something written—that is, the capacities needed to send and receive messages are related to the capacity to read and write. And to say that Drummer's little sculpture was "merely" a form of "marking behavior" is to raise new questions about marking behavior—birds marking out territory with song, and canines with what we delicately call "scent."

Here I pause to consider Gallup's work with primates and mirrors. He thought, among other things, that it was odd that only human beings should have a concept of self, that there should be so large an evolutionary leap. Then he seemed to find that there was such a leap, only it started with chimpanzees rather than people; for he showed that chimpanzees can recognize themselves in mirrors. I find myself as uneasy as Gallup seemed to be, though not so much with the idea of an evolutionary "leap" of this sort as with the idea that a concept of self must be expressed by a certain relationship to mirrors. Chimps do not have wonderful senses of smell, but dogs do, and I would say they unquestionably have a concept of "mine" and "thine," often expressed as perceptions of scent; a dog doing a perimeter check responds differently to his or her own scent than to a stranger's. Perhaps the evolutionary leap, which can go in either direction, I suppose, up or down the evolutionary scale, is to a particular way of perceiving in which seeing is believing.

There are other possible interpretations. Daniel C. Dennet, in *Consciousness Explained,* claims that Wittgenstein misses the point when he says that if a lion could talk we wouldn't be able to understand him. The main point for Dennet is that it is not any particular lion we want to understand, but "lionness," and a talking lion would not be typical, would tell us nothing about "lionness," in perhaps much the same way a talking woman tells us nothing about womanhood.

Another interpretation might come from some branches of the humane movement, in and out of the university, which, like Dennet, reject cases of individual doggie initiative of this sort, though not for being atypical, but rather for being purchased at too great a moral cost. Dogs who are not trained, who do not have grammars, do not behave as Drummer did, and training, according to the humane movement, is inherently coercive.

But! I found myself saying "sculpture," and now, perhaps excessively encouraged by some of the company I keep, I want to say "poem," or at least "proto-poem." In any event, I said "sculpture," as though Drummer's creation were something like a work of art in being intended in a particular way.

So: Imagine Drummer by himself, meditating in this way on relations between himself, me, Texas, and the work Drummer and I do together. Hoping that I would, in Matthew Arnold's phrase, overhear his meditation? Or only later interested in that, as I am only later interested in the response of a reader when I am writing a poem? If it was a poem, then here is what may have happened: Drummer may have begun by wanting to leave a message or mark, perhaps for me, perhaps for heedless young Texas. Or he may have had, as so often we do, an impulse that is halfway between the desire to leave a "message" and something like the diarist's impulse.

I recited all this to John Hollander, who knows a lot about how poems come about, and he noted, in great excitement, what happens if we imagine that at some point Drummer became more interested in the arrangement itself than in the message. Indeed, the more I think about this, about the precisions of the arrangement, the specificities of the relations between the three objects—crate, collar, and scent article—the more this seems to me a reasonable idea. And an intriguing one, for one result of this idea is that Drummer acquires a great deal of authority, or authorship—much more than he would have if he had merely been sending a "message" in the way dogs do when they object to a new pup by tearing into the furniture, chewing up leashes and retrieving articles, and so on.

By the way, someone may want to know why, if it was the arrangement that interested Drummer, he did not add to it any of the other articles from the rich collection in the front of my jeep. The answer, I think, is fairly simple, and not particularly to the present point: Drummer happens to be an extremely gentlemanly dog, and the other articles weren't his. As a footnote to this digression, I should like to say that I once had an Airedale who was remarkably good at picking up odd routines; he played leapfrog with the other dogs, cheerfully imitated Poodles, German Shepherds, Golden Retrievers, and police dogs, could learn a particular route through a set of playground equipment in ten minutes flat, and so on. One evening I thought I would work out a "pickpocket" routine with him and tried to get him to retrieve a handkerchief hanging out of someone's back pocket, and he simply wouldn't. Puzzled, I asked my training teacher about this, and he replied, "Well, that dog isn't a thief." I was much abashed.

Drummer isn't a thief either, which is not to say that he is a submissive dog; he is very interested in his own authority, in people knowing Who He Is. There are those who would tell me that the amount of training I do with him diminishes his authority, but anyone who says that simply does not understand dogs. More deeply, anyone who says that does not understand authority itself. Floating around in literary studies these days is the idea that literature itself is coercive, and that writers are unwitting tools of the state, coercion being the only synonym for power some people have. On that interpretation, Drummer's poem or sculpture puts him on the next rung up the ladder, an oppressor rather than an oppressee. Or else an unwitting tool of the state.

The great poet Yeats wrote in his old age, "We [meaning poets and storytellers—which means in a way all of us] have no gift to set a statesman right," but it may be that poets have a gift to set the statesman wrong, which is why this business of telling dog stories is such a delicate matter whose interior tolerances are so minute, and why I wanted to embark on a study of dog stories.

But I got waylaid by a theory of animal rights. I have avoided for twenty years now coming up with a theory of animal rights, since it did not strike me as a rational thing to do. Still, people kept asking me about it, and one day it happened: there was a theory of rights appearing on the page, which I shall now impose on you. Some of this material has already appeared in print and may be familiar to you, but it is necessary background for some comments I hope to be able to make about a specific kind of law.

I have moved lately, more rapidly than I wanted to, from the idea that language is primarily a matter of exchanges to the idea that rights are also a matter of exchanges, and that the dear, gorgeous fiction of rights embedded in the fact that in this country rights are codified into the law of the land—an astounding idea if you think about it a bit—is a fiction that needs to be reapproached if it is to be salvaged.

When I said at the outset that I think rights has become a largely bogus topic, in and out of the academy, I had in mind largely the fact that rights are generally used these days to justify interventions of one sort and another on someone else's behalf. These interventions are inevitably institutional, and in many cases disastrous, the result of the worst sorts of hypocrisies, I believe—worst in that they are functions of our highest capabilities, our capacity for reading and writing. It is a peculiar fact for me that rights talk nowadays justifies interventions, which tend to take the form of prosecutions and impoundments, since I grew up on the idea, naive and rusty, that rights had to do with being left alone. The failure of this idea is what has led me to my present ramblings.

The question that comes first to my mind is this: What would it mean to say that an animal has the right to the pursuit of happiness? How would that come about, and in relationship to whom?

Understanding the answer entails, first, understanding that not all happy animals are alike. A Dobie going over a hurdle after a dumbbell is sleek, all arcs of harmonious power. A Bassett Hound cheerfully performing the same exercise exhibits harmonies of a more lugubrious nature. Happiness for the draft horse named Pete, a weight-pull champion of international caliber, is not the same thing as Secretariat's ebullient bound, his joyful length of stride. A Border Collie's intelligence, that rich soil of happiness, has to do with balancing and ordering sheep. For the weight-pull horse or dog or ox, happiness is of a different shape, more obviously awesome and less obviously intelligent, for it is at its most intense when the horse or dog or ox goes into himself, allocating all the influences that organize his desire to dwell there in fierce and delicate intimacy with that power, leans into the harness, and makes that sucker *move*.

The liberty horse trainer with her band of stallions dancing about her is another matter yet, for her horses' happiness is a work that for some, better than Rome or Paris, writes one meaning of culture in a legible dance. There are chimpanzees who love precision the way musicians or fanatical housekeepers or accomplished hypochondriacs do, others for whom happiness is a matter of invention, variation— chimp vaudevillians. There is a rhinoceros whose happiness, as near as I can make out, is needing to be trained every morning, all over again, or else he "forgets" his circus routine, and in this you find a clue to the slow, deep, quiet chuckle of his happiness, and the glory of the beast.

There is a sea lion named Algae, of a queenly nature, She Who

Must Be Pleased—"She's so snooty she just sticks her nose in the air and walks off if you don't do it right," says Mark Harden, her trainer. Algae refuses to leave her pool for a job if she hasn't been worked that week, on the grounds, apparently, that she isn't to be handled casually; Harden has learned a great deal about making situations "Algae-proof," which means making situations such that it won't be disastrous to obey Algae's whims. Obey Algae's whims he must, for it is a happiness for most animals to see how many things they can make the handler do. Most people who start training their dogs with the idea that training an animal is a matter of ordering the animal about are quickly reeducated; working with an animal is not a matter of manhandling or forcing the animal (if it were, there would be no such thing as guide dogs or dogs who work with paraplegics), but the handler does have to be as committed to the situation as the animal is.

In speaking of "animal happiness," we often tend to mean something like "creature comforts." The emblems of this are the Golden Retriever rolling in the grass, the horse with his nose deep in the oats, kitty by the fire. Creature comforts are important to animals; "Grub first, then ethics" is a motto that would describe many a wise Labrador Retriever, and I have a pit bull named Annie whose continual quest for the perfect pillow inspires her to awesome feats. But there is something more to animals, something more to my Annie, a capacity for satisfactions that come from work in the full sense—something approximately like what led so many women to insist that they needed a career, though my own temperament is such that I think of a good woodcarver or a dancer or a poet sooner than I think of a business executive when I contemplate the kind of happiness enjoyed by an accomplished dressage horse. This happiness, like the artist's, must come from something within the animal, something trainers call talent, and so cannot be imposed on the animal, but at the same time it does not arise in a vacuum; if it had not been a fairly ordinary thing in one part of the world at one point to teach young children to play the pianoforte, it is doubtful that Mozart's music would exist. There are animal versions, if not equivalents, of Mozart, and they cannot make their gay passions into sustained happinesses without education, any more than Mozart could.

Aristotle identified happiness with ethics and with work, unlike Thomas Jefferson, who defined happiness as "Indolence of Body;

Tranquility of Mind," and thus as what I call creature comforts. Aristotle also excluded as cases of the ethical anything that animals, women, artists, and children do, for reasons that look wholly benighted to me. Nonetheless, his central insights are more helpful than anything else I know of in beginning to understand why some horses and dogs can only be described as competent, good at what they do, and therefore happy. Not happy because leading lives of pleasure, but rather happy because leading lives in which the sensation of getting it right, the "click," as of the pleasure that comes from solving a puzzle or surmounting something, is a governing principle.

In Aristotle, and in other Greek (Athenian, that is) writers, the term "rights" in its modern sense does not come up, but these writers do discuss happiness. Aristotle in particular has it that happiness "is the only self-sufficient good, therefore the highest good," and for him this inevitably meant that to encourage what we moderns call the pursuit of happiness was to encourage the good of the *polis*. If there is anything to this, and if there is anything to Dickens's discovery of the citizenship of the dog, then the good of the (human) *polis* depends on the happiness of animals.

We have a tendency to hear something like "the state" or "the nation" in the word *polis*, and when I first found that Aristotle elevated the *polis* above the individual—I was quite young, and it was the late sixties—I was appalled, and immediately connected that view with his infamous support of slavery. But his notion of the *polis* was not, could not have been, any modern notion of the state or the nation, because the unit he thought in terms of was Athens, a town at the time smaller than the campus of the University of California at Riverside, not too far from the size of Socrates' just, or ideal, city—a few thousand souls, a neighborhood, in short.

Thus, Aristotle's thinking is even more alien to ordinary modern assumptions than his defense of slavery suggests. I don't mean that he was right about everything, only that when he speaks of happiness, and of what is due from whom to whom—that is, of justice, of what we may call rights—he has in mind always someone in particular. In a village or a neighborhood, you have rights, or lose them, in relationship to other individuals, because everybody knows everybody else. This has been the foundation of many bitter complaints about small towns and neighborhoods, of course.

When I think of neighborhoods I have known—certain university campuses, one or two small towns, and some air force bases—and of how rights *naturally* arise in neighborhoods, I realize that every time there is a situation in which it comes about that one person defends or honors another's rights in the ordinary course of things, it also comes about that the relationship between the two people can be indicated with a possessive pronoun. That is to say, these two (or more) people own each other, have each other. Examples are:

Leave her alone, she is my mother!
She is my daughter, and it is my job and no one else's to help her
    find a zither instructor.
I wouldn't say that if I were you—that's my friend you're talking
    about.
Sir, I cannot do that. I cannot betray my men.

It happens that I am more tender of the happiness of my mother, my father, my husband, my child, than I am of the happiness of other people's family members, though of course the possessive pronoun and the responsiveness it carries with it can extend, as when my friend's friend, who isn't much more than an acquaintance to me, lends me money on the strength of our mutual friendship. Thus do the lines of owning, owning up to, possessing someone else through responsiveness to who they are, to what their particular happiness consists in, expand. I do not know for sure what size they expand to, but Plato, or at least Socrates, imagined a city small enough that everyone in it could be on a matrix of possession/friendship with everyone else; there would be no strangers in his ideal city, which is why Socrates thought that dogs could guard it: a dog can know what a neighborhood is.

If I repudiate an obligation given in the fact that someone else is "mine," what I say is that I "disown" that person. In terms I borrow from Stanley Cavell, if I do not own you, own up to you, then I do not acknowledge you, I repudiate you. You cannot have interests or rights in relationship to me unless we own each other.

These days it is not fashionable to say that owning someone is a good thing to do, much less to say that it is a case of honoring someone's rights. When contemporary ethical philosophy, even those parts of it that do not sound like planted letters to the editor, considers the nature of things when one person owns another, the only case that comes to mind is slavery, where persons can not only be disowned— i.e., "freed"—but also sold. This is because we have a sickened concept of owning and owning up, one we are sickened by, whether our hopes started as democratic, anarchic, socialist, or royalist.

A friend who works at an emergency veterinary hospital told me about a vet who devoted with enormous energy and under enormous stress to saving a young Rottweiler from parvo, and then the owner said, "Oh, it's too much trouble, the follow-up care, just put him down." And the vet who had been so heroic screamed, "You can't do that after all I did to save him," but the dog was put down in the midst of one instance of our mad confusions about what owning is. The vet, in working so hard to save the puppy, owned up to the puppy before the puppy had the strength to own up in turn; but the vet was not the legal owner, he was only at that moment what we might call the natural owner. These myriad abrogations and diminishments of something—obedience, owning—for which "marriage" is still one of our best words, if not one of our best institutions, show that indeed the rose is sick at the center of the crimson heart of joy.

But what I have in mind is the kind of possessing in which, while one person can disown another, that person cannot *sell* another. The important detail of the kind of owning, possessing, that I am suggesting as fundamental to a rights relation is that the owning should be reciprocal, and even symmetrical to some degree (though we must be careful with this Euclidean image of symmetry, because symmetry means a certain identity of form that does not hold when actual persons, whether they are human or not, are in question). If, for instance, I have a daughter, then we have rights in each other—it *follows* from my having a daughter that she has a mother. And only rarely can it come about that you are my friend unless I am your friend. One way of understanding the Jesus story is that Jesus was a friend to those who were no friends of his, but that is a visionary affair, a matter of the eternal and the divine; it is the case for me, in general, that I rarely can have a friend if that person does not have me as a friend, even though an act of generosity from a stranger can lead to friendship. It is certainly true of me that I cannot be kind to the entire planet, and I do not believe that any mortal or group of mortals can be kind to the entire planet.

But I have wandered from rights to kindness. The kind of possessive I have in mind is not like slavery. It does not bind one party while freeing the other. Sometimes people will appeal to the idea of ownership to justify abusing someone—"She is my wife!"—and there have been laws that sanctified that position, but I think it is more accurate to say that if I abuse my dog on the grounds that she is my dog, then I do not, at the moment at least, in fact own the dog, am not owning up to what goes into owning a dog, do not understand my own words when I say I own the dog and can therefore do as I please with her. It is another matter if I say, "I own (and therefore know intimately) this dog, and I *know* that he actually prefers sleeping on the porch rather than inside on a comfy couch, because he likes to be on duty."

We can and do disown each other all the time, sometimes criminally, sometimes only civilly, as it were. I may momentarily disown my friend or my child or my husband by saying, "Leave me alone, I'm busy!" And that disowning can become reciprocal in the way our mutual possession of each other was if the rebuffed person responds by pouring syrup on the keyboard of my computer—"I'll show you what comes of being too busy for me!"

When I said earlier that I wanted to be cautious about invoking the idea of symmetry, I was thinking of relationships where there are built-in limitations to the reciprocities involved, and different rights and duties on each side, such as student-teacher relationships, or patient-doctor, or many commercial relationships. (The fact that a local merchant with whom I am friendly might aid or defend me in one sort of situation does not make her a person I can call at midnight as I might a more intimate friend.) The limitations in a given rights relation do not, however, mean that it is not a rights relation.

It might be argued that all rights relations have their limitations, if only because we are all mortal. Certainly the example of Christ suggests to me a large range of limitations. I might forgive a friend a lapse in driving (when I am following her and her sudden stop leads to a dent in my fender) more quickly than I would a stranger's identical lapse, for instance. The stranger does not have the right to expect that from me, though if I do forgive by not caring about the dent, taking insurance information, and so on, we may be in a different (new) relationship.

The relations signaled by the presence of reciprocal possession, the responsibilities and the ties, are not infinite, except for a Christ or some other supernatural being, but they are typically hard to dissolve; I may find it as difficult to give up an enemy as to give up a friend, and in many cases the one becomes the other, as though the logic of the possessive pronoun outlasts the forms it chances to take at a given moment, as though we are stuck with one another, whether as friends or as enemies.

In order for me to be in a rights relationship to someone, the following minimum conditions must hold.

1) I must know the person, have the ability to know that he or she exists.

2) The person must know me, have the ability to know my existence. (Whether or not someone knows my being as I know it is not the point, though there should be some agreement about it; things get thin and precipitous if I believe that you are a murderer and you do not believe that.)

3) The grammar of the reciprocal possessive must apply.

4) Both of us must have the ability to conceive the *right* in question itself. (I cannot imitate Christ in forgiving, cherishing, the entire planet, nor can I claim rights against Christ; that is not what prayer is.)

The ability to conceive that we both must have need not overlap in intimate detail. For example, if it is my puppy to whom I am saying, "Leave that book alone, it's mine!" then the quarrel is not about a book, because puppies cannot know what books are, cannot read. Perhaps it is an old book, bound with animal glue, and the puppy thinks I guard it the way a dog guards a bone or a food hoard, or perhaps from the puppy's point of view the quarrel is about, say, whose chew-toy the object is. The puppy will not be able to follow a disagreement between me and my husband about whose copy of the *Tractatus Logico-Philosophicus* a given object is, in somewhat the same way I cannot follow a dispute between two mathematicians about which of them "had" a certain idea first, and also in somewhat the same way I cannot follow a dispute between two men about "whose" woman I am. And it would be wrong to think that the mathematicians' quarrel about the idea is somehow dependent on intellectual rather than emotional conceptual faculties in a way the second quarrel is not; if, as Hume noted, reason is just another instinct, then mathematics is one instinct highly developed. We call it an activity of intellect, but then so do we call Shakespeare's plays an activity of intellect. Mind/heart dualism, like mind/body dualism, is a sometimes useful fiction, but it breaks down, as do all the wondrous artifacts of our imaginations.

Every person who honors my rights honors and can honor only those rights that person can understand. If there is a constitutional right to privacy, it is only through that right that people whose loves are too alien to mine for mutual understanding honor my right(s) to the pursuit of happiness. And of course, from most people I do not need or require that they understand my work, or even that work is a central happiness for me, only that they leave me alone. They have to know that I exist and (usually) that I am a rights bearer in order to respect my rights, and I have to know that they exist in order to claim my rights. You cannot say, "Leave me alone," or "Send my Social Security check!" or "That's my book," or "I want to become an artist," to nothing or no one (though it may seem to the recipient of government aid that that is what is happening).

The idea of democracy is in part dependent on the citizens of the democracy realizing that the government exists and knowing how to claim rights against it. And as I have said, dogs can know the sort of grouping that was on the minds of the Greek philosophers who began the kind of thinking that led to the idea of a democracy—a largish neighborhood, something my Annie can know the boundaries of as she knows the boundaries of the neighborhood that is Yale, though not the corporation that is (also) Yale.

I do know this much, that the government exists even though this government is not a neighborhood, because I get mail from it and see its "representatives" running about in uniforms. Whether I really have any rights in relationship to the government is less clear, but the idea that I do is symbolized by the right to vote. I obey the government perforce, and in theory it obeys me, by counting my ballot, reading the Miranda warning to me, agreeing to be bound by the Constitution. In practice, the reciprocities are not so clear—I cannot arrest the government, for example, nor can I tax it in quite the same way it taxes me. It is neither so responsive to me nor so respectful in relationship to me as my friends are. It is a problem. My friend obeys me as I obey her; the government "obeys" me to some extent, but not as I obey it.

But at least I know that it exists, which is one reason I do not bark at the mailman.

What kind of thing can Drummer have knowledge of? Well, he can know that I exist, and through that knowledge can claim his happinesses, with varying degrees of success, both *with* me and *against* me, because I know a lot about this pup and am committed to acting on what I know. Someone who does not know the kind of training I do could not, even if they wanted to be very, very kind to him, create the structures within which he finds his meticulous way to very nice work on the figure eight or on a recall at the end of which his feet are as close to exactly parallel to mine as he can make them. The friend who knows poetry well enough to correct me if I show her a poem in which for a moment I fail to keep count is the friend for me, so long as other things are in place.

Drummer can also know about larger human/dog communities than the one that consists only of him and me. There is my household, for example—the other dogs, the cats, my husband. In the time I have had him I have not had occasion to go to my office on campus often enough for him to learn that community, but I have had enough dogs on campuses to know that he can learn that Yale exists, learn it as a neighborhood or village. As I said, my older dog Annie does know that Yale exists, and can tell Yalies not only from "townies" but also, as I learned while teaching there during labor troubles, from other kinds of outsiders, such as union officials.

In fact, in cases where the mail carrier is fully part of the neighborhood, not all dogs bark at the mail carrier, but rather greet him or her as they would any other friend or neighbor. Insofar as "the mail carrier" becomes Drummer's friend, small rights relations can arise between them. Perhaps the mail carrier always slaps Drummer on the back, or perhaps they have some game they play for a few seconds before Drummer extends to the mail carrier the right to enter his property. Rights are embedded in exchanges.

Dogs can and do have elaborate conceptions of human social structures, and even of something like their rights and responsibilities within them, but not so elaborate that you will find a rights relation between a dog and the state, or a dog and the humane society. Both of the latter, unlike a village or neighborhood, are notions that depend on writing, on notations and memoranda, such as the mail carrier's or dogcatcher's uniform, or the seal of the United States government, all of them literary constructs, all of them beyond a dog's ken, which is why the mail carrier who doesn't also happen to be a dog's friend or neighbor is forever an intruder . . . and that is why dogs bark at mailmen.

It is clear enough that rights relations can arise naturally between people and animals. Drummer, for example, can (and does) say, "Hey, let's go outside and *do* something!" if I have been at my computer for several days on end and he hasn't gotten to work. He can (and does) both refuse and accept various of my suggestions, and can (and does) tell me that certain things make him fear for his life—such as the huge white bass drum that appeared out of nowhere, as it seemed to him, on the Green one evening when we were working—and I can (and do) say to him either, "Oh, you don't have to worry about that," and "Yes, I'm sure," or else, "Uh-oh, you're right, Drum, that guy looks dangerous." He can say these things to me in somewhat the same way I can vote—I taught him a fair amount about how to get responses from me. Obedience is reciprocal, and you cannot get responses from a dog to whom you do not respond accurately; I have enfranchised him in relationship to me by educating him.

There is a sense, somewhat obscure, in which I was educated, not only by parents and teachers, but also by the state, but there is no sense in which Drummer was educated by the state. Even police dogs, trained at public expense, are not educated by "the state"; a police dog never learns what his master's uniform means, though he does learn a "beat," which is a kind of neighborhood. I did not, perhaps, at the age of six or seven, have the concept of "the state," but I have it now and can make sense of the idea that I had a public education. I can speak of "my" government, and if it should ever become appropriate, I can even defend my government. Drummer can speak to his owner, but he cannot speak either to or of the state. Therefore the state cannot grant rights to Drummer, cannot be *his* state. Hence it is not an incidental or accidental but a central fact that in practice the only way a dog's rights are protected, against neighbors or the state, is *by way of an appeal to the owner's property rights in the dog.* A dog owner is no more an infallible granter of rights than any government is, but an owner is the only rights granter a dog can know. If something happens to me, Drummer's rights will be a function of the details of the way someone else does or does not fully become his owner, *the owner that belongs to him,* the one he defends and loves and plays his gentle Airedale tricks on. The same is true of children; it does not follow from the fact that some parents abuse their children that children's rights would be strengthened if they were all declared wards of the state. (And we are still learning that declaring all blacks or all women or all *anything* wards of the state does not amount to granting rights.)

People who claim to speak for animal rights and/or animal liberation are increasingly devoted to the idea that the very keeping of a dog or a horse or a gerbil or a lion is in and of itself an offense. The more loudly they so speak, the less likely they are to be in much of a rights relation to any given animal, because they spend so much time in airplanes and on the telephone, practicing what Charles Dickens in one of his usual strokes of genius called "telescopic philanthropy." And the more they do so, the more effective they are in reducing my power to grant rights to my dog. Any example taken at random will do. Consider Ingrid Newkirk of PETA, who urges that domestic animals be spayed and neutered and ultimately phased out. She prefers, it appears, wolves—wolves someplace else—to Airedales, and by a logic whose interior structure is both emotionally and intellectually forever closed to Drummer, she claims thereby to be speaking for "animal rights."

She is wrong. I am the only one who can own up to my Airedale's rights, and he is the only one who can own up to or refuse my rights in relationship to him.

I will now appeal to a poet, Donald Davie, and misleadingly quote only one section of a lovely poem in which the Bird, the Salmon, the Human, and the Angel speak of their happinesses. The poem, "Utterings," ends with the happiness of Sheepdog and Artist.

(Sheepdog/   Knowing your own business,
Artist)   And such a delicate business;
               Uttering it with the promptness
               That such a knowledge gives—
               If anything that lives
               That is able to know it, knows
               A better happiness

In his dog's life than this,
He is welcome to it; most,
I apprehend, know less.

It is a central happiness of Drummer's to know his own business, which is a delicate business. It is his right in relationship to me to pursue that happiness. It is my right, a right I have not so much earned as come into in the course of things, come into even as I was writing this essay, a right I am still coming into, a part of my being and becoming, to pursue my happiness in his work and mine in relationship to him. It is his fate and mine to fall short of heaven in pursuit of happiness, but not, I pray, to lose our happiness, whether to the words and accompanying violence of the state or of charity.

As for Drummer's rights in, say, the state of Texas, where I gave a version of these remarks, there is a law in Texas that goes like this: Say some students are outside the room behaving rowdily and Drummer, who is not accustomed to students, woofs. He now becomes a dangerous dog according to Texas law. Say that after the woof that made him a dangerous dog, someone came in and assaulted me and Drummer disabled my assailant. I would then be subject to a prison sentence of one year. Drummer of course would die. Furthermore, if Drummer happened to be lying down in front of Willard just before the assault, then Willard could be considered to be in custody of the dog and would go to prison for a year.

It was humane organizations that produced the PR that prompted, among other things, the Texas "dangerous dog" law. I have already ranted and raved about this in a book called *Bandit,* so will forbear here and return to the dilemma.

The dilemma is: Drummer's happiness is no business of the state's. He cannot read, cannot vote, and so cannot command the reciprocal possessives in relationship to the state that he commands in relationship to me. Animals cannot make speeches, write retainer checks, or instruct lobbyists. It follows from this that there can be no animal rights movement. Yet the good of the *polis* does, I believe, being convinced by Aristotle and Dickens and Drummer, depend on making room in the neighborhood for Drummer's happiness—that is, his rights relations with me and other persons of his acquaintance. Drummer is a fairly privileged dog, largely because I am well known and his breed is politically correct, and because he is a gentleman most of the time. Nonetheless, he earns each privilege bit by bit, winning over the proprietors and patrons of the local pharmacy, the diner, my travel agent's offices, most buildings at Yale, sundry local bookstores. A law that identified dogs as well trained as Drummer, and that allowed local merchants to suspend health regulations in the case of dogs who have passed tests for street soundness, would do a lot to empty pounds and relieve the terrible confusion the average dog owner in this country faces. It would also reduce the need for police patrols in some areas, since a well-trained dog is the best and safest deterrent to amateur crime—rape, mugging, and so on. The state, as I keep saying, cannot grant Drummer rights, but it can create social space in which the rights relations natural to such an animal can develop.

And all of this because writing is such a tricky thing. I was telling a philosopher one day that dogs cannot recognize uniforms, and he said that was wrong, that he was sure his children recognized members of his family by their costumes. I said, a tad crankily, that I was talking about dogs and not children, and also that I was quite sure that was *not* how my daughter recognized members of the family, because otherwise she would have been pretty confused.

But about that story, the one about Drummer's proto-poem or sculpture. When I am reciting my rights theory, it seems quite plain to me that dogs cannot read and write, and therefore cannot know about cities and corporations, only neighborhoods and such. But when I look at my Drummer story I am not so sure. For after all the splendidly energetic interpretations prompted by his arrangement settled down, I was left with the one that says it was a proto-poem.

A few days later, possibly impressed by how impressed I was by Drummer, Texas began making a kind of sculpture in the house. It consisted entirely of metal objects: a stapler, two cans of peas, several lengths of chain that were waiting to be turned into training equipment, a metal retrieving article, and a bronze figurine of an Airedale, which was set (upright) on top of the stapler, which in its turn was on top of an overturned pot. (I do not know how he got hold of these objects. Texas is a tough guy, and though he was bred in Michigan from German lines, he may belong in a book I saw recently, called *Texas: Amazing but True.*)

And it may be that I need to add to this list of anecdotes another, also involving an Airedale. That dog's name was Gunner. It came about one day that I was working past his suppertime, so he was attempting to prompt me to feed him. He brought me his food dish, which I absently put on the desk, saying, "Yes, yes, in a moment," and went back to my typing. A while later, he returned with a wastepaper basket, wiggling so hard in gleeful appreciation of the joke that he almost dropped his prop. I laughed—some people get tired of Airedale jokes and try to find good homes for them—took the basket from him, and again went back to my typing. Later yet he returned with a tiny silver filigree candy basket, the handle hanging from one of his teeth. And so I got up to feed him, but by now he was into finding troped food dishes, so while I was preparing his supper he brought also an ornate ashtray and a wide-mouthed jar.

The uncanny thing here is that dogs—I am sure of this—cannot read and write. You cannot leave a note for a dog, as far as I know. Yet what Drummer and Texas and Gunner did exists in some as yet unexplored territory of language, of proto-poems and proto-writing, that I am unprepared to name more specifically, for these matters still exist in wobbly forms in my mind. That "proto-poem" is, if not right, then at least not so wrong a characterization does seem clear, but that means that poetry is a very peculiar form of writing indeed—not, for example, something you can make policy with. It is a way of happening to which the poem returns us with refreshment, just as Stevens says, so that we share for a moment the first idea.

From this it follows that poetry, by transcending writing, by being as Thoreau says a second inheritance of language, transcends by demolishing the blunt instrument that thought that depends on writing becomes when we lose our animalhood—as is inevitable and perhaps proper.

And from this it follows that when we teach the five-part essay, for example, we are working against the muse—which does not mean we should stop teaching the five-part essay. This is a fallen world; we get to the muse by working against her, we learn good in a welter of evil, as John Milton says we do. What it means is that writing, with its astounding powers to deprive us of the world directly in front of our noses, and even to make us consider the world well lost for the resulting autism that we call "intellect," is the means by which we return to the world so lost, and even to our own authority, or authorship, within it. The name of the kind of writing by means of which this happens is poetry.

By now you have recognized the lie in my title. I have not produced a theory of language; I have only reported on some uncanny questions that have come my way. The theory of language in question is the theory of the poet/dog trainer, which is to say that it is more an account of what I was driven to think about language, the way I might be driven to God, perhaps by chariot.

So I will close by returning to Donald Davie's remarkable poem "Utterings," which I cite in full in the next essay, the last essay, wanting to give Davie the last word, being in a mood to trust him more than I trust myself. I commend the poem to the reader's attention in a different way here, however. It is a poem of the progress of happiness, and it is structured in such a way that the happiness of Sheepdog/Artist is a higher-than-human and higher-than-angelic happiness—or it suggests that possibility, I believe, and I take leave from that and other details in the poem to read it as an account, or a vision, of both art and training as leading to a higher-than-animal, higher-than-human, and higher-than-angelic happiness because they are disciplines that not only take us into various darknesses and entanglements, including especially the entanglements of writing and of whatever forces prompted Drummer's proto-poem, but take us out of them again, for a while, into a clarity beyond question, or at least beyond our restless questionings of each other and the world.

Job's Animals

Reflections on the Sacred and the Ordinary

*T*ragedies and lies have often been the occasion of my learning
new forms and articulations of joy. Ben Franklin put this differently, by saying that pain is the source of pleasure. John Milton, arguing that bad and even wicked books should not be suppressed, said
that it is our condition that we learn the good in the welter of evil. I
am prompted to say, as others have been, that for us darkness is the
occasion of light. And for me the Book of Job is the greatest, or at least
the most compelling, the most uncanny account of darkness occasion-
ing light.

The author of the Book of Job is the animal trainer's prophet. The
bulk of the speech of the Voice from the Whirlwind is devoted to animals. The first chapter of that Voice, Chapter 38, concerns waves, the
weather, the heavens, the breadth of the earth, and so on, but closes
with remarks about the lion and the raven. Chapters 39, 40, and 41 are
about nothing but what animals are like: the wild goat, the unicorn,
the peacock, the ostrich, the horse, the hawk, the eagle, Behemoth,
and Leviathan.

The question that interests me here is not the question of what
Job "deserved," which the rabbis are more competent to deal with
than I am, but this: Why did the Voice go on and on to Job about the
animals? What was it that Job didn't know? It's not as though Job
weren't a herdsman, a husbandman. You don't have as much healthy
stock as Job had without knowing a thing or two about animals, so
here was no city slicker in the usual sense, and yet God had to remind
him what animals are like. Job was quite upright, apparently active in
community affairs, and would nowadays no doubt be called a humane
man, and God scolds him by letting him know that none of his

uprightness and humaneness makes any nevermind to the ostrich. Which is one way of saying that neither love nor justice is what God has in mind, and that happiness is not to be understood in terms of human uprightness, whether domestic or political.

Harold Bloom has aptly noted that the Book of Job is "not a theodicy, a justification of the ways of God to man." That seems to me to be understating the matter; the Book of Job is as violent an assault on the idea that there is any divine integrity in the practice of justice, indeed on the idea of divine or human integrity itself, and thus also on the idea of the Law as any guide to the divine, as exists anywhere in literature. What is at issue is the uprightness of uprightness itself. You might think that various rumors about what went on in Jerusalem in connection with the condemnation and execution of Christ by all those upright Romans constitute such an assault, but those tales leave us with the comforts of love and friendship and divine approval in the wake of the destructive distortions of righteousness. Job, on the other hand, is told in no uncertain terms that his uprightnesses are but pedantries beside the sort of thing God can have in mind—a sort of thing revealed in contemplations of animals.

When Job says in the epilogue (Chapter 42) that he understands this, he is summarily restored to a condition of even more respectability and uprightness—restored to everything, that is, that God's servants the horse and the ostrich and so on ignore, as though it didn't matter that uprightness does not matter. If Job's enlightenment, in the form of the Voice from the Whirlwind, weren't so thundering and theatrical, there would be little to choose between his story and a thousand others, from teachers of the *Tao* and admirers of Buddha, about the unhappy carpenter who reaches true enlightenment and then just goes on as before, carpentering. Bloom calls this epilogue, in which Job gets his wealth back and then some, "pious tampering," as though he expects the story to have a more natural or plausible ending of the kind often commended to students in creative writing classes, and there is no doubt something to his observation. There is always something to Harold Bloom's observations. However, the epilogue to Job satisfies me as well as anything I can imagine when it is understood in light of what God wanted Job to know about the animals.

But first we should understand what God was not saying. The Voice certainly wasn't recommending that Job go out and be like the ostrich or the unicorn, for instance. Nor was it claiming that it was itself the ostrich or the unicorn or the horse or Leviathan—a point worth stressing, because Bloom sets up a parallel between God's (Yahweh's) nonhuman servants and what he calls Yahweh's "peculiar vagaries, as when he tries to murder poor Moses at the outset of the prophet's reluctant mission, or . . . when he rapes Jeremiah." This is misguided. God is mainly concerned with how the animals are beyond human wisdom and justice, beyond human uprightness. One of his examples of the ways of Dwelling is the ostrich, who

> . . . leaveth her eggs in the earth, and warmeth them in dust,
> And forgetteth that the foot may crush them, or that the wild beast
>   may break them.
> She is hardened against her young ones, as though they were not
>   her's: her labour is in vain without fear. (39:14–16)

By the way, it is hard to chide an ostrich, as I learned one day in an ostrich-handling class. One of the students asked the instructor a standard beginner's question in animal work—whether the males or the females are harder to handle—to which there is usually a helpful answer, such as "The males bite and the females kick." In this case the instructor merely said, regarding the line of eight-foot-tall birds advancing upon the class with baleful glares, "Well, that's pretty much up to the bird," who laboreth in vain and without fear.

It can be a joy to labor in vain, perhaps, and what is interesting about the Book of Job is not the problem that arises when God doesn't turn out to be as restrained and kindly as benevolent governments are supposed to be, but the fact that his servants labor in vain, without fear. For the ostrich, it seems, that is her piety.

Presumably—Bloom's discussion of Job is sketchy, but I don't think I am here doing damage to its fundamentals—Bloom sees Yahweh's ostrich as he sees Leviathan, and as he sees Yahweh. He writes, "I take it that Job recognizes the reality of Yahweh's extraordinary personality after the voice out of the whirlwind has completed its message, a recognition that is the resolution of the book." Since the resolution directly follows Chapters 39 through 41, which are all about animals, Bloom leaves us no choice but to make the identification—ostrich and Yahweh.

The book in which these remarks of Bloom's occur, *Ruin the Sacred Truths,* is indispensable for anyone who cares about animals or children or poetry and other things that do not yield easily to injunctions about uprightness, and especially for anyone wanting to puzzle out the bizarre social and political assaults currently under way against virtually everyone in this culture who has a genuine relationship with animals, and the connection between those assaults and the forces that are turning our universities into what Bloom calls "temples of societal resentment." There are a multitude of reasons that I find the book indispensable, for example, in my role as director of training and narrative consultant for the National Pit Bull Terrier Defense Association and Literary Society. But facts are facts and must be acknowledged, at least by animal trainers who care to preserve their sanity, and the fact is that Bloom's book gives us a reading of Job that is afraid of animals.

Not only afraid of animals, but exactly afraid of them because there is in the animal world no acknowledgment of human merit or justice as created by books and institutions. Or such is my interpretation of the way Bloom's parallel between the animals and Yahweh the crazed rapist and murderer is given, as a deep assumption, as something that needs no more mention than does the author's need to breathe while he writes. I do not mean that Bloom himself is afraid of animals; I do not know his emotional habits. But his pages on the Book of Job *are* afraid of animals—which does not make *Ruin the Sacred Truths* any less an invaluable work of genius, much needed in a bad time for America. Still, Bloom doesn't know animals, and the author of the Book of Job did.

The animals in Job are neither murderers nor rapists. The vagaries of the Yahweh who behaves with terrifyingly childlike menace have nothing to do with the animal traits that the Whirlwind Voice commends to Job's attention. God's servants are not deviant, depraved, unpredictable, whimsical, nefarious, villainous, or unjust. If they were, Job would have gone entirely mad, and not even a prophetic author could have prevented it.

I have heard tirades about animals that sound remarkably like the tirades of the Whirlwind Voice. They are familiar to me as a mostly oral genre that has recognized canons, within which there are recognized masters of the genre. They are in my nonbiblical experience instructive tirades, just as they are in Job, and they are quite often on the topic of all the illusory human values the animal in question does not care about. Dogs, for example, do not care all that much about pleasing people, and true trainers compose tirades about this because when some idiot decides that dogs do want to please, that idiot will eventually, unless distracted, get into killing dogs who reject the idiot's expressions of approval and pleasure. The tirades I have in mind are often apparently mysterious, oracular, unfriendly, and come from an intricately conceived rage of narrative against idiocy. They are of necessity literary rather than scientific or philosophical, because science and philosophy, and history for that matter, are relatively powerless against the Tar Baby of pious illusion, just as Philip Sidney said they were.

And in a true trainer's vocabulary, "idiot" never means "harmless idiot."

I will return to Job, but first I should say that there is nothing unusual about a great intellectual failing to get the first thing straight about animals, and that quite often fear seems to be the basis of the ignorance. The philosopher Donald Davidson, for instance, who is not as extraordinary as Harold Bloom, puts an inexplicable amount of energy into denying that dogs can think, and his grounds seem to be identical with the grounds that prompted the Athenians to call non-Greeks "barbarians." The word "barbarian" means, roughly, "barker," and the idea is this: If I can't understand a Frenchman, it is because the Frenchman is irrational, cannot think or talk. Davidson cannot understand dogs, and blames a canine failure of rationality rather than his not happening to know how to talk sense to dogs. This is oafish, or at least parochial, but what is interesting is not that a philosopher should have oafish moments, just as anyone does, but that Davidson is so strenuous in his denials. What is he afraid of? The unpronounceable, perhaps, or that there might be minds and thinking out there that are inaccessible to him, that his knowledge might be human, finite.

The academy has always been a hazardous place for trainers and others interested in animal minds, even when they are otherwise academically respectable; consider Bougeaint, the Jesuit priest who, in a period when the church and the academy were still pretty much in bed with each other, was excommunicated for writing a book in which he said animals could think. The oldest surviving book in the Western world on dog training, Xenophon's *Cynegeticus,* is animated by the author's exasperation with the academy. He opens by informing us at length that the knowledge of dogs is a gift given by the gods to the heroes, for their greater glory, the implication being that it isn't a knowledge given to everyone, especially not, say, to educators, as Leibniz (who was not a member of the academy) in effect confirms in *Discours sur les beaux sentiments:* "Those who urge that in the education of children everything be done according to nature have not sufficiently observed nature. Let them study horsemen and sportsmen who train horses, dogs, and birds."

All well and good. But I should now confess that one of the minor reasons academicians don't know what is going on with animals is that people who do know tell lies. The major reasons have to do with some vagaries of language and intellect beside which the vagaries of Bloom's Yahweh are nothing, but in the middle of these vagaries of the human mind, trainers tell lies and people are misled.

For example, one day I was talking with Mark Harden, a chimpanzee and wolf and tiger trainer, about temperament. Temperament is, among other things, the working ability that is either there in an animal or not; it is the stuff animals make worlds out of. It is the reason we put "In God We Trust" on our money, another trainer said to me one day. Just as the weather causes an Iowa farmer, contemplating his corn, to contemplate God, so the obdurate facts of temperament cause an animal person to recall in Whom we can trust. Job raised camels, asses, and oxen, all animals valuable chiefly for their working talents, their temperaments.

The study of temperament is the study of all the things we care about that animals don't care about. Not everyone is ready to know this—to know, for example, that love doesn't matter very much to dogs but trust matters enormously, which is the main reason many dogs take to biting people who "love" them. So as I said, one tells lies, as Mark Harden did one day. He and I were having a discussion about the wonders of temperament, how the trainer's art is in part a matter of getting this right, and about the ways one must give oneself up, often, in order to get it right, when a reporter called to ask Mark how he got his animals to do all those wonderful things. He said, without missing a beat, "Food rewards." And went back to telling me that while you might begin training tigers because you are in love, you must progress beyond love, to respect and admiration, or you will get killed, or nothing will happen because the animal will be indifferent to you.

This is the sort of thing God brings to Job's attention. It is not merely that Leviathan is hard to hunt down, but that the unicorn, say, is indifferent. God tells Job, basically, "Go try training a unicorn and then come talk to me about it" ("Will the unicorn be willing to serve thee, or abide by thy crib?"). The important point about the unicorn, I think, is identical in spirit to the passage about the wild ass immediately preceding: "He scorneth the multitude of the city, neither regardeth he the crying of the driver. The range of the mountains is his pasture, and he searcheth after every green thing" (39:7–8). It is not that the unicorn is miraculous, but that this is a wild animal, one that did not follow us when we went East of Eden, into the cities. And Job was a farmer, and would have known that wild animals do not care about the city or the tabernacle.

The Anchor Bible gives "buffalo" here instead of "unicorn," by the way. As a footnote I would like to say that I use "unicorn" for the reason I rely on the King James Version in general, since it is likely that the translator of this passage was summoning, by contrast to the unicorn, ideas of what it is to train a horse that are specific to the English Renaissance. The King James Version was translated by people who inherited the extraordinary revivals of the knowledge of animals—of classical horsemanship and dog training—that are among the still inexplicable mysteries of the sixteenth century in England. Hence it is informed by a trainer's myths in a particular way, a way that I can read.

Job had camels and oxen and asses and dogs—animals that have to be trained—and in 30:1 he complains that he is now mocked by men whose fathers he would not have let handle the dogs of his flock. I do not know if these were herding dogs or guarding dogs. Chances are that Job's dogs, like David's, were guarding dogs, dogs who would stay with the flock, because it is impossible that writers who are as good on the subject of animals as David and the author of Job should have something as wonderful and complex as a true herding dog and not mention it. Either way, the likelihood is that when Job makes this complaint he is invoking an idea of a great deal of intelligence. Saying that a man is too dumb and depraved to work sheepdogs is not like saying that he is too dumb to take out garbage; it is more like saying that he is too depraved to learn a craft such as silversmithing or to honor philosophy's queenly commands. The "children of fools, children of base men . . . viler than the earth" (30:8) are people who cannot train a sheepdog. (This is a trainer's book, as I keep saying.)

And God points out to the owner of camels, sheep, sheepdogs, and oxen that he cannot train a unicorn—or even a buffalo. He also points out to the owner of five hundred donkeys that he can't herd or train wild donkeys. There are nowadays people who can train wild animals, including buffalo, and they are a very, very tactful and noble lot, at least among their animals. A buffalo does not feel pastures or any other civilized artifact to be safety, to be home, and is as likely to charge through an electric fence when he hits the tingle as to back away from it. A horse, by contrast, will accept human approval, human acknowledgment, and will recognize some tasks as partnership activities. A horse will make friends, even though human love and approval are for so many horses irrelevant to friendship. Not so the buffalo, the giraffe, the zebra, and the unicorn.

Or the wolf. It is possible to train a wolf, and for me the procedures are similar to those I use in training a dog, but the difficulties are not. Even the most messed-up, dingbat, rotten nasty dog in the world, the one who goes for your throat as soon as you say good morning, is immediately, *immer schon, toujours déjà*, prepared for the possibility of friendship, and that is what it means to say you can work with a dog. A dog who attacks you out of hand is not indifferent to friendship but refusing it, and *thereby* knowing and acknowledging the possibility.

A wolf does not refuse friendship, because for the wolf it isn't there to be refused in the first place. Wolves have no word for it in their language. Hence working a wolf is a light, delicate matter of tremendous precisions of response. If a wolf has been socialized young, she will not be particularly dangerous to handle, even though she has teeth that can go through your arm like scissors through paper. The problem with the wolf is that she does not care for your love. She responds to praise with about as much welcome as a cat responds to being sprinkled with a water gun. Human love and praise are alien to her, so if you don't build into your relationship with the wolf, step by step, a language of relation whose meanings she will accept, she just isn't there. It is not like a scene from *Rambo*, training a wolf. It is more like training a cloud or a dream or a shadow. I sometimes wear silk to work a wolf, to put myself into the right frame of mind. And when you are done, when you have trained the wolf, you do not have any more than you put in. Her acceptance of you does not transfer to other people without more formal work, and there is not the bountiful offering of spontaneous elaborations of what you teach her that makes dog training so rich and complex. (Still, I should add that there are people who work with wolves, meet them on their own ground, turning from the usual forms and energies on which domestic lives and friendships so often depend. Job was not one of them, which is nothing against Job, as the ending of his book shows.)

So when the Voice tells Job that the unicorn does not have a working temperament, it is reminding him that there is a vast world of significance, meaning, and earthly—that is, ordinary—divinities that is outside of the nobilities, charities, and righteousnesses of Job's condition as an animal husbandman. This cannot be understood if what the horse trainer does is confused with what the prison guard or the collector of instruments of bondage and discipline does. In order to train a horse, or a camel or a donkey or an ox or a sheepdog, you have to make peace for a while at least with the attributes of ha-Shem, one of the many names of the ineffable name. You don't have to know what these attributes are, exactly, but you do have to make your peace with them. You have to go forth into animal training stripped, to some extent, of your righteousness, perhaps not as Job was stripped, by Satan, but rather by the fact that your animals, whether wild or domestic, are present someplace else, outside of righteousness, earlier than love, nearer to heaven—and this is not reassuring.

There are people who describe training as a process of discussing with animals the attributes of God, a discussion in which the human listens as much as she talks. A shepherd who failed to respect his dogs, then, would not be a bad shepherd—he wouldn't *be* a shepherd, because his dogs would tell him where to get off; you can't coerce a sheepdog who is doing a four-hundred-yard outrun and thereby performing one contemplation of ha-Shem. So the shepherd whose dogs won't herd for him would be impious, would be the ignoble fool of Job's complaint. Respect for the ideas of God as they show up in animate creation is built into the farming Job does, and when Job complains about the base nature of those who mock him, those who lack the attentive pieties demanded of the shepherd, God does not deny the reality of the virtues so named. What he says is only that even all that respect is not enough on which to found commentaries on ha-Shem.

You might say that what God tells Job is that he is not capable of being kind, of fully desiring kindness, toward the whole planet. And incidentally, when someone who is bent on being kind to your animals walks into your kennel or stable or wild-animal training compound, that is when you have to take special care to protect your animals, because they may well die if the kindness succeeds. This is why trainers do not want humane cops around, persons sponsored and authorized by irreverence for the extent to which creation is a matter of so much more than any one person knows. In the Woodland Park Zoo in the state of Washington, such "kindness" turned the birds loose in winter, and all but two or three of them died of exposure within a hundred and fifty feet of the aviary. I know less about animal rights activities in laboratories than I do about the damage they cause in the world of training, but I did have to leave off teaching a writing class one day at the University of California to help round up some frightened macaques. The situation was urgent enough for me to abandon a classroom because the macaques would have died on the loose in one or more of a number of horrible ways. They had been "freed" by people who pitied them, but pity is another uprightness the unicorn, the ostrich, and the macaque do not find compelling as we do.

In a lifetime of work with animals I have never known moral outrage to help a single animal. Ever. I am not saying that *I* know enough to decide what ought to be done with all animals, only a few. I am saying that there is more on the earth than any of us knows, and that it is interesting to me that in Job ha-Shem is moved to speak about animals to, of all people, a farmer and (successful!) overseer of many animal trainers.

God says the unicorn does not have a working (domestic) temperament. When you understand temperament, when you understand that the desire to work is not given in categories of justice or duty, you learn things about the mind that you don't learn as well in other ways. You learn about differences, you learn that the imaginative foundation, the *ur*, of the world of the ostrich is different from the *ur* of the bulldog, and that both are different from yours.

Difference. Trainers have to be prepared for the differences. And the trainer knows that there is no such thing as IQ, there are only the various shapes of desire, and that when these are instructed and activated, you have what Heidegger called *Weltbildung*, although he denied that animals were *weltbildung*, or "world-making." The philosopher does not have to know that there is such a thing as temperament, as that particular activity and antic of difference, but the trainer has to know it. The trainer has to know, for example, that the unicorn's refusal of the kind of handling the horse accepts and actively transforms and makes part of his world is a function not of the unicorn's being too stupid to understand what the horse understands, but merely of the unicorn's desire, and therefore his IQ, not being in that landscape. Desire and passion and IQ are one for the trainer.

It turns out, by the way, that while you are listening to a trainer's detailed discussion of how a certain lion made manifest in the actuality available to him various emphatic insistencies of temperament, it is hard to remember, much less understand, what Heidegger might have meant, or thought he meant, when he said, "Das Tier hat keine Welt, auch keine Umwelt" ("The animal has no world, nor any environment"), and thus no spirit, no *Geist*. Derrida founds his criticism of Heidegger's ontology in part on Heidegger's curious idea that animals are *weltarm*, "poor in world." Here again, it must not be supposed that Heidegger's idiotic remarks about animals are in any way unusual. In fact, it must not even be supposed that a philosopher's idiocy about animals has anything to do with philosophical greatness.

And here again is Mark Harden, talking about the sort of thing the Voice tells Job. "Tigers do not care about your love. They do not crave your approval. They also do not fear your disapproval. What matters to a tiger is the way a tiger walks, and if you don't know everything about how a tiger walks, you will find yourself getting in the way and you will get hurt. Of course, you're probably going to get hurt anyhow, but you will not survive if you think that your love is to the point of anything you will ever see in a tiger's eyes. You have to understand your cat."

Understanding. Mark and his animals understand each other. Indeed, the continuous flow and play of understanding between human and elephant, human and serval, human and lion, is what prompts me sometimes to think that a place such as the training compound in Thousand Oaks is as close to paradise as people get. That is, it is a place of return to the ease of mutual recognition that is figured, troped, as the unfallen hymn in Book 4 of *Paradise Lost*. The ease of this understanding is the ease of great skill, the result of discipline, and is not inheritable in the way athletic ability is, but it is ease and it is understanding. Understanding of the exact ways and reasons of the chimpanzee's desire for a soft-shoe routine. Understanding of the exact sinews of the lion's rolling pace, the pitch and revolution of his roaring.

This understanding is in sharp contrast to the talk of animals one hears from persons who are notably active in the humane movement. Their catechism is given in Jeremy Bentham's "The question is, not can they think but can they suffer?" The constant citation of Bentham, along with many other details, makes it as plain as anything can be that what interests some people is not the joy and intelligence and difficulty and difference of animals, but only their pain. Someone who does not care about the wit of a wolf, someone who is indifferent to a wolf's giddy antics and is interested in the wolf only if something in the wolf can be seen to fester, is not my idea of an animal lover. The love of animals is not professed in a catechism of their suffering but in uncanny catechisms of their joys.

Of course, we know from the trainer's own mouth that there is something beyond love that animates him. And we know also that he lied to the reporter. It is therefore important for me to harp on the fact that there is such a thing as a sometimes brutal politics of who gets to have what opinions about what animals are like, and that while this politics is not the *cause* of the generally idiotic nature of institutionally approved beliefs about God's servants, the various kinds of idiocy that the prophet of the Book of Job is refusing to give authority to in his account are related to each other. Not identical, but related, perhaps second cousins. Job complains that those who castigate him for his purported offenses against righteousness could not train a sheepdog—he says that they are the sons of men he would disdain to set among the dogs of his flock—and Mark Harden's colleague and partner Hubert Wells complains that his castigators could not get a Labrador Retriever to come when called.

As I have said, I am reading King James, where the unicorn is contrasted to the horse at a moment of wondrous intellectual and literary and practical achievement with horses that may have begun when

Henry VIII went to Italy and was so enchanted with the horsemanship he saw there that he became the first English monarch to hire a horse trainer. (He also sent off to Italy, in effect, for cabalistic advice about his divorce.) In the English Renaissance, the cooperative nature of the horse was a figure of his nobility and courage. Obedience was not then pictured as it is now, as a case of one person having command over another, but rather as two persons or creatures bound together by a common goal or ideal. And it is important to recall that Sidney, Shakespeare, and Spenser all wrote with a lively awareness of the significance of Bellerophon's having fathered both the art of poetry and the art of horsemanship when he bridled Pegasus. In the opening of Sidney's *Defense of Poesie,* the horseman is the poet, equally at a loss to account for the worth of what he does in terms acceptable to the YMCA and the Chamber of Commerce.

Let us look at God's servant the horse. I do not have the scholarship required to claim that Job 39:19–25 was translated with any particular Elizabethan text in mind, though I doubt it is an accident that it is preceded by the horses of *The Faerie Queene,* of *Venus and Adonis,* of *Henry IV,* Part 1. All I want to do here is to report that the horse God describes as his servant is an ideal working horse. This is not Black Beauty we are looking at, this is no humble and wistful recipient of blows from an alcoholic cab driver. He is more like the great John Henry, who even in retirement at the Kentucky Horse Park awes visitors with the fierce and joyful indifference in his eyes. Or like the Piebald in *National Velvet,* who careened madly around town until taken in hand by a fourteen-year-old girl with a passion for difficulty and competition equal to the great horse's. The horse in Job 39:19–25 is like Man o' War or Secretariat or the mare Touch of Class, about whom people speak in tones of awe once they have seen her jump, because she doesn't care about anything but getting the job done, getting over those huge Olympic courses.

The horse in Job is a war horse, not a jumper or a racehorse, but he is metaphysically identical to the Border Collie who doesn't care about you unless you are able to help her achieve her goals; to the chimpanzee Willie, who had some socialization problems but would do anything for the sake of the exact; to horses I have met who are more than a little skittish and rough to handle around the barn, but who will die for you if you enable them to do their work. Such a horse may push the panic button if someone paints the truck too loud a shade of yellow, say, but is unstoppable on course. I have known horses of this nature who were never calm, who were always terrified until they learned that there is such a thing as a horse show, and as soon as they caught sight and sound of the show, they were transformed. Just so is God's servant, and of course God isn't only saying he understands these things—he is saying he is the source of these things.

> Hast thou given the horse strength? hast thou clothed his neck with
>   thunder?
> Canst thou make him afraid as a grasshopper? the glory of his nostrils
>   is terrible.
> He paweth in the valley, and rejoiceth in his strength: he goeth on to
>   meet the armed men.
> He mocketh at fear, and is not affrighted; neither turneth he back
>   from the sword.
> The quiver rattleth against him, the glittering spear and the shield.
> He swalloweth the ground with fierceness and rage: neither believeth
>   he that it is the sound of the trumpet.
> He saith among the trumpets, Ha, ha; and he smelleth the battle afar
>   off, the thunder of the captains, and the shouting.

I have met this horse, ha-Sus shel ha-Shem, and his brethren more than once. You characterize such a horse just as the Voice from the Whirlwind does here. You might say that he spooks like a baby if a butterfly flits by, but put that sucker in the Puissance class at Madison Square Garden and watch out! And you understand, as a daily, ordinary fact about such a horse, that, to paraphrase the Voice, "He smelleth the contest afar off, the announcer and the applause, and he sayeth when he hears the sounds of the horse show, Aha!"

If we can say that in the passages about animals something is urged upon Job, some understanding he did not have before, one good word for that would be "cynicism"—in its original sense, that is, as inherited from the Cynic philosophers, Diogenes and others. The word "cynic" just means "dog," and one way to interpret cynicism is to say that a cynic doesn't believe in anything that an animal cannot understand. The Cynic philosophers reverenced, not animals themselves, as near as I can tell, but the knowledge of animals, that knowledge being a way of knowing the divine. Not all seekers after the divine have thought this way; in Frances Yates's book *The Occult Philosophy in the Elizabethan Age,* the dog is said to represent, mostly in Dürer, the sleeping senses—the senses that must sleep, that we must be freed of, before we can learn the true secrets. My tendency is to side with Cynics, or at least to suspect that they would be willing to entertain this idea: Knowledge of animals, which is knowledge of animal happiness, is knowledge of the divine (though not the only knowledge of the divine), in part because knowledge of animals, work with animals, is one place where we can escape the confusions, or what Wittgenstein called the bewitchments, of language. A place also where many mysteries of ethics can be revealed, though perhaps to little earthly purpose, or so the worldly might argue.

A cynic in this sense is not someone who just doesn't care, someone with blue bags under his eyes and sartorial immorality, but is rather someone who cares deeply about what animals can understand and care about. This leaves in a great deal more than you might think, because animals are not only pretty sharp but are also capable of caring about and acting in a wondrously various range of worlds and ideas, including ideas of God. But not all worlds and ideas.

For instance: Police dogs can easily be taught the concept of a weapon, and good ones recognize as weapons objects they haven't previously been introduced to, and often do so better than their human handlers. Bomb dogs can find explosives they have not been worked on, and can do so while ignoring various other kinds of equipment in building and area searches. So a cynic has got to believe in weapons, because dogs do. But as I have said elsewhere, police dogs are not so good on abstract categories—they flunk out on uniform recognition. You cannot teach a dog to draw conclusions about someone from clothing; neither L. L. Bean nor Brooks Brothers means anything to a dog. Thus, if you wanted to pull off a heist by dressing up as a rabbi or a priest or a New Haven cop or a Yalie, you would not be able to fool a good police dog, who would see through your disguise as though it weren't there, because for the dog it isn't there. Literally.

Notice that you could quite easily fool a philosophy professor or even a dog trainer who has lost track of her dogs. Not forever, perhaps, but long enough to pull off a heist. A philosophy professor has advanced conceptual faculties and so knows a uniform when she sees one, and usually knows the uniform better than she knows the wearer of the uniform.

The devoted cynic, then, is just someone who says that uniforms don't mean very much. The cynic is left free by this discipline to believe in courage, loyalty, God, and the worth of philanthropy, and even, as Socrates tells Glaucon in the *Republic*, justice and wisdom.

There are worlds, worlds of speaking and knowing, in which it is an *ordinary* fact that horses love their work the way a schoolboy loves his pie or a Kentucky colonel his rye. Worlds in which it is a fiery but ordinary fact that there are dogs such as one Goliath, of Louisiana, who weighs seventy-four pounds and would rather be out pulling more than ten thousand pounds than anything else on earth. Worlds in which horses might be a little spooky about some of our arrangements, our yellow trucks, but when it comes time to do their jobs have their necks clothed in thunder. None of this need be terrifying, unless it terrifies you to realize that the ostrich is not interested in your mercy, and that Secretariat and John Henry and Rin Tin Tin are never going to be impressed by your pity, though perhaps by your generous kindness.

To honor the happiness of the horse of Job 39:19–25 it is necessary to have a battle or a horse show, and to desire that battle yourself in order to match the kind of being the horse is. To be kind to a Border Collie is to herd sheep, or to find some work that enables the Border Collie to articulate her eerie capacities. Trainers are supposed to know this, but even lion trainers may sometimes forget in the midst of their tribulations that there is more on the earth than the lion trainer's kind of kindness; and a trainer is not always wise enough to contemplate temperament when the reporter calls, or to refrain from the attempt to tell the reporter about the kindness and desire of tigers and chimps. Job, unlike any commentator on the Book of Job in my ken, does appear to have known enough about animals to know this, and he is restored, as I said in the beginning, to more of the uprightness and justice that are rejected by the Voice from the Whirlwind. Which Voice could be the conscience of any good trainer saying to the trainer, "Quit yer bitchin'. You don't hear Secretariat or Rin Tin Tin weeping and moaning like that, do you? They know their own business and stick to it."

Now I must turn to a poem of Donald Davie's, "Utterings." It is in five sections, in each of which there is a voice. Just a voice, no occasion, not even a whirlwind. There is first the voice of the Bird, who speaks with the same inarguable authority as the Voice in Job, to utter the happiness of the Bird.

> (Bird) To flex in the upper airs
> To the unseen but known
> Velocity of change
> That both prevails and gives—
> If anything that lives
> That is able to know it, knows
> Better to bend to the press
> Of need and so command it,
> Him I envy, his
> So much more strait duress.

The ordering of the poem perhaps gives us leave to read the next section, in which the Salmon utters a happiness, as part of an ascending hierarchy of happinesses.

> (Salmon) Pressures, pressures of water,
> Of running water, because
> As needs must downward driving,
> Define imperatives.
> If anything that lives
> That is able to know it, knows
> Better than I do the spine
> Set taut against the grab
> Of gravity, that thing knows
> More happiness than mine.

The next higher happiness, that of Man, sounds not unlike the happiness of Job.

> (Man) Making your own mistakes
> And living the blame of them, making
> The same ones time after time,
> Which nobody forgives—
> If anything that lives

> That is able to know it, knows
> A better happiness than
> This—and he is Legion
> That thinks he does—he is
> Disranked from the branch of Man.

Higher yet than the happiness of Man is the happiness of the Angel.

> (Angel)   On us no pressures, none.
> Adoration is
> Not required, but what
> Each one desirously gives.
> If anything that lives
> That is able to know it, knows
> A better happiness, then
> The frame of the world is askew;
> I share the happiness
> Of salmon, birds, and men.

The Angel is not, of course, disranked from the branch of Man for knowing a higher happiness, because angels are not in rank with Man to begin with.

However the delicately and guilefully implied hierarchy in the poem is to be read, we *are* given as the last happiness, and possibly the highest in this sequence, the happiness of Sheepdog and Artist.

> (Sheepdog/   Knowing your own business,
> Artist)   And such a delicate business;
> Uttering it with the promptness
> That such a knowledge gives—
> If anything that lives
> That is able to know it, knows
> A better happiness
> In his dog's life than this,
> He is welcome to it; most,
> I apprehend, know less.

Thus the artist is disranked from the branch of Man, *by* Man.

What Job learned, what God had to teach him by pointing out to him what was beyond him in the flight of the hawk, the fierceness of the horse, the indifference of the ostrich, was his own business. The great animal trainer who has dealings with—not with the secular world, because when we are speaking of animal trainers, or of poets, as Bloom rightly indicates, there is no more point in deciding where the sacred leaves off and the secular begins than there is in deciding where one half of the earth leaves off and the other begins, so what I mean is: The great animal trainer who has dealings with the profane world, the world created in, say, the Fall or the Tower of Babel, when the animals and our words were torn from each other so that we actually have to teach a dog to come when called, must occasionally learn Job's lesson. The significance of domestic animals—of dogs and horses, of the sheep (and presumably sheepdogs) and oxen and asses and camels to whom Job is restored as custodian—is that through respect for them, through a discipline of admiration, one of whose names is training, we can come, momentarily, perhaps in spiritual danger or perhaps not, to a higher happiness than that allotted to our species. Acceptance of that knowledge entails acceptance of one's own limitations, and poetry and animal training are, of course, disciplines of exact limitation. The hawk trainer does not complain at how God has made the hawk but learns to fly her. The horseman does not weep upon discovering that Touch of Class does not love him but learns to fly with Touch of Class. And then and only then do the sacred and the ordinary transcend the artificial boundaries given to them by the ideas—the very idea!—of the profane and the secular. Then and only then does happiness as a creature sharing the planet with other creatures become knowing your own business and uttering it with the promptness that such a knowledge gives.

I do not mean by this that God's ways or the ostrich's ways or any human way is justified, whether by the Book of Job or anything else. We are free, the ostrich is free, and God is free, and freedom can never, as the French philosopher Emmanuel Levinas so correctly says, be justified, though it can sometimes, briefly, be rendered just.

But I have not been talking about justice. I have been talking about a few of the ordinary divinities of the trainer's world, which consists of a work with ways of Dwelling that are not given in the canonical categories of human justice. For a city slicker—someone like me, that is—it is not easy to come to unmediated awareness of the servants of ha-Shem, and too swift an entry into such awareness may well be dangerous for some minds, which is probably why understanding of and kindness toward animals is not given in the Commandments—it is harder to understand animals than to love the Lord thy God. It is hard to know and work with the Dwelling that is an ostrich, but fatally easy to come to imagine that one has unmediated awareness of cruelty, and thus to become a loser in the kindness wars; for to imagine that you have privileged knowledge of such intimate matters as what kindness and cruelty are is to practice the sin of pride, a fatal sin that I have been trying to avoid throughout my remarks, with how much success it is not up to me to decide.

The kindness wars are wars over who gets to *say* who is kind—Job or his comforters, for example—and they are wars in which there are no human winners, only losers and survivors. Job is one survivor.

Goodness and kindness and uprightnesses of all sorts are, I think, aspects of what Levinas calls our freedom—the vast exteriority of the self whereby to be is already to announce, act, articulate, titter or swashbuckle or withhold or greet or fail to greet, the world and all of its Others. Levinas says, arrestingly, that our freedom can never be justified, only *rendered just*. Thus kindness is part of our freedom, like breath, and unjustified (something I suspected early on when I got old enough to encounter the state in the form of grammar school).

But if our kindness is part of our freedom and unjustified, it can perhaps, for various periods and in various large and small clearings, be rendered just. Kindness is not a source of happiness until, like any other aspect of the spirit, of life, it becomes educated, rendered just. In order to be kind to an animal, you have to know that animal; Proverbs 12:10 says that the righteous man knows his animals and that the tender mercies of the wicked are cruel—a wonderful and mysterious moment, the identification of "tender mercies" and cruelty. When kindness is an achievement, the words for it in Job are "uprightness" and "righteousness." Job, we are allowed to believe, is a man whose kindness has been rendered just (from which it follows, by the way, that freedom is not justice) but not rendered global. Job has not got the temperament to behave justly toward the ostrich; that is not a possible topos for his kindness. In this, he is not so much a prefiguring of Christ as a presentation of the dilemma—the intolerable contradiction, an image as of Babel, that created the pressure that produced the idea of the kindness of Christ as the hitherto unsuspected third term that releases, placates, the dilemma, or so some say. In any case, neither Job nor the New Testament gives us any reason to suspect that any attempt to make our kindness or happiness global can have any but the most disastrous political results.

So I like to think that the terrible pieties of the animals in Job—Behemoth, say, who can drink leisurely because "he trusteth that he can draw up Jordan into his mouth" (40:23)—are the rebuke to moral excesses. Hence, in citing the ostrich's vain labors as the case of her piety, or Davie's Sheepdog and Artist as the case of their happiness, I am warning myself against my own incomplete piety. Job's uprightness was complete, and that mattered, but his piety was not, any more than ours is or ever can be. Our morality comes to a halt just as our knowledge does against the tremendous range of pieties and happinesses by means of which animals are, and are building their worlds.

And it halts, too, against the tremendous range of divinities and pieties—hazardous pieties, glorious pieties, unsuspected and unlikely happinesses—by means of which people are, and are building their worlds.